T0385264

KIKU

KIKU

聴く

The Japanese Art *of* Good Listening

DR HARU YAMADA

First published in 2025 by Headline Press
an imprint of Headline Publishing Group Limited

1

Image Credits
page 125 – Jean-Louis Grall, CC BY-SA 3.0 <https://creativecommons.org/licenses/by-sa/3.0>,
via Wikimedia Commons, redrawn by Jason Cox, Atomic Squib Illustration
page 213 – top: Dr Mazen Abudari; bottom: Mr UMEKI Takamori
page 218 – Jason Cox, Atomic Squib Illustration

Cataloguing in Publication Data is available from the British Library.

Hardback ISBN: 978 1 0354 1181 8

Designed and typeset by EM&EN
Printed and bound in Great Britain by Clays Ltd, Elcograf S.p.A.

Headline's policy is to use papers that are natural, renewable and recyclable
products and made from wood grown in well-managed forests and other
controlled sources. The logging and manufacturing processes are expected
to conform to the environmental regulations of the country of origin.

Headline Publishing Group Limited
An Hachette UK Company
Carmelite House
50 Victoria Embankment
London EC4Y 0DZ

The authorised representative in the EEA is Hachette Ireland,
8 Castlecourt Centre, Dublin 15, D15 XTP3, Ireland (email: info@hbgi.ie)

www.headline.co.uk
www.hachette.co.uk

Contents

Prologue:
Listening Intelligence

No other life form turns noise into sound, sound into language, then language into understanding quite the way humans do when we listen. As a sociolinguist growing up in different places and languages, I've been fascinated with the way people navigate their day listening to language systems that code the world in such dramatically different ways. It's difficult to pinpoint the exact time this curiosity began, but it might have been that day when I was sitting in a bus on my way to a primary school in Tokyo, wondering how come the Japanese don't have more accidents when they call a green traffic light *blue*?

It was the day I discovered that there's a cost to being a daydreamer, particularly at the back of a public bus on the way to your first day at primary school, because you're likely to miss the announcement of your bus stop. If you've ever been to Tokyo, you'll know that all of the thousands of intersections in the vast metropolis look pretty much the same. This is especially true if you're seven years old and fresh off the boat from having lived for three years in New York City, at a time when you had to rely on your inner GPS.

If you miss the announcement, you miss your stop. The auditory cortex, the hearing part of your brain, might have heard the sounds that manifested as an announcement, but if you were thinking about blue traffic lights instead of listening for the announcement, the complex translations of mechanical vibrations into electrical impulses that comprise your hearing would have all been for nought. Since you heard the announcement but didn't listen for it, now you're at the wrong bus stop and lost.

Listening helps you gain the information you need to navigate successfully through your day, not only to get you to your destination but also to learn about the people you meet along the way. Listening connects you to people the way it connected me to the kind man in the suit who gave me a ten-yen coin to call home so I could eventually get to school that day, albeit in my mother's giant station wagon and not on public transport like everyone else. Listening isn't a perfect and foolproof fix-all for the ailments in the world, but it is an intelligent human navigation system that helps you discover places and the people in them.

Listening helps you to understand another person and the way they are trying to relate to you. This starts the moment you identify that the sounds just delivered to your auditory cortex are being made by a human voice, which kickstarts the listening energy you need for identification. Do you recognize this person? Do you know the words in the language they are speaking? Initial listening investigations may seem basic, but they form the foundation that allows you to do things like respond to a voice you can identify, choose the level of formality of the interaction with someone whose voice is less familiar, match the emotional energy of the person and ultimately decide whether it's important to keep on listening – or not.

When we stay in conversations, we listen to words, or what linguists call the 'surface level' of language that is explicit and audible, but our listening intelligence helps us to search into the 'deep structure' that sounds out relational and cultural meanings, too. Human listening navigation is capable of going far beyond allowing us to get off at the right bus stop. This book explores the practice of the kind of listening intelligence that allows us to reach the deep structures of meaning in communication when we are relating with someone.

I stumbled across this kind of listening many years after the missed bus stop in Tokyo; this time in London, in hospital, after I fell off a scooter. I'll tell you about this accident in chapter one, but here, I want to first tell you about the listening energy I discovered in the hospital that inspired the main idea for this book – it all came down to one tiny Japanese character brought over by Empress Suiko's emissaries from China to Japan in the fourth century. Pronounced 'kiku' 聴く, this treasure of a word for listening is comprised of smaller characters that together generate the secret alchemy of listening: an ear 耳 on the left and fourteen 十四 hearts 心 on the right, conjuring a person listening with the energy of fourteen hearts.

The image of Listening with Fourteen Hearts is important because it opens us up to the idea that there are many listening channels we can dial into – you'll find five of them in the first foundational chapter and the remaining nine in the chapters to follow. The amplitude of listening is vast because it isn't just an auditory experience, but a visual and tactile one that extends out into personal, relational and cultural reaches. Listening with Fourteen Hearts is practiced in surround sound, synthesizing the human voice and language we hear through all our sensors.

In our listening journey here, we'll echo the expanse. Sourcing from my own sociolinguistic research and that of others, I include personal stories that recount the nomadic life I led until I settled in London, where I live with my French partner and family. These stories are intended to conjure the idea that language cultures aren't confined to country or region, but include the much larger reaches of conceptual spaces, like generation, work and social style. As you go about your day recognizing the listening you're employing, amplifying and shifting into, I hope you can enjoy reacquainting yourself with your own hearing and listening practice, the way I did when my son remarked how each train station in Tokyo had a signature melody. While I'd heard those jingles composed for blind passengers to tell them where they are many times, I'd forgotten all about them. Every person has a signature tune to their voice we learn to recognize when we get to know them, but Listening with Fourteen Hearts is rediscovering that voice time and again.

As we cast a wide net with our listening, we're also going to go deep to rediscover the listening intelligence we have been developing since before we were even born. We need this skill, sometimes cast as the mere 'receptive skill', just as much as our productive speaking skill, the better-known side of our everyday communication. While technology and public speaking has been grabbing our attention, our listening has been there, consistently acquiring information and showing up for us, sometimes even while we're asleep.

To help you reacquaint yourself with your listening energy and intelligence, the ten chapters in this book are each headed by a Japanese character that hints at the meaning of each chapter the way the characters must have in the fourth century for Empress Suiko when her emissaries brought the first wave of the writing system over from China. Superimposed on spoken Japanese, the characters that visualized the ideas of the time were also their coded technology.

By contrast to the ancient tech, at the end of each chapter you will find seven practical takeaways to observe, reflect upon and practise in your daily listening. Some of the takeaways define the listening competencies that you might not have known you have, while others might be a new way of thinking about listening. These insights are followed by three exercises for you to try out. I hope that these exercises, along with what you read in each chapter, inspire you to give your listening the attention it deserves. It's my hope that you'll share these ideas with friends and family and rediscover the joys of listening that's part of your everyday living.

In a nationwide poll of 1,112 US women by the Associated Press and a petcare company, one third of the women surveyed said their partners were worse listeners than their pets.[1] When I first read this finding, I thought it was a terrible indictment on those non-listening partners – you know who they are. But then I saw this study was done in conjunction with a petcare company and I took my own advice on Credibility Listening, that I talk about in chapter four and have come to interpret this study to mean that two thirds of the women surveyed in the study actually did benefit from human listeners, while the other third benefited from pet listeners. If we assume that half of the world is comprised of men, we could conclude that something like 17 per cent of couples think their pets are better listeners than their partners. On the whole, then, perhaps the study could mean that humans aren't doing too badly at listening after all, but maybe we could take the pressure off some of those pets. Since listening is for everyone's benefit, we need to help out that 17 per cent, especially since most of us know someone who would count themselves part of it.

This book is for you and anyone else you want to help discover their fourteen energies of listening – for the ultimate purpose of staving off the noise and misinformation no one wants, and, instead, cultivating a practice of listening to the music of those important to you.

1

Listening with Fourteen Hearts

Listening with Fourteen Hearts[*]

One autumn Saturday in London before the school term began, I was racing my daughter on a scooter when the front tyre jammed and shot me out over the handlebars. On landing, my jawbone dislocated, morphed into an arrow and pierced through my eardrum to the lining around my brain, causing my head to break open and leak CSF, hospital language for cerebral spinal fluid.

This sort of thing would typically require a simple surgical procedure, assisted by an artificial ventilator connected by a tube running down your nose and through your windpipe, which is designed to help you breathe. In my case, however, it did the opposite and punctured a lung, requiring draining tubes out each side of my chest so my lungs wouldn't fill up with fluid and drown me. Due to the failed earlier intubations, I then needed a tracheostomy tube fitted, which meant

---

* Etymologists have theorized that 'kiku' 聴く is either fourteen hearts 十四心 or ten eyes and hearts 十目心, with the character for 'four' on its side read as 'eyes'

an incision in my throat to provide direct access to the ventilator. Unfortunately, the tube was threaded just beneath the vocal cords, preventing my voice box from doing what it is supposed to do, which is to open and close to produce sound.

With two hoses draining my lungs, nine drips inserted into my arms and feet, and a ventilator clapped onto my throat, I was already not the best version of myself that I had been hoping for that autumn. But over the course of a month, this version degraded further still. It started with what sounded like an electronic hissing in my left ear, which I initially thought was the sound coming from the 24/7 fluorescent lighting torture in the ICU. I'd eventually find out, though, that it wasn't the lighting, but a newly acquired hearing disability called tinnitus.

Tinnitus comes in lots of different manifestations but, from what I have since learned, they are all uniquely horrible. As a kind of phantom reaction to the newly acquired deficit, tinnitus mourns a hearing loss by composing its own noise. It turned out that my hissing was made to compensate for the absence of what phonologists call 'voiceless sibilants' or 'fricatives', or s- and f-sounds for normal people – which, by then, I was pretty sure I wasn't. Instead, muted and hearing impaired, I was a sociolinguist turned recording device without a microphone or speakers.

Under duress, though, I learned that humans fight to survive. Motivating me were my two children, six and seven, who became the driving focus for me to get out of the ICU. With hindsight, I think this drive developed because the hospital is an isolating place made more real when your extended family is scattered abroad – in Japan, the United States and France. Furthermore, despite my overzealous drive to go home, the other thing I learned during my time in hospital was that while it is hard to get people to listen to you when you actually have a voice, it's even harder when you don't have one. A voice can get someone's attention, especially if you can turn up the volume and increase its frequency. Separated from this voice action we typically call 'shouting', though, when you're in the ICU, you're really just a silent bedwarmer, sidelined to the attention of hospital staff who keep repeating the mantra: 'You can only be discharged when you can breathe on your own. Hospital policy.'

Deflated by not being heard but not defeated, I was startled awake one morning by a blood-sucking vampire who went by the hospital name of phlebotomist. 'Good morning,' they said in a really loud voice into my good ear. Sleep deprived from the fluorescent lights but still eager to find out the information I needed to get back home, I grabbed the yellow pad the ICU had furnished me with and got on-task to ask: *How long is this going to take?*

To answer me, the phlebotomist used what we call non-verbal language, holding up a pointing finger with one hand while the other drew blood. Still new to hospital language, I had no idea if the phlebotomist was telling me that the bloods would take a minute to draw, or if this was standard phlebotomist-speak to tell people who had cracked open their head to wait. I'd guess now that it was the former because the phlebotomist next used what we used to call 'good bedside manner' and told me how nice my handwriting was. 'Aspiring to be a doctor, I guess?' they asked. But it was after I answered back, *No. Aspiring to get out of this place*, that the phlebotomist replied with words I'll never forget: 'Soon,' they said. 'You can't stay here on holiday forever.'

3

Years later, the phlebotomist's line has stayed with me, not just because it made me laugh, but because I suddenly made the connection that it was listening to the people around me that was going to help me get better: the medical information about surgery scheduling, prognosis and aftercare, of course, but also the funny comments from the phlebotomist telling me I was 'on holiday' and multiple visits by family members skirting visiting hours to respond to my grievances with videos of kids doing their homework and cleaning kitty litter. By showing me those 'silly videos', my sister and partner weren't just listening to my gripes about going back home, but also supporting me with the motivation I needed to get better enough to 'breathe on my own'. In addition to the medical team, it was this steady supply of reinforced human connection, practised as Everyday Listening with Fourteen Hearts, that was what helped me regain the fitness I needed to get back on my feet.

Listening can not only help bolster your physical health but also the many personal, social and cultural channels of health we will explore throughout the book. I had to find this out the hard way, waiting a month to get the notice of a discharge from the ICU, then getting a lump in my throat (where the hole for the ventilator was) when saying goodbye to the phlebotomist and the rest of the medical team. But enjoying the benefits of Listening with Fourteen Hearts doesn't require falling off a scooter, or even anything near as extreme as a head injury. What it needs is just a gentle reminder to reacquaint with the fourteen channels, starting now.

Your Fourteen Hearts

I got the idea that not all listening occurs on the same channel when I first started my research into listening. Deconstructing two Japanese characters that are both pronounced 'kiku' but have distinct meanings, the first character we're calling 'Listening with Fourteen Hearts' 聴く, and heads this chapter, tunes into the channel of *a person*, while the second character, that we'll call 'Informational Listening' 聞く and heads the next, focuses on *listening to language, content, task or topic*. When we talk about listening, we generally think we mean this channel of Informational Listening, where the character 聞く is composed of an ear 耳 positioned between a pair of gates 門, like a person pressing up an ear to the gates trying to gain information from the other side.

We use Listening with Fourteen Hearts and Informational Listening on different channels. The first involves listening deeply for personal, relational and cultural voices while the second involves optimal listening for surface information, typically expressed in language. Flash back to the London ICU and you can imagine my family and me using Informational Listening to understand the medical diagnosis, results of the surgeries and the prognosis going forward, while the phlebotomist, family and I participated in Listening with Fourteen Hearts in focusing on each other's voices in our daily living experiences. We use both these listening channels and more, but in our day-to-day listening, we tend to value Informational Listening more, in part because Listening with Fourteen Hearts is harder to describe and grasp, and in part because our education at school and work reinforces the idea that it's this 'productive' channel of listening that is important. Here we challenge this idea and start with the lesser-known but powerful five channels comprised in Listening with Fourteen Hearts that provide the energy to tune in to other channels.

Japanese character-readers weren't the only people who were privy to the idea of fourteen listening hearts in early times. Greek philosophers too had apparently thought of this kind of listening, calling it 'meta', where the original etymological meaning for the word included the senses of *with*, *beyond*, *after* and *among*. Meta Listening was communication that works *with* speaking to enable us to hear beyond what words say about our reality, *before*, *during* and *after* we say them, and always exists somewhere magically in the space *amongst* humans.

Listening with Fourteen Hearts is a synergy of art and science. It's a provision of health that supports our personal well-being but also our physical health. As one of the longest and most comprehensive studies of human development, the Harvard Study of Adult Development found that listening can protect against chronic diseases and mental decline,[1] and a study in the cardiologists' journal *Heart* found that the risk of coronary heart disease and stroke decreased as much as a third for those who felt heard.[2] Because the five foundational channels of Listening with Fourteen Hearts, like the other channels of listening, start with a physical hearing that fuels their energies, let's first talk about your hearing powerhouse that drives your listening.

Your Hearing Powerhouse

Our auditory system is designed as a first line of defence. A loud bump in the middle of the night can startle you awake and instruct the release of stress hormones like adrenaline, noradrenaline and cortisol to prompt you to react through the fight or flight response. As your 'startle reflex' switches you on, your airways open up and your blood gets pumping, you are alerted to a potential threat, real or perceived. To determine the actual level of threat, your listening intelligence kicks in as soon as you have a moment to consider it. When that morning alarm goes off, we startle awake before our listening kicks in and we press the snooze.

Even more interesting is the listening we do at the other end of the spectrum from our startle reflex in our auditory system – our hearing tells us to listen for sound but also its absence, too. That bump we hear in the middle of the night followed by silence, or the people we expect to hear at the other end of a video conference and don't. We don't like it when we're expecting to be able to hear sound and we don't. 'You're on mute! You're on mute!' You know the drill.

Like our other perceptions, we tend to think of our hearing in absolute terms – 'I heard you!' – but hearing is actually a sensor that works across a range. The spectrum of hearing is an important concept because our sensors are heightened when the alerts are at the extremes of the range. We notice low audibility at the other end of a call, and say, 'Uh, hello? I can't hear you,' even when we have heard something but it's too low to qualify as hearing. Equally, we notice sounds that are too high in volume or pitch and hurt our ears. While

7

we notice these pressure points at the extreme ends of our hearing range, we often don't pay attention to the sounds in the normal range when we can generally assume our hearing is functioning normally. This was pretty much my attitude until I got tinnitus from the accident and was sent to see an audiologist for post-trauma hearing therapy.

When I told my audiologist that although I'd been going to the optometrist since I was twelve just to have diagnostic 'checkups' even when everything seemed okay, but that this was my first ever visit to the audiologist, she said that, sadly, I was pretty typical. Even though we make hygiene visits for our eyes and teeth, we don't look after our hearing in the same way. This is likely due to the cultural value we place on youthfulness, and although vision loss can also be age-related, we view hearing loss as a particularly shameful marker of being old and in decline. The stats at the end of this chapter, though, show that you don't necessarily have to be old to suffer from hearing loss. So the first order of business is to have your hearing checked if you haven't already. You will be contributing to dispelling the stigma at the very least and rewarded for becoming better attuned to the amazing instrument you have that protects you.

Your hearing isn't just a heroic protector that keeps you out of danger but also an extraordinary system that ignites your listening. Starting on the outside of your head and going into your brain, your auditory system begins with the two satellite dishes we call 'ears' that act as antennas that capture sound. Once the soundwaves are caught, they are then sent through a two-and-a-half-centimetre-long ear canal that finishes at your ear drum. Although the ear drum in the middle ear is an astonishingly tiny, one centimetre in diameter instrument that stays that same size from child-hood to adulthood, its demure size featuring three of your body's tiniest bones has the important job of drumming up vibrations, which it will pass on through an oval window to the snail-shaped organ that is your inner ear.

Called the cochlea, the tininess of this pea-sized organ also belies its awesome power. Inside this miniaturized hyper-hearing centre are bundled groups of hair cells that lie swirl-ing around like anemone in a sea of sensor corals, waiting to sense the drummed-up mechanical sounds and change them into electrical currents. Next time someone tells you that you can't change things, think of the mind-bending change that goes on in between your middle and inner ears every time you hear something.

And as we approach the end of the hearing trajectory, your auditory system performs one last, breathtaking feat. These electrical charges are sent along the auditory pathway as fre-quencies to the hearing part of the brain called the 'auditory cortex' – the enchanted place where our hearing blooms into listening. Says the ecologist John Muir:

> A few minutes ago every tree was excited, bowing to the roaring storm, waving, swirling, tossing their branches in glorious enthusiasm like worship. But though to the outer ear these trees are now silent, their songs never cease.

As sounds persist after you've heard them, that's when your listening starts. There, in the forest of your listening, an electrical storm of associative memories matches the sounds you've heard in prior encounters to begin listening to what you are hearing now.

We know from the Greek description of the 'meta' in listening that Listening with Fourteen Hearts is always ahead of hearing and behind it simultaneously. To be able to auditorily listen, we need to be able to hear a sound in the present and match it with a memory of a sound we've heard in the past. The extraordinary human ability of listening isn't new – it has been around for millennia. Saxon hunters in the fifth to eleventh centuries used it when they listened out for their prey. We know this because in Old Saxon, an old form of English, the word 'listen' was pronounced 'hlysnen', and actually meant *listening-for*. Like us today, Old Saxons didn't so much *listen-to* anything as *listen-for* it. We recall sound from memory to recognize it in its current environment. Listening in the present is the repeated process of drawing from auditory hearing in the past and listening for it in the future. And that begs the question, what are we listening for?

Your Human Voice

When I asked a cochlear implant surgeon to explain why hearing is important, he laughed and said, 'Well, it's because it allows us to do what we're doing now and listen for the human voice.'

Our hearing helps us to identify the human voice not only when someone is speaking, but also through the noises humans make when they shout, sing, laugh and cry. We can hear these kinds of energies humans create in their vocal tracts because we're endowed with the ability to decipher volume and sound frequency, that we decode as pitch. Humans can verify that what they are hearing is another human voice by detecting an average human speaking volume that occurs somewhere between fifty and eighty decibels (dB), and a sound frequency range between twenty and twenty thousand hertz (Hz). Ultrasounds show we detect this human speaking range in volume and pitch from when we are around four months old in utero, making babies the top hearers of the human voice by the time they are born.

Like car value, though, unfortunately human hearing begins to decline once it comes off the lot. But, as if by compensation, we gain the skill of listening instead. Even though the adult human hearing range is inferior to a baby's and a teen's, and pales by comparison to the top ten animal auditory superstars in the list below, we rival them all and possibly surpass them in our ability to listen and bring meaning to the pitch of cries and, eventually, language. Volume and Pitch are two of the five channels that we listen for in sounds to assess the quality of a human voice, alongside timbre, which we explore next.

Auditory Superstars

Animals have truly amazing auditory equipment. Here are the top ten contenders selected and adapted from the websites, Hidden Hearing[3] and BioExplorer[4]:

1. The greater wax moth can hear ultrasonic sound frequencies at 300,000Hz, 15 times higher than the highest sounds humans can hear at 20,000Hz.
2. Bats hunt at night using echolocation, squeaking then using the echoes to navigate, sometimes to catch moths.

3. Owls are night hunters, too, and have specialist ear locations on their heads to pinpoint prey to great accuracy.

4. Elephants can move herds to shelter, having heard the sound of a storm 10 kilometres away.

5. Wolves are the best long-distance hearers and communicators. They can hear from a distance of 6.2–9.9 miles (10–16 kilometres) away. Their domestic descendants, dogs, also have a hearing range far superior to humans and can hear you coming home long before you're at the door. Growing up, I had a cairn terrier we used as a kind of seismo-alarm because he knew an earthquake was about to hit Tokyo about half a minute before we did.

6. Cats have superior hearing ears managed by three dozen muscles per ear that allow them to rotate their ears towards sound and away from noise.

7. Horses use a lookout to protect their herd. They also hold their ears forward to show attentiveness and tip them downwards to show excitement or fear.

8. Dolphins and sharks use echolocation to create sound maps that guide their navigation. A shark has electroreceptor organs called ampullae di Lorenzini that allow them to detect weak electrical fields, helping them to locate their coordinates and navigate thousands of miles across waters, crossing in excess of 20,000 miles (32,187 km), from Africa to Australia and back.

9. Rats have super-powered hearing that can help pinpoint the source of food but also their predators.

10. Pigeons have ears beneath their feathers and can

hear sounds as low as 0.05Hz, allowing them to detect storms and seismic shifts that help them navigate away from natural disasters.

Listening with Fourteen Hearts 1: Timbre

The first kind of sound in the human voice we listen for is timbre, the highly personal quality of human vocal sounds we can perceive. Once we hear a voice and identify it as human, we begin listening by studying its timbre. Recognizing timbre gives meaning to a particular person's voice and allows us to identify them. In other words, if we know a person's voice from having heard it on repeated occasions before, we can ID that person by the timbre of their voice.

In fact, the timbre in a human voice is thought to be so unique to a particular person that some banks use a voice recognition security check as an alternative to eye or finger-print identification. Although we can never actually prove that no two people have an identical voice, as far as we know, your voice is unique to you. What is arguably more important than the ID checks banks use, though, is the unique voice you recognize in family members and close friends.

Recognizing the unique timbre in someone's voice is important not just because it identifies someone but also because it starts the back-and-forth of listening and speaking. When you identify that the person who just said 'Hello' is your dad, for example, now it isn't just a security check but the start of two people in communication. As the human voice conveys messages by using language, it also broadcasts meta-messages about how someone is feeling. When the voice of someone you know changes tone, you can understand something about how they are. Just the other day, I over-heard someone say in a restaurant, 'Oh my god, they'd better hurry up. He's starting to talk in that Dad-is-hungry voice.' The timbre in someone's voice can act as a weathervane, allowing you to listen for someone's well-being, especially in people we know. But as you cultivate the practice of Listening with Fourteen Hearts, you can also learn to recognize subtle changes in the voices of those you know less well, too.

Listening with Fourteen Hearts 2: Amplifier

Some languages like Mandarin Chinese have tones and formalize them in their language. Four different tones dis-tinguish the four meanings of the word *ma*, that can mean 'mother', 'hemp', 'horse' or 'scold'. Hearing tones in a tonal language like Mandarin Chinese is necessary for understand-ing the language, and not hearing them means that you could end up misunderstanding a key message or mistaking someone's mother for a horse, which is generally not ideal in any language culture.

In spoken English, tones aren't formalized in the verbal language and fixed to sounds to differentiate word mean-ing. Instead, English speakers use tones to establish the mood or vibe of a conversation and can be specifically used to draw attention to the intended meaning of a word – for example, by stressing a syllable in the word to provide emphasis. In greeting your mother, for instance, you can say, 'Hello, mother', 'Hello, MOTHER', 'Hello, MOther' or 'Hello, moTHER'. Unlike in Mandarin Chinese, your mother would still be able to understand you are addressing her in every one of the greetings. She might, though, hear a different tone of voice in each one, especially if the way you address your mother on an average day is different from the one you just used. Depending on how you normally greet your mother, saying 'Hello, MOTHER', loudly and accenting the whole word might give your voice an angry tone, while placing an accent on one syllable or another in saying, 'Hello, MOther' or 'Hello, moTHER' might give your voice a tone of contempt. Of course, only your mother will know how she heard your greeting and only you know the way you actually meant it, but part of being fluent in any language is also being able to listen for and understand tone of voice, like the Amplifier you just used. As a listener, being able to understand an Amplifier is important because it can help you interpret what someone is saying in relation to you.

So even though missing tone of voice in English might not result in the misunderstanding of language the way it does in Mandarin Chinese, it might result in someone being unable to understand what's happening to the relationship in the context of the moment. For the listener, a tone of voice like the Amplifier is a navigation marker that prepares us for what might happen next. Will she continue to be angry? Should you put the kettle on? Tone of voice supplies subtle information about someone's personal and relational every-day well-being so that listeners can evaluate and navigate next steps in the conversation as it rolls out.

Like English, the Japanese language is also not tonal. And like the English language, Japanese uses tones to communi-cate relational information. However, instead of emphasizing words by turning the Amplifier up, the Japanese language turns the dial down to create emphasis by staccatoed syllables. As you might say, 'Oh. My. God.' in English, Japanese hold sounds down between syllables in words for emphasis, saying things like '*sug.goku oishii*', meaning, 'it really tastes good', but with the emphasis on 'really', sounding out the English equivalent, 'It REAlly tastes good'. Because listeners notice emphases at both extremes of the range, Japanese listeners pay attention to the silent pausing between syllables. In prefacing the comment with eyes opened wide and sucking in air to add a surprised tone of voice, a speaker expresses their relational message for the listener to understand and enjoy. Amplifiers create emphasis, but also amplify the experience to include the listener.

Listening with Fourteen Hearts 3: Shifter

In both English and in Japanese, we use voice and language to emphasize things that matter to us. If after a daughter greets her mother and says, 'It raiiined!' stretching out the vowels and calling attention to the fact that it rained, her mother would be able to detect the relative shift in the wailing pitch between 'rained' and the mundane, flat pitch of the preceding word 'it', to hear a mood change for the people in the conversation – for example, if the daughter is annoyed because she didn't bring an umbrella and she got wet. A tone of voice can be a Shifter that signals a change in the atmosphere between people.

As in English, Japanese speakers also use the tone-of-voice Shifters by drawing out sounds, but because a shift in the mood of the relationship is important for the listener to know, a speaker might add an explicit tone marker at the end of the sentence to signal the shift. The two most frequently used tone markers in Japanese are *ne* and *yo* where *ne* means, 'right?' and *yo* acts like a word with an exclamation mark in English so that *ame futta yoooo* sounds like, 'It raiiined!' in English.

In any language, listening competence isn't just about understanding its words (as we'll learn more about in the following chapter on Informational Listening), but about understanding the tone of voice that supplies personal and relational meaning. It's how people can reproduce verbatim what someone else said, like the fact 'it rained', and still not understand what they meant if they didn't listen for and interpret the amplifier or shifter that demonstrates that *they're mad it rained.* Fortunately, first-language listeners of all languages can become competent in both language and tone of voice without even trying – we'll see in chapter three on Soft Listening that we learn a good part of our listening skills outside of formal academic training.

One example of the tone-of-voice shift we know and take for granted is signalling a different meaning by changing the intonation at the ends of sentences. As listeners, we know that the English language typically uses a falling pitch at the end of a sentence to make a statement and a rising pitch at the end of a sentence to ask a question. Many other languages use these same patterns of pitch in creating statements and questions, although some, such as Japanese, use language rather than tone, for example, using the word *ka* to act like a question mark and explicitly clarify that a sentence is a question in speech. When typical pitch patterns are in operation, listeners of English know they can focus on the content – the words – of the statement or question. But first-language listeners of English also know that if they hear a pitch shift, like a rising pitch at the end of a statement, or a falling pitch at the end of a question, these are tone-of-voice signals that the sentence can have other added relational meanings.

Here's an example. Let's say your grandmother takes a fall and your mother tells you 'She's going to be okay?' using the rising pitch of a question instead of the typical falling pitch of a statement. From the statement 'She's going to be okay?' you can understand the literal message that *your mother thinks your grandmother is going to be okay*. But with the rising pitch at the end of what is otherwise a typical statement sentence, your mother is also sending you three additional meta-messages:

1. She hopes your grandmother is going to be okay.
2. She is worried and not sure whether your grandmother is going to be okay.
3. She wants you to be okay with this information.

The first meta-message expresses the statement with some uncertainty and tells the listener that what the speaker is saying isn't fact but a sincere hope; the second meta-message emphasizes the speaker's own worry, while the third shifts into a relational concern to express worry about how the listener will manage what they've just learned. Using a questioning pitch in place of a standard statement pitch can send multiple messages beyond the explicit contents of a message. When you're a Listener of Fourteen Hearts, you are presented with the opportunity to listen for all three messages and not just the literal informational one.

Where adding a questioning pitch at the end of a statement adds multiple senses to the content of a statement, flattening out what could be a grammatical question can create a bantering tone. If instead of your grandmother taking a fall, you take a spill on the kitchen floor and a family member, seeing you're more or less alright, says in a flat tone with the discrete words 'Are. You. Okay.', you know they are not asking if you are actually uninjured but playing at a kind of subverted empathy. We'll talk more about banter in the chapter on Social Listening, but for now, remember the phlebotomist who bantered to me: 'Soon. You can't stay here on holiday forever.' Using a deadpan falling tone on top of language that referred to being in the hospital as 'on holiday', their humour worked to deliver the meta-message that they knew I wanted to go home. When someone's meta-messages are spot on, that's when you feel heard.

Listening with Fourteen Hearts 4 and 5: Volume and Pitch

I once took part in a professional development workshop that used an ice-breaker called 'Glad-Sad-Mad', a technique used to train actors to trigger emotions in performances. The facilitator explained that while actors are typically asked to use prior memory to trigger the emotional states of gladness, sadness and anger, we would find these emotions on video and discuss them as a way of getting to know one another.

As it was an entirely new kind of ice-breaker for many of us, it took us a while to settle in on one participant's video of football chanters in a pub. Initially, a volunteer classed the chanters in the selected video as *glad*, and as a group we hummed back our agreement. But as the video rolled on, the chanters' tone changed. Focusing more on the individuals of the group, we heard some of the chanters were shouting more than singing, while others were crying more than chanting. Now we weren't sure anymore whether the chanters were *glad*, *mad* or *sad* until someone suggested that perhaps the chanters' team had lost a match. Now we had a potential meaning to listen for, we could reassess the whole range of emotions the chanters were expressing.

The class reviewed the video again and reflected on how we frequently observe a range of emotions that are in fact multidimensional. Our emotions are often mixed, complex and difficult to classify in simple terms, but of course that doesn't mean we shouldn't listen for all of them. When we first see a smiling face and hear their laughter, we're likely to listen to and identify that emotion as gladness, like we did for the chanters. But as we listen for and consider what we hear and see, we're likely to better recognize middle-of-the-range, nuanced variations.

We recognize emotions best in their extremes, where our emotion reader matches excitation ranges on the extreme ends of Volume and Pitch. The emotion listeners can identify most accurately is anger, because the vocal manifestations usually occur at the high volume end. When a listener hears a person shouting and expressing themselves at the end of the speaking range that typically measures above ninety to one hundred decibels, their startle reflex switches on, adrenaline shoots through their veins and their muscles contract to protect themself from the potential threat, in the same way they would if they were physically assaulted. Anger is the emotion humans read best because our listening processors are on a danger watch for volume outside the usual range, whether screaming mad or seething quiet.

We're next best at recognizing sadness in the glad-sad-mad series but, once again, only if it is expressed on the high intensity end of the tone-of-voice gauge, with large variation in sound frequency, which humans translate and listen for as pitch. Crying, with its strong pitch variation, is the emotion we listen for and recognize as sadness, even if we can't see the person and register the associated facial expressions. Just as we listen for the shift in intonation in sentences to understand a shift in mood, we listen for shifts up and down in Pitch to judge a baby's mood.

We said earlier that babies are great at hearing and detecting pitch with a broader range of frequencies, but that adults might have the edge in listening to and understanding a baby's cries. A study of parents and non-parents showed that adults can differentiate babies' cries – for example, in requesting help, pointing to an object or protesting.[5] As adults distinguished different baby cries, they were able to vary their responses according to voice to be able to help the infants. Listening is, then, not only being able to hear a cry but also being able to navigate a beneficial response through considered listening.

As a listener, it's satisfying to be able to attend to a physical discomfort and fix it – the relief a baby feels when their discomfort is alleviated is palpable to the attending adult. It's also natural to want to be able to relieve someone's emotional discomfort when we perceive it. But in the face of many of the emotions we recognize as listeners, we aren't always able to supply an immediate fix. Everyday conversations are much more complex than the response of feeding a hungry child, and the resolution isn't so much in fixing them as showing up for them through deep listening attendance – Listening with Fourteen Hearts – because it's in the full action of listening to someone that ultimately makes them feel heard.

Seen, Heard and Understood

Before I cracked my head falling off the scooter, I used to regularly quote the great Zen master Dōgen Zenji's teaching on empathy in seeing the world as you: 'Fools see themselves as others. The wise see others as themselves.' It felt like a handy way of repeating the mantra of empathy, that it's important to be able to step into other people's shoes. Explaining it, though, did often make me wonder if you can really do such a thing as know how someone else feels by stepping into their shoes. It seemed to me that other people's shoes are hard to fill and you can never really completely feel the way someone's shoes fit them. It was only after my stay in the ICU that I realized that what the Master was actually saying was not that you need to step into someone else's shoes, but into the in-between relational space between you and them when you listen. This was demonstrated by the phlebotomist, who, as someone in the ICU on a daily basis, could share my discomfort of being there and my wish to go home. Listening with Fourteen Hearts is a way of stepping into and showing up for a person in that in-between space.

The idea that listening takes place in the space between two humans is written into the Japanese characters for the very word, 'human' 人間. Composed of the character for 'person' 人 and the character for 'the space-in-between' 間,* it implies that every listening experience presents the opportunity to

---

* Like informational listening, the character for 'the space-in-between' has gates, but instead of an ear pressed up to it, there is a sun 日, as if to conjure *light coming through from between the gates.*

step into the in-between space between two people so that you can gain a little more insight about another person. A Zen Buddhist like Master Dōgen Zenji might tell you that it's in this in-between space where you can find the stillness of true sound – silence. What we actually say and listen for in a really good chat isn't as important as the feeling we walk away with that comes from the energies of a mutual Listening with Fourteen Hearts. If you've ever answered the question, 'What were you talking about?' with, 'Oh, nothing', smiling about the heartwarming chat you've just had, you've probably felt seen, heard and understood in that in-between space, having experienced Listening with Fourteen Hearts.

Listening with Fourteen Hearts for the Human Voice

Our listening has the capacity to identify the timbre of a human voice and distinguish one person from another as we can listen for and learn more about them in that moment through their volume, pitch and any changes in amplitude or other tone of voice. When we tune in to a person's voice, we can further identify whether a shouting stranger or a crying baby might be glad, mad or sad – or, as is often the case, a complex, changing mixture of many emotions. As voice triggers the release of a cocktail of neurohormones for listeners that prompts us to hear people, it activates Listening with Fourteen Hearts to see and feel them in the in-between space where we join in together.

Although empathy has become an overwhelming if somewhat judgemental term that is required of someone to be a good person, in its plain form it's really something we do intuitively when we're hanging out with the people we care about in our everyday listening. By listening in the channels of Amplifiers, Shifters, Volume or Pitch, we can hear all sorts of complex emotional priorities and relational tones of those we tune in to in our shared in-between spaces. Empathy is listening out for hungry dads and daughters who talk about 'moTHERs' when they're not at their best. It's how we understand family and close friends we frequently interact with, but also others we're about to get to know. When a person catches our attention and calls on us to listen, our fourteen channels of listening provide us with all the bandwidth we need not only to recognize who they are, but also to feel out what's happening in their day.

Listening is how we attain the level of power superstar animals gain with their hearing. Like the greater wax moth that can hear at fifteen times the frequency of humans, the wolf that can hear a call up to nearly ten miles away or the shark that can use their hearing echolocation to navigate from Africa to Australia and back, we can listen to potentially soak in and relieve grief, disarm anger or show up and go the distance. Ultimately, what I learned in the ICU was that listening with Fourteen Hearts isn't just so you can breathe on your own – it's so you can share that sentient space and live together with others.

7 Listening with Fourteen Hearts Competences You Might Not Know You Have

- You have a **startle reflex** that hears loud sounds and alerts you of danger to keep you safe. You can also hear loud volume and a wide frequency range and interpret the neurohormonal expressions as the emotions of anger and sadness respectively.

- You **listen for** voice more than you listen to voice by making associations between what you've heard before and what you're hearing now, and this is how you translate your hearing into listening.

- You can listen for **Timbre** to recognize the voice of someone you know.

- You can listen for **Amplifiers**, such as emphasis in accented words in English or staccato words in Japanese, to get a sense of what matters to the speaker.

- You can listen for **Shifters**, changes in intonation that can indicate relational messages of empathy or subverted play. A shift from falling to rising intonation in statements can signal a relational meta-message about the people in the conversation. A shift from rising to falling intonation in grammatical questions can signal irony or banter.

- You can hear **Volume** and **Pitch** and recognize simple emotions. You can hear anger in amplified volume and sadness in pitch shifts.

■ When you listen more deeply, you can understand more complex emotions that are best experienced in empathy in the in-between space rather than 'fixed' through advice.

3 Listening with Fourteen Hearts Applications

- **Voice ID game:** The next time you gather with family or friends, close your eyes and see who you can identify by voice. How is your voice ID? What do you hear in the voices of people you know well? A friend once told me that one of the small things they enjoyed the most is having friends over and hearing the happy tones of friends' voices interacting from another room, even when they couldn't actually hear what was being said. What are your favourite things about listening to familiar voices? Can you tell what they're talking about even though you can't actually hear what they're saying?

- **Listen to a baby cry:** Is the baby crying hard in a loud volume and/or is there a lot of pitch change up and down the soundwave frequency? Can you tell what the baby is crying for?

- **Listening-channel check-ins:** Observe how you listen using these five Listening with Fourteen Hearts speech channels in one of your next listening experiences. Do voice ID and listening-channel check-ins with your friends to spark conversation and to get to know your closest people even better.

5 Listening with Fourteen Hearts Listening Channels
- Timbre
- Amplifier
- Shifter
- Volume
- Pitch

Don't Forget to Get Your
Hearing Hardware Checked!

The World Health Organization (WHO) reports that over 1.5 billion people globally live with some degree of hearing loss. While nearly one third of people over sixty-five experience disabling hearing loss, this isn't something that just affects older people. An estimated 34 million children have hearing loss, of which 60 per cent is due to preventable causes, such as infections and medication, and about 1.1 billion young people aged twelve to thirty-five are at risk of having noise-induced hearing loss due to recreational exposure.

Hearing loss can creep up on you. The Royal National Institute for Deafness say most people start to lose their hearing at around the age of forty. As many as one in four US adults who reported excellent to good hearing were found to already have hearing damage.[6] In the UK, one in six people have some degree of hearing loss, and many more don't know it.

The big cost of hearing loss isn't only the billions spent in health and educational treatment and support. The biting personal cost is that when you lose your hearing, you don't just lose a few hair cells and nerve fibres, you also lose your listening. When your cochlea and auditory cortex don't get to play and process sounds anymore, your listening stops hearing music the way it used to.

Fortunately, there's help in the form of modern technology and cutting-edge hearing aids. There are hearing aids today that look just like earphones. No one has to know you're even wearing them. It's funny, though, since despite the availability of hearing tests and aids, studies show that people don't listen! Even in the UK, where a hearing check is free, people wait on average ten years before seeking help for their hearing loss and often only after a third party has brought on an intervention.

The good news is that while studies show that hearing loss can lead to depression and increase the risk of dementia by up to five times, treatments like wearing a hearing aid can reduce the risk of any of these outcomes.[7] Being able to hear so you can listen to know what's going on in the world around you in all its detail is as important as being able to see it. Chances are you probably don't have hearing loss, but as my audiologist reminded me, prevention is better than treatment. Get your hearing checked so you can take full advantage of your listening.

2

Informational Listening

Listening at the gates

Listening helps us find things. When our phone rings, we know where it is. When an announcement is made at the airport, it helps us to find our gate. At home, at work and at play, we ask about things and listen to find an answer. As one of the most intelligent tools humans have cultivated, listening helps us to find language to track the information we need.

Without our listening intelligence, we can't find the most basic information we need. I learned this the hard way, at first in a New York City kindergarten and then in a primary school in Tokyo. At four years old in NYC, I found out that you can't find anything without the English language, and then three years later in Tokyo, I discovered the same thing, but this time in Japanese! Picture a seven-year-old following the instructional fingers of her classmates helpfully pointing down the hall from her primary school homeroom towards the toilets. She heads off in the right direction to three signs above three identical doors and, feeling a little like a contestant in one of those game shows, randomly chooses a door to go through, only to find that instead of the toilet she's desperate for, she has ended up in the principal's office!

Remember the story about how I missed my bus stop and got lost on my first day of school in Tokyo because I was daydreaming and didn't listen to the announcement? Well, now that I had arrived at school, I still had to figure out how to find my way. Because my mother had followed the recommendation of the Ministry of Education that decreed that children didn't need to be able to read Japanese characters until they entered primary school and other students' parents didn't, they could read the sign for 'Toilets', for example, whereas I couldn't. So there I was, making the brutal discovery that without language, you can't find the right doors to get you to the place you want to be.

Language gets you the information you need, whether by reading written text, by listening for auditory information in the form of language and voice, or by visual and tactile information made available through nonverbal language. We'll talk about nonverbal language in chapter five in more detail, but here we explore Informational Listening that gives you access to intelligence you didn't have a moment ago by means of a spoken language. Like a password, Informational Listening gives you admittance to *listen in from outside the gates* to all the coded words available to its communicating members. That's the meaning of the character for listening that heads this chapter.

Language has boggled the minds of scholars from a variety of disciplines for millennia. Linguists, lexicologists, literary critics, psychologists, philosophers, sociologists, anthropologists and neurobiologists have all grappled with the complexities of language alongside those who have examined its use in politics, marketing and business. When we explore language use, we analyze language as 'information', a word with Latin roots that carries both the senses of *shaping* and *communicating* language. In other words, 'information' is shaped and communicated language, and in this chapter, we'll talk about both these senses while exploring the formal study of language and the processes of shared information in action.

One scholar who forged the way in understanding how we actively onboard information was Nobel Prize laureate and economist Daniel Kahneman in his systems analysis of thinking fast and slow, which explains the two modes our brains use to process information and make decisions. Piggybacking on his idea, we can understand the Informational Listening channel as also composed of two modes: one for listening fast to find information in simple language – like picking up an announcement in a train station – and one for listening slow to find relational meaning in the more complex language information supplied in conversation.

To listen for and understand informational language, we need both modalities, and to find them in this chapter, we're going to first try and find where language is located in the brain. From there, we will journey on to observe language the way lexicologists do, as words we store in our minds. Once we have explored the words we listen for, we can fast forward to look at an example of how machine language mirrors us in listening fast, and then end the chapter by uncovering a key principle that ultimately makes listening for information between two people work in listening slow.

Listening for Informational Language in the Human Brain

The brain is the place where language is born. That has been the theory of neuroanatomists since the seventeenth century, when the study of listening for language as a science began. A pinnacle moment on the path to finding the hearing brain in neuroanatomy is often attributed to nineteenth-century physiologists Eduard Hitzig and Gustav Fritsch, who were conducting experiments on dog brains to identify different perceptive areas within the larger thinking cerebral cortex. In the same era, anatomist Richard Heschl then located an area in the temporal lobe of the brain now known as the 'Heschl's gyrus' that was thought to be responsible for our auditory hearing. The scientific community agrees that this area – now more commonly referred to as our 'primary auditory cortex' – is generally the part of the brain that hears and processes language.

Around the same time in the nineteenth century, acousticians were studying how sound travelled through substances like air and water. Connecting the wave theory of sound that emerged from these studies to the physiology of hearing, the physicist and physician Hermann von Helmholtz explored sound in instruments, giving detailed descriptions of important qualities such as vibration and resonance. Advancing the idea that the ear perceives pitch by breaking down complex sounds, it was von Helmholtz who introduced the idea of timbre and the unique quality of sound we talked about in the previous chapter.

Meanwhile, neuroanatomists were deepening their debate

on the exact location of language in the brain. Correlating patients exhibiting language difficulties with compromised parts of their brain, the neuropathologists Carl Wernicke and Pierre Paul Broca advanced the idea that auditory processing happens in two different parts of the brain, one dealing with language production and the other with language comprehension. They reached these conclusions based on patients who had brain injuries in the left frontal lobe near the motor cortex and presented with problems in language production, for example, in forming words and fluency, while patients who had injuries in the lateral fissure of the temporal lobe retained physical fluency but produced language that was incomprehensible. As a result of the work of these scientists, the condition of language loss called 'aphasia', with difficulty in physical fluency, became known as Broca's aphasia and the condition of language loss with difficulty in producing comprehensible language became known as Wernicke's aphasia, the kind of language loss that would most significantly impact our language comprehension.

Though both of these theories of language location in the brain were absorbed into neurology-related fields today, they are contested on the grounds of variability across patients. Indeed, diagnostic instruments like magnetic resonance imaging (MRI) and functional magnetic resonance imaging (fMRI) that investigate ongoing metabolic activity in the brain have since discovered that no two brains work identically. Some patients with language loss, for example, were found to be able to recover language, while others couldn't. With every new study, we are discovering that brains differ between individuals and are even more complex and plastic than we have previously thought.

Today, investigators of language in the brain tend to think of its representation as fluid and interrelated in neural pathways. Although the Broca's area is still thought to be mainly responsible for speech articulation and long-term encoding of words into memory, and Wernicke's area is responsible for sound and meaning recognition, instead of strictly fixed areas in the brain, the areas are conjured as occurring in dynamic communication, explaining more plausibly how our brains synthesize information from other receptive sources such as vision to listen and comprehend language in its entirety.

This all helps to explain our brains' versatility in processing language. However, while the human brain is equipped to cope with a vast amount of information, it isn't infinite and doesn't perform its best when overwhelmed. For the human brain to be efficient, it needs and optimizes for listening comprehension. Listening fast and slow each provide their own modality of optimization, and here we look at each in turn.

Listening Fast and Listening Slow

If you've ever lost a child in one of the world's busiest train stations, you'll know that the first stress reaction isn't fight or flight – it's freeze. Thankfully, while I was debilitated by my fright coma, nature rolled up its sleeves and sent in its best panic hormones. As adrenaline expanded my airways and pumped around the extra blood needed to focus on my search for my suddenly missing daughter, my auditory system got ready by calling up what linguists call a 'selective auditory attention'. Loaded up alongside the adrenaline, selective auditory attention dials down background noise and homes in on the focus of your attention in that moment. For me, standing in Paris's Gare du Nord – the third loudest train station after Shinjuku in Tokyo and Grand Central in New York – it was listening for any potential announcement about my seven-year-old.

To optimize the efficiency of listening fast, we target information. Information is the priority, the *what* of our search. When we are listening in this mode, we can obtain the information quickly without much concern for anything or anyone else. Our focus is as singular and clear as a radio searching for a channel. As we exclusively target information, our listening selectively dials down background noise and actively drives out distracting ambient sounds – like the hum of people milling around in a noisy train station.

Obtaining this singular focus isn't easy, though, because competing sounds vie for your attention. Whereas you can be in relative control when you're listening to a friend in a noisy café, or in a video call where the platform controls and selects your auditory attention by reducing background noise and enhancing the voice of the speaker talking, you might not be able to gain this advantage in a noisy train station where other sounds call out at the extremities of your hearing range to catch your attention. It isn't just announcements that are designed to hover slightly above the ambient noise, at something like one hundred decibels, sirens too cut through background noise and interrupt whatever is the current focus of our attention.

Volume just outside the upper end of our hearing range is designed to get our attention. A siren that blares out above a hundred decibels is an alarm signal that is specifically aimed at agitating psychological excitation[1] to force us to take notice. It's because we know that sound at any volume that features at the extremes of the intensity measure of excitation, high or low, good or bad, music or noise, wedding bells or fire alarms, draws our attention that humans shout. A siren is a mechanical noise shouting, *Stop what you're doing and get out of the way!*

Now here's where it gets interesting. Because when our listening fast mode is on and we hear a siren, we'll react and conform to the generic meaning implied in the direct instruction. We'll get out of the way in traffic, instantly obeying what the signal tells us to do. But as soon as we give ourselves time to listen slow, we begin to personalize the meaning of the instruction. Overlapping with the focus of the signal is your own focus on whatever you were doing as you heard the siren, like driving to work or looking for your daughter. As you begin to reflect on your immediate reaction to the sound when you were listening fast, this is when you begin listening slow. When you begin to consider your own concerns, you personalize the generic sound of the siren to continue about your way, which in my partner's case means *follow the ambulance so you can drive faster*, or in my case at the train station meant hearing the siren in my daughter's voice 'Neeno neeno' to get back on the task of finding her.

Like the timbre in a loved one's voice, sounds and language motivate personalized associative memories to recall, which help us remember them better. Researchers found that personalized informational cues significantly enhanced recall compared to the generic ones.[2] Our listening slow system is smart because it knows that personalized memories are the ones we most vividly remember. Personalized listening is what makes generic information most relevant to our very particular situation in the here and now.

In Informational Listening, you activate your selective auditory focus to recall generic meanings, honing and updating them with each new experience. The morning alarm on your phone might come with a factory setting that generically means *Wake up!* when it goes off. On mornings when you have an early meeting to attend or a flight to catch, your personalized meaning is likely to correspond with the factory setting. You'll probably listen fast and promptly wake up. But on another morning when there isn't a morning meeting and you're working from home, you might listen slow and stay in bed a little longer as you make the alarm sound relevant to the schedule of your day. You might personalize the alarm you hear to mean you can have five more minutes in bed, which means you'll likely hit the snooze!

We grow our collection of meaning-sounds – whether it's the timbre of a voice, a tone of voice, words in a language, or even an automated sound like the washing machine telling you it has finished – through this process of attaching a meaning that is updated in each new episode of experience. Learning the sounds and words we need for Informational Listening is a kind of forestation project that populates our internal dictionaries with personal meanings alongside generic ones. In listening fast, we need a selective auditory focus, but in listening slow, we draw on the resource of our lifetime experiences to make what we are listening to relevant to us. Like two currents in a river, the systems of listening fast and slow complement each other in our search to grasp words and their meanings in Informational Listening.

The spoiler alert to my lost-daughter drama is that I found her, or else I probably would be too devastated to tell the story. I actually found her twice – once by listening fast to the announcement and the second time in person by listening slow in the back-and-forth verification that finally physically connected me to my daughter in the handover. I'll tell you about how I listened slow to mind the other person in addition to myself personally in more detail in just a moment, but first let's take a moment to look at the 'what' of informational language when we're listening for and focusing on the generic meaning when we don't have to mind the personalized meanings of the people in the conversation. We'll start with words and continue on to grammar, because although words and grammar are misunderstood for their stuffiness, they are the stuff in language that together dress it up and make meaning in conversation.

Building our Word Forest

In Japanese characters, 'word' is written as 言葉, literally meaning *spoken leaves*. As the final expression of a tree, leaves are how you recognize a tree, just like a voice is how you recognize someone you know. Spoken words are also how you recognize a language. To someone who doesn't know the tree, all the spoken leaves of a language sound the same. But to someone who does know the tree, each leaf is different and together they make up an impression of the tree. As word forest managers who look after various language tree varieties, humans tend to more than 7,100 spoken languages in the world, according to the language database, Ethnologue;[3] at the same time, however, about 90% of these languages have less than 100,000 speakers. Historical linguists who study the origins of languages and how they relate to one another visualize them as branches of a language family tree. English is part of the Indo-European language family, so that from the perspective of a historical linguist, every time you're listening to words in English, you're listening to the word leaves on the Germanic branch of the Indo-European language family in the forest of human language trees.

Another way of classifying a language is by compiling a list of words that comprise it. Linguists call this collection of words a 'lexicon', which, translated from Latin, roughly means *spoken words we use together*. When a lexicon is categorized for reference purposes, today we call it a 'dictionary'. Although we think of dictionaries as written rather than spoken because we see them in print, the word 'dictionary' descends from Latin *dicere*, which means 'to say', so dictionaries are actually meant to represent spoken language. Words in dictionaries are generic spoken word leaves which we personalize by using them. This means that when we listen fast to track spoken words where we don't have to mind the other person, such as in announcements, we listen for their generic meanings. But when we listen slow for words in conversation, we are trying to understand the personal nuances of one person to another that go beyond the generic meanings. It's because we aren't identical or generic talking dictionaries that sometimes we think we're talking about the same thing when actually we aren't.

Early English dictionaries were intended primarily as a description of the language for learning purposes. One of the oldest English lexicons was curated by English grammarian and poet John of Garland in 1220 when he was teaching at the medieval University of Paris, but the earliest English language dictionary we know about is Robert Cawdrey's *Table Alphabeticall* published in 1604 with some 2,543 entries, which can still be found in the Bodleian Library in Oxford in its fourth edition. Cawdrey said the purpose of making a dictionary was to facilitate the understanding of 'hard usual words'. By 'hard', Cawdrey probably thought about words less commonly used and by 'usual', he likely meant words used in everyday speech. 'Hard usual words' were the words you would hear from time to time, but not all the time. Arguably, one the most famous collection of hard usual words in English can be found in Samuel Johnson's dictionary published in 1755, which is still on display where he lived off Fleet Street in London. Dr Johnson's *A Dictionary of the English Language* was in use until the mother of English dictionaries, the Oxford English Dictionary, more commonly referred to by its initials as the 'OED', was published in 1884.

By 1989, the OED had expanded to a 20-volume, 21,728-page dictionary, but the third edition published in 2010 is said to have some 600,000+ entries, dwarfing the number of words of its language competitor across the channel. By contrast, the fortieth edition of the most widely used single French-language dictionary, *Le Petit Robert*, contains 60,000 words. Ironically, one of the reasons English dictionaries have many more entries is because of the influx of French words into English that took place during and after the Norman Conquest in 1066.

In practice, though, any theory of language dominance based on number of words in a dictionary is silly because, as every Scrabble player is aware, we don't know all 600,000 words in the *OED*. The most comprehensive analysis of common words an average first-language speaker of English 'knows' was conducted by lexicographers examining a text database of more than 2 billion words in the 'Oxford English Corpus'. In simple terms, a text corpus is like a library of texts that researchers use to study language. The top twenty-five of the 2 billion words listed comprise about a third of the words we know and use most in written English, suggesting that in everyday speaking, we tend to emphasize the *usual* side of Cawdrey's Alphabeticall dictionary rather than the *hard* ones, meaning that we know many more words than we habitually use.

Furthermore, while we can get some sense of the most common words we use, and presumably read, by analyzing written records of words like those found in the Oxford English Corpus, finding out how many spoken words we actually use and hear is notoriously more difficult, originally because of the logistics of transcription. However, even when machines took over the tasks of transcription and tabulation, lexicographers still had the major challenge of how to account for meaning. For example, although it's easy enough to count the word 'fly' as two words, as in the insect and something travelling through the air, how should lexicographers consider words in their grammatical variations? Are 'fly' and 'flew' two words or one?

So here's where grammar can step in to resolve the dilemma as a powerful instrument of language that at once helps us constrain it with its rules and at the same time generates a potentially infinite number of combinations of words in a sentence. Specially, grammar carries meaning, and if you're a first-language learner you know intuitively what a second-language learner of English learns analytically, namely that 'fly' and 'flew' are in present and past tenses respectively. They are two separate words with two different meanings. A plane that *flew* in yesterday means something critically different than a plane that *flies* in today. Only if we disregard the conjugation and count 'fly' and 'flew' as two words, what about the 'fly' that can be used in the present tense to mean future action – for example, if you say, 'I fly tomorrow'? What second-language learners would have learned as the present simple tense can be made to indicate a scheduled future event, which adds yet another meaning to the concept of *fly*.

Complicating matters further, words don't only have literal meanings. They have idiomatic, metaphorical and personal ones. To say *something flew* may mean that it moved quickly, and not necessarily while airborne. She *flew* out the door. Time *flies* and, apparently, so did my daughter at the Gare du Nord, according to the kind man who gave me the information, 'She flew that way.' Sadly, after a 360 visual search, I was able to ascertain that she had indeed *moved quickly* through the crowd because she was nowhere to be seen. Words are difficult to tally because they have grammatical but also situational meaning in context.

Undaunted by such challenges of counting words, Professor Marc Brysbaert of Ghent University took on the challenge of tabulating the average number of words a person knows, finding that the US American participants of his 2016 study could identify 42,000 words by the time they were twenty and 48,000 words by the age of sixty.[4] But although identifying a word might mean we've 'heard of' the word before, it still might not mean we 'know' its meaning (or all of its meanings). It's perhaps why other estimates came out much lower, with the *Economist*'s 2013 study of US Americans stating a vocabulary knowledge in the order of 20,000 to 35,000 words,[5] and lexicographer and TV adjudicator for *Countdown* Susie Dent echoing the idea that while adult vocabulary can reach 40,000, most first-language English speakers limit themselves to around 20,000.[6] Regardless, 20,000 words still sounds to me like a lot of words to use and listen for, given that I struggled with acquiring 2,000-plus characters upon my return to Japan.

Knowing more 'hard usual words' is undoubtedly useful in winning Scrabble or Wordle battles. More importantly, perhaps, is that psychologists believe that a large vocabulary eases a listener's 'cognitive load' – in listening, this could translate to the idea that the more words you know, the easier it is to make out what someone is saying. Despite the cognitive easing we gain from knowing more words, however, English speakers and listeners communicate most frequently with very few, as you can see from the list of the top twenty-five most used words in English.

Top 25 Most Used Words in English[7]

1. the
2. be
3. to
4. of
5. and
6. a
7. in
8. that

9. have
10. I
11. it
12. for
13. not
14. on
15. with
16. he
17. as
18. you
19. do
20. at
21. this
22. but
23. his
24. by
25. from

Unsurprisingly, perhaps, these aren't the hard, erudite words but the connectors of our language we think of loosely as grammar. Grammar plays an important role in helping us say what we mean and personalize what we want to say. As the top contender in the list of most commonly used words, 'the' helps specify a particular thing that, a moment ago was the general thing, 'a' – it helps personalize what the speaker, who goes by the tenth most commonly used word, 'I', wants to say. In listening, we systematically analyze these small, seemingly insignificant pieces of grammar to obtain the information we are searching for.

Grammar makes our language efficient, helping to optimize listening fast and making it unnecessary to have an extraordinary number of words to say what we mean or a huge repertoire of vocabulary to listen for and understand what most people say. Despite the popular belief that correlated large vocabulary to intelligence propagated in some social circles until the early parts of the twentieth century and still resurfaces in various guises today, knowing a greater number of words doesn't automatically result in better language listening comprehension, and having a larger vocabulary doesn't make the language users more listening competent either.

In fact, almost to the contrary: what the large size of the English language dictionary imposes on listeners is the greater possibility for misinterpretation. With 1.456 billion speakers, the English language is the world's most commonly used language, a lingua franca adopted as a common medium of communication between speakers with many different first languages. What makes the English language so important today is that second-language learners of English comprise a critical three-quarters majority. Compare this 75 per cent of the total number of English speakers learning it as a second language to, say, Mandarin Chinese, whose second-language speakers make up only 18 per cent. The fact that the majority of English-language speakers are bilingual means that when we are listening to English, it is often in the context of people who bridge other language cultures.

The fact that second-language speakers of English are the majority is important not only for researchers of intercultural communication, but for all listeners of the English language, because in conversation, we often assume we're listening to the same 'English' when actually we aren't. Numerous studies

Top 10 Languages Spoken in the World as First and Second Languages 2024[8]

Language	L1 First-Language Speakers	L2 Second-Language Speakers	L1+L2 Total Speakers
1 English[*]	380 million	1,135 million	1,515 million
2 Mandarin Chinese[†]	941	199	1,140
3 Hindi	345	264	609
4 Spanish	486	74	560
5 Modern Standard Arabic[‡]	0	332	332
6 French	74	238	312
7 Bengali	237	41	278
8 Portuguese[§]	236	27	264
9 Russian[§]	148	108	256
10 Urdu	70	168	238

[*] Excluding Creole languages   [†] Excluding other varieties of Chinese
[‡] Excluding dialects   [§] L1 + L2 total is rounded

demonstrate that knowledge of another language and its culture can impact the way a person speaks and comprehends a second language. We typically notice these different 'Englishes' through accent and regional expressions; however, we'll see in a later chapter on intercultural communication that cultural language can transfer from one culture to another at much deeper levels, creating the potential to wreak all matter of confusion and misunderstanding.

The three-quarter majority of second-language speakers of English places an important demand on both the speaker and the listener, highlighting the idea that what they mean may not necessarily be heard that way by the listener. We know that personalizing meaning already makes it difficult for two people to have the exact same word meaning, and this mismatch is magnified in interaction in English because of its diversity of speakers. The upshot of this is that listeners of English are likely to be exposed to many non-generic meanings of words, that contain personal but also cultural meanings, making us vulnerable to misunderstanding the way we are in intercultural listening where communicators think they're talking about the same thing when actually they aren't. We'll talk more about intercultural misinterpretations in chapter six, but for now we need to keep in mind that the availability of the English language is also what makes it open to miscommunication.

The high number of second-language speakers and the sheer size of the English language drives the need for clear language production on the part of the speaker and openness of interpretation on the part of the listener. Especially in situations where interpersonal familiarity amongst the communicators is low, a speaker can minimize misunderstanding and help their listeners by being simple and clear. But the onus of communication isn't solely the responsibility of the speaker and a listener can promote better rapport by remaining open to the idea that any ambiguity in meaning can be explored in further conversation in the manner of asking, 'Is this what you mean?', a question which might not be most appropriate to ask in the immediate here and now but taken up at a later point in time. The hunt for informational meaning can take time. It can be fast or slow – a tracking number or a negotiated understanding about someone we are called upon to use in a listening opportunity.

Tracking Fast in Informational Listening

In order to listen fast for informational language, we need to target words we know. If we didn't, we'd have to search through those 20,000-plus words we know magnified by some gruelling factor of combination that grammar enables. Even twenty words can generate an unwieldy number of sentences, which in theory could number something like 10^{20}, or 100,000,000,000,000,000,000.[9] Memorizing all possible sentence combinations so we can understand what we hear isn't practical – it would truly take us billions of years to say and understand all possible sentences in the human language. Fortunately, our brains don't work like this because we learn a finite number of rules of language to generate an infinite number of sentences, a skill that first-language speakers of English acquire mostly before formal schooling. We are wowed by machines we think of as fast processors but actually, machines are modelled on us. Humans can listen fast, and we listened this way before machines did.

In 1956, long before AI, the mathematician and linguist Noam Chomsky and mathematician and physician Marcel-Paul Shützenberger published a theory of information that proposed a model to explain how humans are able to generate an infinite number of sentences. Though little known outside of academic circles of the time, the Chomsky–Shützenberger model would ultimately influence not only the development of computational linguistics and AI, but also enable computers to simulate and understand human language. By assigning meanings to words and grammar, and creating instructions for what words came next and where to find them, the Chomsky-Shützenberger model was the first major step in teaching machines how to 'talk' and 'listen'.

One simple machine application that the Chomsky–Shützenberger model influenced is information extraction. Information extraction has several modes of search algorithms, but the one that we can use to understand how we listen fast is called 'hashing'. Whereas other linear algorithms go into a pool of data, say, of 20,000 words, and look up every one, a hashing search takes a shortcut, specifically tagging a word with coded data instructing on where to look for more specific data. When I asked an engineer at a tech company how a machine 'listens', they explained that computers simulate the fast listening humans do by selectively matching typical word patterns with those in their database. By searching the surrounding context of a word, a computer can approximate its most likely meaning based on things like the frequency and rarity of its occurrence in its database, a little like hashing the name of a train destination in a scheduling announcement. Because you are listening for a specific word and tracking it through your selective auditory focus, when the announcement comes on over the loudspeaker, you can easily find the information you need.*

When we track a word in listening fast, we scan its context the way we have taught machines to do. We regularly

---

* The fact that machine language was influenced by Professor Noam Chomsky's work is hugely ironic because he sees human language as aesthetic and nothing like what machines can do.

rely on early information to predict what could happen next, for example the electronic white noise similar to the sound of tinnitus in my left ear that comes on when the broadcast system turns on at the Gare du Nord. From my personalized past experiences of announcements in train stations, I know a routine train scheduling announcement is frequently preceded by a jingle, and I'd be delighted to hear that generic jingle if I'm about to catch a train but less so when I'm looking for personal information that concerns my daughter.

That's why a pause in the system after it turns on instead of a jingle feels promising. There's meaning in words but also in the pauses that separate them. What comes before a hashed word can be predictive of what's coming next in informational language, whether it's a word, a shift in tone of voice we discussed in chapter one, or even a pause. Whatever the signal we use to track and listen fast for our message, it happens in the blink of an eye, or what neuropsychologists have variously computed as something of a mere 200 milliseconds.[10] For me, what that meant at the Gare du Nord, after I hashed my daughter's name in the announcement, was to hear the words that told me they found her, accompanied by the following instruction: 'Would her mother please come and collect her at the information centre.' Listening fast explains how we can optimize getting the specific information we're searching for, although it can't actually explain what it feels like when you find your daughter and her Hello Kitty sandwiched between two gendarmes, Remington 870s at their chests. For that memory, forever stored in my personalized database, I thank my lucky stars, because hardly any other memory reminds me of the benefit we can gain from listening slow.

Listening Slow

At the information desk at the Gare du Nord, I breathed again having been reunited with my daughter. But I next had to complete a successful security check to verify I was actually the person they called out in the announcement. This involved a conversation, which wasn't as straightforward as the generic etymological meaning of the word 'con' and 'verse' of *putting together verses* might lead us to believe. Humans don't talk in full sentences with all our words arranged in perfect grammatical fashion, although they might follow critical rules that affect meaning, like English sentence order of subject, verb and object (SOV). First-language speakers are mostly not conscious of grammatical rules and we often leave out words, or repeat them in fits and starts, and sometimes even use gesture as if words are redundant or hard to find. What's amazing, though, is that even as we do this, listeners can decipher what we're trying to say.

Three important researchers of listening and language help explain how listeners can understand things when the informational language is incomplete, absent or even sometimes contradictory. We've already mentioned psychologist Daniel Kahneman, whose work with his colleague Amos Tversky explained the systems of thinking fast and slow. We borrowed Kahneman's thinking systems here to understand how we listen fast for informational language, using shortcuts like hashing, and how we listen slow when we need to process the information and weigh our decisions. When we hash a word and listen fast, we don't need a full sentence. When we think slow and reflect on what someone tells us, on the other hand, we have time to fill in the missing pieces to understand what the other person could have meant, by matching what someone says to what we have stored in our dictionaries, which are not only filled with information about words, but information about the different ways in which people can actively use those words.

Here's where our second influential scholar, the philosopher of language J. L. Austin, was revolutionary. In his 1955 Harvard lectures, Austin advanced the idea that we actually 'do' things just by saying things. He explained that words are 'speech acts' that can accomplish things – like a religious marriage by a priest proclaiming, 'I now pronounce you husband and wife'. Once heard, we can surmise that the action has been fulfilled.

Austin identified seven basic functions of language in his theory of speech acts:

1. Assertions that state or describe something.
2. Questions that ask for information.
3. Commands that give orders or instructions.
4. Promises that commit to a future action.
5. Apologies that express regret or remorse.
6. Invitations that offer or request participation.
7. Rejections that refuse offers or requests.

In reality, there are more than these seven speech acts, but like Cawdrey's 'hard usual words', these are the common functions we use every day, the rules of sentence grammar of things we say. If someone says, 'I feel bad about not being able to come', you can understand they mean number five, an apology, even if all they say is 'I feel bad' and not 'sorry', and they don't supply the rest of the sentence, or maybe even just send you a nonverbal signal of dejected puppy-dog eyes. By referring to our dictionary of functions, we're able to understand what someone is saying even if they leave out the information in words.

Next time you're out and about, just observe the number of times you use any such 'usual' functions in your everyday listening. Common are numbers six and seven, invitation/ rejection. If you ask your co-worker, 'Hey, can you go for coffee?' and they reply, 'I have to finish something', they know you've invited them for coffee, and you can listen and understand that they have rejected the offer even though they haven't said so in words. Thankfully, they were gentle in letting you down and didn't reply, 'No, I cannot go for coffee with you,' even though that would be a more accurate, if literal, response. Our ability to listen slow kicks in to help us understand the function of rejection even without the direct language that tells us 'no'. Listening slow allows us to x-ray sentences and see through to their intended functions even without the literal words.

At the information centre at the Gare du Nord, the security officer asked, 'Can we see some ID?' It's easy to see that the officer's speech act is a generic question that conforms to the second function in Austin's list, but also the third function, a command. Like the Glad-Sad-Mad emotions we talked about in the previous chapter, our speech acts are often combinations and blends which we can recognize as listeners. As I responded by showing my personal ID, I said 'yes' to the question and complied with the command because I knew that this was a crucial step in being reunited with my daughter.

As a series of functions we act out and respond to, human language is an attractive model for machine language. Call-

54

ing what humans do 'natural language processing', or NLP for short, computational linguists and AI programmers have admired us so much that they have modelled machine language in our image. Today, NLP has AI applications in the traditional areas of machine translation and information search, but programmers are also pushing the boundaries to explore language in the listening slow areas of speech recognition and sentiment analysis. While machines and their programmers love human language for much of what we do in listening slow, we admire machines for the human-like language that they can process infinitely faster than we can. For example, when you ask a question of a search engine, it will return results in far less time than it would take a human brain to understand the question.

Philosopher Paul Grice is our final language expert who can help us understand how we accomplish the feat of listening for informational language even when that information is sketchy. Grice theorized that listening for and understanding indirect, vague or even off-topic language is possible because of something he called 'the Cooperative Principle' that suggests that communicators have an implicit agreement to cooperate with each other to ensure meaningful communication. Grice's Cooperative Principle consists of four 'maxims' communicators needed to fulfil in any interaction:

- **Quality:** say what you believe to be true
- **Quantity:** say what you have to say in the right amount
- **Relevance:** keep to the topic in hand
- **Manner:** be clear and avoid ambiguity

Grice proposed that in conversation, it's safe to assume that most people are actually trying to communicate something and that they'll try to stick to doing this using the optimal manner of the cooperative principle of being truthful, relevant, clear and appropriate. Grice's Cooperative Principle advances the ubiquitous idea that humans bank on cooperation as a way of making sense of everyday conversations. Grice argued that the assumption of cooperation is what helps communicators understand the function of information, so that if a work colleague replies, 'I have to finish something' to your invitation to go have coffee, you can understand the informational function that they are turning you down, if ever so cooperatively, without explicitly using the word 'no' or saying, 'I can't go'. 'I have to finish something' has the implicit function of denying your request and the only way you can make sense of it is to assume that your colleague is cooperating in the conversation and saying something relevant to reply to your invitation.

Informational language that comes from an announcement is different from informational language that comes from interacting with another human because in listening to announcements we do not have to mind another person. When we do have to think of another person, though, we need to manage the relational aspect of the informational language, too. It's often why we deviate from saying exactly what we mean – to uphold social politeness principles that negatively value rejection. Because we see rejection as uncooperative, we devise ways of saying no to soften the impact and sound like we're not saying no even though we are.

The Japanese are famous for being unable to say no. In a study comparing Japanese and American bankers' conversations, I identified ten distinct ways the Japanese say no without actually using the word or even saying anything using words. In fact, as in English, one way to reject something is not to reply. If a listener-turned-speaker responds with something that sounds like (but isn't) a no, then they are breaking the maxim of Manner in the Cooperative Principle of being clear and unambiguous to be more convivial and socially friendly. Part of being cooperative in conversation is knowing how to gently skirt the rules in the interest of tact.

When the Cooperative Principle is put into jeopardy, a listener is called to level up their reading of what's happening, as I once was on the Zurich autobahn, when a man in a black Mercedes chased me down, pulling up alongside me to motion a gesture I mistook as some kind of inappropriate invitation. As I drove faster and faster to get away from him, he increased his speed to go above the speed limit, too. This was curious for me, because the Swiss, like the Japanese, are stereotyped as rule-abiders. When I pulled off the autobahn and stopped at a light the man pulled up alongside me and lowered his window. As I looked straight ahead to nonverbally communicate what I thought was the fairly universal function of rejection, the man upped his ante with another stereotypically curious act and began shouting out his now-open window. Forced to listen, though, I then finally realized why he was tailing me. 'Your tyre is kaput!' I heard him say, using the number one function in Austin's list of assertion to tell me that my tyres were dangerously low! Rather than being inappropriate, the man was being informative and kind. Informational Listening involves competence in recognizing the signals that alert us to its functionality.

One alert signal we discussed in the previous chapter is amplification. Shouting as the driver did on the autobahn is an amplified tone of voice that goes outside of the normal speaking range to signal something is out of the ordinary. Like turn-signals on a car, listeners use such indicators to notice informational language that doesn't conform to our typical expectations. By listening for Amplifiers, Shifters and any other change in tone of voice, we can deploy our Listening with Fourteen Hearts to inform our understanding of informational language – but in considered time, so we can work out its function that may not be immediately obvious. When you're listening by *doing* language like this – and you do it all the time – you're allowing yourself time to listen slow to get a better grasp of the immediate situation.

Hare and Tortoise

We have been collecting informational language through listening experiences our whole lives, gaining supporting evidence for the auditory cortex to integrate the information it hears with other perceptions, and then sending out the processed information to other parts of the brain for further language processing. Somewhere in these language regions lie our generic dictionaries, ready for sharing in social relationships, so that we can grow our personal dictionaries of meaning in sounds, words, grammar and pauses as we hash words to obtain information fast. Our ability to track words and find information has proven to be so compelling that we now have technology made in our image that does what we do but even faster.

It's easy to get mesmerized by speed and fast information, but fast isn't always better when we're trying to understand other humans through the language they use. We recognize this when misunderstandings arise, which surprisingly occur just as much between people who know each other well as between those who don't. Spellbound by the speed of machines, perhaps we've become good at fast-tracking information at the cost of listening slow for the information we need to understand each other in cooperation.

In our practices of listening going forward, we need to complement the tech gains we have made in fast information processing with slow, considered understanding. Everyday listening is a delicate mashup of Aesop's fable of the hare and the tortoise. We love the hare for its speed and wit, but we also admire the tortoise for its slow persistence.

With an awareness of informational listening competencies, we can have both. In obtaining information you need here and now, think train platform announcements, listen as fast as the hare. You know what you want and what you're listening for, and it's satisfying to know how to obtain that kind of information fast. In conversation, though, give cooperation its due time to flourish. To get to know someone, always remember to turn on your inner tortoise and listen slow – it could help you see the implicit meanings that aren't in the words. By using both systems of listening, fast and slow, listeners can optimize the ability to be both hare and tortoise, and find the information you're listening for.

聞く Listening for informational language is gaining access to get inside the gates. In the words of Austin, it's a way of doing-listening that allows us to learn because, as the great Dalai Lama once said, talking is about repeating things you already know, but listening is about learning something new. Starting from my first day back in a Japanese school, I learned the 2,000-plus characters you're supposed to know to be able to read a paper. And though I confess I did find myself back in the principal's office, it was for different reasons. Since then, I've taken to heart the lesson I learned that listening for informational language is important in our learning journeys, whether we want to obtain simple information quickly or gain understanding about someone over time. Listening fast and listening slow: we need them both to optimize what we learn when we meet informational language at the gates.

7 Informational Listening Competences

- Listening helps us find out about things and people through **selective auditory attention** so we can zero in on what we need to find and tune down background noise.

- We give generic and personal meaning to the information we listen for, and attach our own social importance to the things we listen to.

- We listen fast and listen slow. To optimize listening for informational knowledge, we need both systems.

- We listen fast to obtain simple and specific information we want to know – for example, the platform number of the train we're taking.

- Like humans, machines also use 'hashing' to help us to listen fast. We hash words to listen predictively.

- We listen slow in cooperation to understand indirect language and fill in gaps in conversation.

- Humans listen for speech acts to understand underlying functions of language, such as promises and requests, and to pick up on politeness and implicit meaning in conversation.

3 Informational Listening Reflections:
Find things fast, discover people slow

Take time in your day to think about whether you're listening fast or slow:

- Were there any words you recently tagged/hashed to obtain information you wanted fast?

- Reflect on a time you used or heard a rejection without actually saying 'no'. How did you do this?

- Notice other times you listen slow to supply all the missing words for the informational language to be complete and understand what someone is saying.

3

Soft Listening

初心者

Novice Heart Practitioner

'Coochy-coo', we say in what developmental linguists call 'baby talk'. Then we listen. We wait for an adoring face to answer back. You know the one. It's because hardly any person listens to us the way a baby does that makes them so irresistible. If you want to study the way to win someone over, don't study C-suite executives but babies that make you the absolute centre of their auditory and visual focus instead.

Babies put you first because they put listening first. For the baby listener, listening not speaking, is at the start line. This begins in utero and by the time they are born, a baby's hearing range beats adults' hands down. Babies can hear at the extreme ends of the human hearing range of about 20 to 20,000 Hertz, a bigger range than what most teens can hear. But while their hearing ability is superior, it's their listening intensity that is enviable. When you were a baby, you were a shining example of Zen Master Dōgen Zenji's vision of empathy in Listening with Fourteen Hearts – of seeing others as yourself.

You could argue that seeing others as yourself is easy for babies. Not long ago, when they began hearing, they were hearing their mother as themselves. In the womb, a human foetus learns to hear what's going on in the outside world at somewhere between sixteen and twenty-five weeks into their gestation. Unable to see outside of the womb, their lungs filled with amniotic fluid, hearing has about a five-month lead on vocalization, which is typically expressed at birth as a cry only after expelling the amniotic fluid that has been in their lungs.

Hearing for a foetus means something slightly different than it does for a newborn. Sound comes to them by way of vibrations in a mother's amniotic fluid, so they are actually hearing an echo of what their mother does through the soundwaves in the fluid. A foetus and mother, literally joined together by a single cord, actually hear the world as one. Perhaps it's why the word for 'together' 一緒 in Japanese is made up of two characters, 'one' and 'cord', that conjure an image of how, when two people are together, they are connected by a single thread.

So yes, when babies are born, perhaps it is easy for them to apply their Zen master skills in the outside world, now not only hearing a speaker as connected to them by a single cord, but also listening to them by that same connection. When a baby first starts listening to a caregiver speaking outside the womb, it's a natural progression to keep listening to the caregiver as themselves. As the fruit of their highly intensive and personalized twenty-week hearing training in utero, their excitement on discovering the wonder of this new in-person listening is infectious and demonstrated by their wide-eyed expressions, raspberries and leg kicks.

In this chapter, we'll explore how a child acquires Soft Listening, a learning skill they develop before their verbal language acquisition. We'll begin by looking at why humans need Soft Listening and how this early learning in many ways resembles the way songbirds learn how to sing. We'll then spend some time understanding how children learn to listen for language, exploring the critical period of listening for a first language based on neurological research and reassessing how we might appreciate copying as a form of listening.

Home is where babies learn language, but it's also the source of the energy they'll need for a future of Listening with Fourteen Hearts for informational language. You'll discover a key learning skill you have hidden inside you as a Soft Listener, and how children systematically harness it in language using what developmental psychologists called 'fast-mapping'. Fast-mapping is an important foray into the way we develop what linguists call a 'semantic field', a set of words with related meaning. We'll see how semantic fields build the way we conceptualize the world and influence the way we learn and listen. Our chapter finishes by suggesting a way of incorporating the Soft Listening we had as children into our everyday listening to revitalize our communication.

Altricial Listening: Songbirds and Humans

There have been many systems used to distinguish between living organisms. One interesting classification that developed in the early part of the twentieth century is the altricial-precocial spectrum. This categorizes species by the degree of development at birth or hatching and their subsequent dependence on care. The word 'altricial' comes from Latin and means 'nourishing'; it refers to offspring that require nurturing after they are born. The word 'precocial' is also derived from Latin and means 'early ripening', referring to species whose young are relatively self-sufficient at birth or soon after hatching. Horses, deer and some bird species like duck or geese that can feed themselves and follow their parents only moments after birth fall in the precocial range of the spectrum, while rodents, humans and birds – especially songbirds – fall in the altricial range, since these animals require care and feeding from their caregivers in order to survive.

Songbirds are a highly illustrative altricial animal. When songbirds hatch, they develop their songs by first listening to the songs of their caregivers, then practise by mimicking their usually male parent's song. Studies have shown that not only is learning the parent's song crucial to their survival, but also that the chicks' learning is better consolidated when they interact with live teachers the researchers call 'tutors' than when they listen merely to recorded songs.[1] Songbirds that were deprived of their parents' songs and left without feedback presented incomplete songs that did not match their parents'. From these studies, we can infer that altricial songbirds learn to listen to their song in the company of their parents.

Like altricial songbirds, human babies learn both voice and language through their caregivers by way of interactive experience. Altricial humans model themselves on their caregiver's voice and speech at that point in utero when their ability to hear begins to develop.

Crying is a baby's first vocalization, although initially it isn't part of their learning to speak but an expression of their own personal discomfort and distress. It's only when human babies begin cooing and gurgling that they first show signs they are trying to make songs like their caregivers do, only they don't yet know that this is the precursor to language. When a baby first listens to adults use 'baby-talk', they tune in to the exaggerated sing-song tone to learn its melody so that they can eventually deliver a language like English. 'Good morning. Did you keep us up all night? Yes, you did!'

The atricial human baby starts to reply to baby talk at about three months old, in the form of coos and gurgles, like a songbird's first notes, which sends the relational meta-message, *I'm listening. I heard you.* A baby's coo demonstrates simultaneous listening and talking the way adults do when they back channel 'uhuh uhuh' to demonstrate their listening and show they are switched on and focused on someone's voice. Babies, though, demonstrate this kind of intense listening all the time, which is exactly how they can make adults feel that they are the centre of their selective attention.

As babies learn to respond to the voices of their caregivers, they begin to focus on short spurts of sound that are segmented by pauses. When eventually they begin to reproduce these sounds, to the adult ears, they first sound like babble. But babbling is an important listening-to-speaking transformational period of language learning that helps babies learn what linguists call the 'prosody' of language. Prosody is the general rhythm and song of a language we make by expelling breath through our voice boxes. In other words, babies learn language by hearing the whole melody first rather than by learning notes one by one, the typical way adult second-language learners do. 'Ma, ma, ma' and 'ba, ba, ba' are the refrains they'll hear, listen for and rehearse to eventually arrive at the segmented words 'mama' and 'baba' in conversational language.

When a baby starts to babble, this is usually the point at which adults say they are starting to 'talk'. Babbling can start as early as nine or ten months in a baby's first year outside the womb and is an important stage in a baby's listening and speaking development. That said, each baby's development is highly personal, and while growth charts provide an interesting gauge for milestones averages, they sometimes produce more anxiety in parents than they merit. We know that a child will eventually learn something in the range of 20,000 words in their operating language. This begins at home, the heart of first language learning and the epicentre of learning to listen.

Learning Soft Listening at Home

Two decades ago, I used to get the strangest looks whenever I discussed how Japanese business relations were based on what I previously called 'sweet interdependence', which, together with the acquisition of language, provides us with the two key ingredients that make up Soft Listening. Back then, when there was no understanding of emotional intelligence, anything that had to do with human feeling was systematically checked at the door before going to work. Although discussions of feelings and emotions did exist in the careful confines of classes like Stanford Business School's Interpersonal Relations class, they were amiably called 'touchy feely' and somewhat sidelined to the study of business management and 'real' business. The idea that the kind of closeness that existed at home when we were babies should exist anywhere outside still caused a lot of discomfort.

This chapter won't suggest going into work and hugging your boss, but it does challenge the idea that Soft Listening can only be enjoyed by babies and people around them at home.

Soft Listening draws on the power that is fostered when we first learn listening. There are conversations and interactions in our adult lives in which we let the other person take charge, the way adults do with children, and children do with adults when they use Soft Listening at home. In communication, one way to let the other person take charge is to let them become the speaker. As they talk, we assume the role of the Soft Listener and keep generating the relational soft power from the space in between the people in the conversation.

Soft Listening is employed in the Japanese context of 'sweet interdependence', a relational feeling of reciprocal nurturing that can have wildly positive or negative outcomes, depending on how it is used. Sweet interdependence, or just 'sweetness', is a transliteration of the Japanese character *amae* 甘え, a concept that has been variously translated as 'indulgence' and 'dependence'. Although it has some elements of both of these words in English, it doesn't include the human weakness implied in either of them.

Amae occurs in a range of feeling; it is the ageless and inclusive sweet spot where a nurturer and nurtured can both taste its sweetness. *Amae* interdependence can be observed not only between a mother and her child and vice versa, but also outside the home and between adults, for example, the appreciation a colleague shows by their willingness to learn from another at work. *Amae* has a powerful, if sensitive, sensor that when expressed or experienced in too great or little amount can also easily make an indulger spoiling or aloof, or an indulged person selfish. For example, when an adult in a close relationship doesn't indulge in *amae* and holds back, the Japanese call this behaviour *mizukusai*, which literally means 'smelling of water' and implies an emotion that isn't at its fullest. It's watered down. Used for someone who is behaving inauthentically in an overly reserved manner, it's as if they had diluted a good cup of sake. I was recently called *mizukusai* when I apologized to a friend who paid for something for me.

When we are learning to listen as babies, we indulge in boundless Soft Listening, the kind of relational *amae* and sweet interdependence that isn't limited by social convention the way it is when we become adolescents and then adults. With multiple demands placed on them, adults cannot indulge themselves in limitless *amae*, and so its expression is suppressed and regulated by their social groups. Luckily, though, in cultures where interdependence is celebrated even as adults, we can find novel ways for rekindling the old sweet interdependence we had as children.

In a trip to Japan during the pandemic, my family was theoretically only allowed a fifteen-minute visit with my father. Usually, when I begin to tell this story, most people nod knowingly at the rule-bound nature of the Japanese, especially in times of crisis. And yet when the head nurse walked in at the fifteen-minute mark to hear my father boasting to his grandchildren at the foot of his bed about his school days, she didn't expel us all as I feared she might. Instead, she used her discretionary power to break the rule about visiting hours and allowed us to stay for the rest of the day. As tenderly as the child who listens to their grieving grandmother and comforts them by sitting on their lap, the simplest action of bending the rules to accommodate the occasion can soften the hardest rules designed to promote public safety and efficiency. Soft Listening is what we sometimes call 'giving in', a way of prioritizing *amae* interdependence, and putting the relationship first.

Turning up Soft Listening Amplitude for Language

Even babies and their caregivers don't have sweet interdependence turned up full twenty-four-seven. Humans turn down their *amae* channel so they can turn up the other key channel in Soft Listening: learning through language. After acquiring a sense of language prosody (music), atricial human babies begin the voracious acquisition of the amazingly complex and intricate instruments of grammar and meaning.

Some amount of interdependent *amae*, though, can be instrumental to a baby's learning of grammar. Unlike with the sure-fire language-learning motivation killer typical of traditional formal language-learning that teaches a rule and then how to apply it, researchers have found that creating opportunities for language acquisition using a wealth of emotional and relational connection like the one that fosters sweet interdependence between caregivers and children, promotes better retention.[2] For example, in a study where participants were asked to recall words associated with and without emotional content, participants were better able to retain words, and more accurately recall its source, when these words were associated with emotional content than without it.[3] It's not surprising then that babies are better learners of their first language than classroom-language-learners of a second language, since the former experience a host of direct and relevant emotional experiences in interaction with their caregivers on a daily basis. We learn best in Soft Listening environments.

Critical Period for Language Listening Acquisition

Although research on language development has been traditionally biased towards speaking, one area that has focused on a baby's listening intelligence is whether or not language-learning has a biological expiry date. The standard answer has historically been affirmative – neurologists have claimed that there is a critical time period in which the brain is primed for language learning. Although some studies end the critical period at age seven or eight, before which it is claimed that a language can be learned and spoken as a first-language speaker would without an accent,[4] the generally agreed optimal time for child language acquisition first identified by neurologist Eric Heinz Lenneberg is before puberty, when the brain is observed to be hyper-plastic and most adept at linguistic processing.[5]

Still, like the milestones of first-language acquisition, language proficiency 'without an accent' varies widely from person to person and depends on the context of learning. Just within the petri dish of my own family, for instance, my mother learned English after puberty at eighteen, outside of Lenneberg's critical time period. Most of her listeners though would agree that she spoke English without a Japanese accent, but instead with a recognizable southern lilt since the first English-speaking place she lived was the US state of Kentucky.

Although listening for language and the resultant vocabulary acquisition isn't a marker of human intelligence, we're often told that it is. This is reinforced in everything from spelling bees to public speaking in work contexts; we reward the idea of using big words well at school and in the workplace. Driven by the idea that a child with a broad vocabulary is likely not only to be intelligent but also successful, schools have traditionally prioritized speaking skills and let listening skills fall off the list.

Vocabulary still remains a marker of developmental intelligence, and one researcher who set out to track language development in children by counting the number of words they spoke was Klaus Wagner. Sewing in a mini microphone bug into nine-and-a-half-year-old Theresa's blouse in 1972, Wagner recorded some 804 minutes of running speech, calculating that Theresa spoke a total of 28,142 German words a day. While it was debatable whether Wagner's quantification led to estimating a child's intelligence, most German listeners of the recording agreed that Theresa demonstrated a proficient command of the language even at the young age of nine.

It's difficult to know what Wagner's study means in universal terms of a child's language development and intelligence – not only because it is challenging to say how many concepts Theresa knew by counting the number of words she spoke, but also because an 804-minute recording is likely to produce a different word count if made in a different language, like English. The linguist David Crystal points out, for example, that the word *Einbahnstrasse* in German translates into three words in English but has the same concept in either language, denoting 'one way street'.[6] This helps support the idea of our last chapter that the number of words you know doesn't correlate with your intelligence, as that would mean the English speaker who heard and understood the three words is more intelligent than a German-listener like Theresa, who only understood the concept as one word.

As with adults, children listen to new words and listen for old ones primarily to learn and consolidate their listening comprehension. As the debate about the critical language acquisition period rolls on, listeners can keep in mind that many of the early studies into this area were experiments set up in laboratories or based on patients who were not healthy individuals, like the wild child, Genie, who, found in Arcadia, California in the United States at the age of thirteen, having been isolated and deprived of human language contact, wasn't able to achieve proficiency in her first language. It's important for caregivers teaching and practising Soft Listening to know that Genie had developmental hearing and listening challenges from severe social neglect, and not because a caregiver didn't get around to reading her a bedtime story on Wednesday and Thursday nights because they were working.

In fact, in stark contrast to caregivers, who may worry about how best to aid their development, children usually take on first-language acquisition with almost alarming nonchalance, making music of language with their own prosodies, then learning word chunks. Some language pedagogists argue that babies around the world have a universal and natural progression to the acquisition of sounds, starting with voiced vowels like 'a', 'i' and 'u', and then combining them with consonants to form easy words like 'mama'. The idea that a baby's first word is one that refers to their primary caregiver is a tantalizingly appealing theory for caregiving listeners to which I confess I fell prey, only to be humbled by my firstborn, whose first word was not 'mama', or not even the second candidate for most-likeable caregiver, 'papa', but 'conco', short for 'Concorde', the supersonic passenger airliner that operated from 1976 to 2003. It was a hard reminder for both his caregivers just how important it is to understand milestones and statistical probabilities of first words for what they are – averages and typical examples that sometimes don't match your own children's language and listening progress. Since then, I've updated my dictionary understanding of listening for a child's first words to include the personal entry learned through Soft Listening – that it was highly possible that in his early days of gestation, the supersonic sound of Concorde ripping across the London skies was amongst the first exciting sounds he listened to and intrigued him most.

That said about typical first words, from about sixteen weeks onwards, a typical baby begins not only to produce sound clusters but also becomes a keen listener of them. As the start of a long process that unfolds over their first years, it's the early days of the practice of learning to recognize words. One of the first words a baby comes to appreciate is their own name, which a caregiver uses with high frequency and exaggerated intonation in their baby-talk with them.

The social interaction involved in a baby hearing and listening to their name is important to their Soft Listening because being called by their name is the first instance of in-person face-to-face identification outside the womb. Listening for their name becomes the eventual demonstration of recognizing how someone else recognizes you. As a baby hears their name, they turn their heads towards the person who is calling them as practice towards understanding that this other person is not them. Because mother and baby are no longer physically connected, listening helps the baby stay connected and learn about the caregiver as a social person. By listening to their caregiver in their first operational language, babies connect and listen for their own name to set the stage for more sophisticated communication later on.

As a baby learns to recognize themselves as the referent of their name, they begin to understand that communication is composed of speakers and listeners. This first step into Soft Listening for language eases the baby into the world outside the womb, where they first learn that there is a prosody in language, meaning there is a relational tone of voice that takes the listener into account and one which will ultimately support the words in the operational language. As their babble takes on the feeling of a melody ready for lyrics, it's how, at ten to fourteen months, they begin supplying words to the tune they've learned.

Although it's hard to remember what language sounded like to us before we knew how to segment what we heard as words, we're likely to have heard words the way we hear long compound words, like 'hippopotomonstrosesquippedaliophobia', which ironically is the fear of long words. We don't know what the first words we understood were, but short, 'easy' words like 'mama', 'dada', 'baby', 'milk', 'bye-bye', 'hello', 'no', 'yes', 'dog' and 'cat' are the likely candidates. Ask your family what words they first heard you say and share these with friends. The discussion might provide interesting insights into what your earliest interests were, which no doubt levelled up a considerable amount in year two, when Soft Listening for language goes into overdrive.

Level Up: Year Two and the Development of the Semantic Field

With a strong listening foundation, children often have a serious vocabulary spurt in their second year, recognizing not only words that mean things and people they can point to in their environment, but also words of action, such as 'come' and 'go'. In their second year, children also begin to take on abstract and conceptual information about place, quantity and time, demonstrating their acquisition of this listening knowledge by speaking them out loud. 'Here'. 'More'. 'Again'. Armed with a new arsenal of vocabulary they can manipulate, a child's listening appetite increases exponentially until they reach the two-word combo stage developmental linguists call 'telegraphic speech', like 'come here' and 'no more'.

When a child combines their newfound knowledge of telegraphic speech and tone of voice, their sentences suddenly begin to sound more like the adult sentences they have been listening to for a while. As seasoned language learners, children learn to manipulate the words they have listened for in two-word telegraphic phrases like 'more' and 'juice', combining them with a rising intonation to form the question, 'More juice?' or a falling one to create the function of a demand for their caregiver, 'More juice!' Eventually, with multiple listenings of their caregiver, children learn the word 'no', one of the most powerful words to use in telegraphic speech: 'No more!' 'No go!'

The telegraphic phase of speech development coincides with a critical developmental time period called 'the terrible twos'. Matured beyond the point of recognizing themselves in the mirror, they develop the consciousness to see themselves from another person's point of view. To provide evidence for this soft learning, they use their telegraphic speech to assert 'Chris more juice'. Eventually, in the second half of the second year or so, children begin to grasp the abstract grammatical concept of substituting a personal pronoun for their name, such as in 'Me more juice'.

Learning to Grow a Word Forest in a Semantic Field

As children's appetite for words keeps expanding throughout the second year, they actively develop new strategies to listen for and acquire words. In the last chapter on listening for information, we talked about how a word in Japanese is written as 'a spoken leaf'. One way linguists believe children expand their listening amplitude is by developing what they call a 'semantic field'. A semantic field is simply a set of words with related meaning, like a forest of word trees with a shared theme. For example, the semantic field of the word 'tree' might include its physical components 'trunk', 'branch', 'leaf', 'root' and 'bark'. It might also include words that indicate what the tree produces, such as 'seed', 'fruit', and 'sap', and more complex ideas like 'canopy' and 'photosynthesis'.

Semantic fields are highly sensitive to culture. A Japanese person's semantic field of a tree is likely to be influenced by the written character for *tree* 木 where two trees joined together as 林 means 'woods' and three combined trees 森 means 'forest'. Words in a Japanese dictionary aren't categorized alphabetically but by semantic fields, like some of the ones we've already talked about so far – tree 木, gate 門 or heart 心.

An awareness of semantic fields is important in developing an understanding of how we listen because it helps us see how we conceptualize words, not in isolation but in connection to other words and ideas. When we listen to someone talk, we don't hear each word in isolation but connected to other words in the same semantic field. In other words, every time we hear the sounds 'ma ma', we don't only listen for and conceptualize the concept of *mama* but also *baba*, too.

A baby does the same except that in the beginning, they are learning the concepts in the semantic fields for the first time. By babbling the sounds 'ma ma ma' and 'ba ba ba' they set up hypotheses they'll test in further babbles and confirm with feedback from their caregivers and observations through other sensory cues like visual and tactile listening that complement their auditory listening. For example, if a caregiver articulates the word 'tree' while pointing at a tree in the woods, a child connects the word they hear to the tree they see that the caregiver has pointed out. If a caregiver says, 'Look over there, your brother is standing like a tree,' your semantic field of trees might next overlap with your brother's as well as other concepts that entail the rigidity of the tree. Over time, as each word is connected to other words in their own semantic field but also those of the others, the forest of words become more richly interconnected.

As children gain experience in their developing semantic fields, they begin to use a learning tool developmental psychologists call 'fast-mapping', a cognitive process whereby initial associations between new words and their meanings are rapidly formed with only limited exposure to the words. For example, if a child hears a word and sees an unfamiliar object like a book, they can quickly associate the word with the book even if they have only heard the word once. Although a child's initial understanding of a fast-mapped word may be imprecise, that doesn't matter because they will have the occasion to refine their definition. Even if they call a magazine 'book', they'll later have the opportunity to learn that some bigger but thinner and floppier books are called 'magazines'. Fast-mapping is like the draft of a word, or a definition of the word in beta – a concept we'll come back to in a later chapter. While some linguists theorize that children are born hardwired and pre-programmed to produce language and fast-map, others argue that they learn to do this through repeated exposure to the words of a language. While the jury may still be out on exactly how a child learns to conceptualize words before reproducing them in their own speech, both theories help explain how children build their own personal dictionaries first before they learn the generic meanings outside the home. We learn to listen for voice and informational language at home and then confirm, modify or expand what we learned when we get to school and, much later, at work.

Semantic fields expand to include names and its attributed character traits that build the way we perceive the world. It wasn't until I went to university that I learned the true ending to the Aesop's fable 'The Ant and the Grasshopper'. The story I had listened to was my mother's soft-telling of the Japanese adaptation of Aesop's story called 'The Ant and the Cicada', where the ant and the cicada were entirely different characters from the original story. Instead of closing the door on the grasshopper and leaving it to die as it did in 'The Ant and the Grasshopper', the ant invites the cicada in at the end in gratitude for having entertained it all summer with song. Soft Listening approaches learning semantic meaning as what people value in their world rather than as a measure of correctness. It involves the process of learning and updating, inviting active engagement in retaining new information, but also the energy to be supple enough to augment, modify or change prior information we have learned. Sometimes, listening involves unlearning.

Soft Listening: A Revision of Copy Cats

World over, we think of child language learners as copiers, by which we mean they mimic actions they've seen and repeat words they've heard. When we think of children copying adult words, we often conjure a child producing an inferior version of the word an adult said, diminishing it through the action of copying. But like a DJ that curates and delivers music by other artists, or a filmmaker that adapts a novel, copying is a form of reproduction that demonstrates something that has been listened for – a way of personalizing what we are learning.

A friend who trained as chaplain at Yale New Haven Hospital shared a transcript of conversations used in a hospital setting whereby chaplain–patient engagements are shared with the supervisors and peers. In one conversation, a patient expresses their gratitude for the chaplain's listening attention by reflecting that they should get together with their family to practise the kind of Soft Listening the chaplain practised with them more often. My friend said the 'copying' the patient was intending on doing was one of the highest forms of compliments a chaplain could hope for.

Copying plays a key role in a child's development of listening skills. By observing their caregivers, family and playmates, children learn about how selective auditory attention works and, at the same time, how to personalize and orchestrate language when it is their turn to talk. This new learning takes energy, which children expend by using all the sensory feelers described in the Listening with Fourteen Hearts character 聴, their eyes and ears, but also the energy of their mind and fourteen hearts. When we copy the words of a language, they pass through the semantic fields in our brain as neural signals, which we hone through repeated exposure to listening and listening again.

Over time, our copied productions that recall past listening observations become increasingly nuanced to meet different environments, enabling us to use the context of the situation to predict what might happen next. Having already received positive feedback for listening for voice and learning that returning a smile after the 'coochy-coo' is likely to lead to more conversation and longer play, we might continue doing so to create longer bouts of conversation, which linguists call 'turn-taking'. It's how children learn the repetitive back-and-forth process of adult turn-taking, not only copying adults but also being interactively encouraged by them to continue the conversation and keep it going.

Studies in early childhood education show that the interactive quality of turn-taking found in activities such as reading together with children sharpens their listening skills to deepen language comprehension and broaden their voice. By simulating turn-taking in conversation, taking turns in reading can copy and re-enact interactive repetition to enhance Soft Listening skills.

Turn-taking is crucial in adult social dialogue: copying the practice helps the child understand its mechanics not only to speak in turn but also to listen. Turn-taking from the perspective of the speaker might be the I-go-you-go turn at talk, but from the perspective of the listener, it's the much more complicated demonstrated response of I-think-this-is-what-you-meant-so-this-is-how-I'm-replying. Caregivers can teach their children turn-taking by giving them the space to process what they heard and pausing for a reply. In infancy, a child's response might be a coo or a gurgle, but later those coos will develop into more complex words or feeling gestures of demonstrated listening.

Japanese children learn turn-taking for talk, but they first learn to emphasize turn-taking that demonstrates their listening. Called *aizuchi*, the two characters that compose the word in Japanese literally mean 'fellow' and 'mallet', and conjure a blacksmith hammering out a sword, much like two people hammering out a conversation. Japanese use *aizuchi* like the 'mhm, mhm' back-channel cues English listeners use to demonstrate that they are present and following people in a conversation, practising Soft Listening. This demonstrated listening for voice is very similar to what babies do when they are first listening to their caregiver, and remains intact throughout the child's development and into a Japanese adult's life.

Amongst the most heart-warming of Soft Listening bonding rituals are caregiver–child interactions in bedtime rituals like lullabies, prayers and bedtime stories. One of my favourite videos of a bedtime story shows a Japanese father reading and then pausing for his son to demonstrate his *aizuchi* listening. A big hug theoretically ends the father's reading session, as the two celebrate their interdependence and the son's mastery of demonstrated listening feedback. But more laughing ignites as the son asks for another reading, repeating the favourite word of *amae*, sweet interdependence spoken by children all over the world: 'Again!'

Incorporating the Child Learner's Novice Mindset in Adult Soft Listening

Moving countries every three years in your childhood isn't something I would recommend, but my early nomadic experience was not without its benefits. One particularly useful tool nomadic children learn to use to survive different cultures, languages and school systems is the deployment of a 'beginner's mind' of approaching each new experience as if it were the first. Although a beginner's mind is a formal concept that comes from the Zen Buddhist word 'novice heart', written as 初心, and composed of the character 初 to represent 'apprentice learning' and 心 to represent 'heart', I prefer the translation 'novice mindset' that headlines this chapter with the added agent 者 who practises the novice mindset, because it articulates the idea that someone with agency is intentionally practising the novice mindset, rather than the beginner who just happens to be starting a role. A novice mindset is an intended practice that requires the effort of adaptation experienced by many nomad and immigrant children.

One of the first memories I have of learning with a novice mindset took place in the doorway of a New York City pre-school. The bell had rung to end our recess and as we dragged ourselves to the doorway, the other pre-school class came pouring out. First to the door, I let everybody come out, until Megan told me something then bumped past me. Even though I couldn't understand a word of English then, like the dog in the cartoon trying to understand what their owner is saying by the speech bubble above their head filled with exclamation marks, I could more or less tell what she was saying with the volume of her voice: *Get inside!* Then, looking over my shoulder to confirm my listening understanding, I saw what the others were doing and copied them. It was a simple exercise in allowing my novice mindset to adjust to the situation then discover that what I initially thought was highly individualized mayhem was rectified in the classroom where we were all back together in what then seemed like the most sensible way for returning to the classroom on time.

Listening with a novice mindset helped me learn about and adapt to a new culture that emphasized entering and exiting a building through a personalized means rather than through the socialized means of group culture. To adapt to this new culture with the individual as a focus, I used Soft Listening, observing what I saw and heard around me, and then copied the information I had learned that day. This action of moving with feedback information is what some superhearing animals do when they echolocate. When bats listen to bounced back soundwaves, they can navigate in the dark. When humans copy other humans, we too can learn from bounceback information the way I did in the New York kindergarten, which, as anyone who has lived there will attest, is no small feat!

As an adult, a novice mindset can also open the mind to learning about new voices and information. Although it's difficult to call up the novice intensity you once had as a child, you can reactivate your novice mindset by listening to both the voices and the echoed voices of those around you. Soft Listening with a novice mindset can help us step into the present space to take on information afresh, accompanied by the resilience to face challenging topics and understand different people we don't yet completely comprehend. While a novice mindset doesn't mean that misunderstandings won't ever arise or that we'll be achieving understanding at the snap of our fingers, it does mean we can update and cultivate a listening practice with which we can learn and grow.

So, in summary, amongst the many Soft Listening strategies children first learn, there are three important ones that are based on the sweet interdependence, *amae*, that is the nest egg for listening to learn. Soft Listening helps us learn to take turns, back-channel and expand our semantic fields. When our open-mindedness towards learning helps us develop our novice mindset, we can use it to approach each new listening experience as if it were the first. As a way of building readiness for new information that allows us to have more tolerance for uncertainty, a novice mindset has the potential to onboard change effectively, copying as we go along to get closer to our learning goals, and ultimately creating the wonder that is so often the biggest reward of learning.

Founder of the Center for Communicating Sciences at Stony Brook University, Alan Alda, says that listening is actually allowing ourselves to be changed by another person. Implicit in Soft Listening is the trust we place in someone else, despite the risk of being changed by them. In an ideal world, we wouldn't need to gauge that risk, but in our actual, in-person world, where the currency of interdependence is volatile, we often do. It's why alongside Soft Listening, we need Credibility Listening, the stream of listening we'll discover next.

7 Soft Listening Discoveries

- The language acquisition process that occurs in the first few years is a crucial part of human intelligence and listening. Babies develop their hearing between eighteen and twenty-five weeks of gestation, and have a larger hearing range than adults but require caregivers for survival.

- Babies learn Soft Listening based in *amae*, or sweet interdependence, to accelerate their learning of both voice and language.

- Although babies learn their first language from its music or prosody, they eventually learn the cognitive process of word meaning by developing their semantic field, which they expand through rapid fast-mapping, a process that enables them to use multiple sensory cues to quickly form associations between the new words they hear and their meanings with only limited exposure. Fast-mapping can be seen as an early form of listening fast.

- While traditional studies in neurology define a critical time period for a child to acquire a first language, the brain is plastic and there are many variations.

- Back-channel cues, called *aizuchi* in Japanese, form an important listening strategy children use to demonstrate they are listening.

- The benefits of copying are underrated. Copying is an example of demonstrated listening.

Soft Listening

- The Zen Buddhist practice of a novice mindset approaches each new listening experience as if it were the first. Novice Listening can help us to keep our options open so we can consolidate new learning and remain malleable.

3 Soft Listening Practices:
Activate and Enhance Your Novice Mind

■ Are there some habits or tasks you approach with a
novice mindset? List them to see if there are other
related ones you can also transfer this mindset to.

■ Have you ever tried using a novice mindset at work?
For example, reflect on what key wonders a child
would walk away with from a presentation and how
they might be used to inspire further action.

■ We often hear people say, 'I'm the only adult in
this situation' as a way of saying they are the only
responsible one. In those times of conflict, what
if, instead, you said, 'I'm the only child in this
situation' as a way of seeing the situation as one that
needs an intuitive, adaptable or playful perspective?

4

Credibility Listening

信頼性

Credibility

No one likes to be deceived. Deception violates the Cooperative Principle of communication and creates long-lasting feelings of mistrust in a listener that are hard to shift. An elderly friend who I consider my auntie said she had fallen victim to a telephone scam. My first reaction was to tell her all the usual things we tell people to avoid scams. I warned her that there was language to listen out and hash for – the Japanese correlates of words that claim quick overnight successes and life-changing products, like 'game-changer', 'disruptive technology', 'revolutionary', 'paradigm shift', 'groundbreaking' and 'world-changing'. But as my auntie chimed along, 'I know, I know', I realized what she needed now was Listening with Fourteen Hearts, an understanding ear about what had happened to her.

I also realized that the best time to avoid a scam is before it happens, and to do this we need to hone our competence in Credibility Listening so we can detect whether what someone is saying is a truth or a lie in progress. Ideally, this means we won't end up losing money in an insurance fraud like my auntie did. This chapter won't promise you'll never fall victim to a scam again, nor will it make you into a human lie detector. We'll discuss whether there is a guaranteed way of telling whether or not someone is lying by their unconscious expressions in the next chapter on nonverbal listening, as lie detection through body language is certainly a part of the story, but let's begin with the idea that we have an inbuilt critical sensitivity that allows us to get an overall reading on the truth–lie spectrum – a Credibility Listening gauge that alerts us if something sounds fishy.

In the same way you can recognize a person by the timbre of their voice, you can tell when something sounds off, too. The word 'tell' is an interesting one in English, in the same semantic field as 'say'. While both report information, our auditory focus of attention is on the speaker in the word 'say', while it is on the listener in the word 'tell'. Tell is a relational word that implies there is a listener to hear it, which is why we tell truths and lies rather than saying them. In Old English, the word 'tell' meant 'relate', but also 'count', meaning the speaker is relating a reality they have analyzed. This relating and counting – or recounting – of an analyzed reality is what happens when we tell a story, a truth or a lie. It's because truths and lies aren't opposites so much as they are at the extremes of a range that makes them so amenable for manipulation.

Credibility Listening can help us see the details of a truth or a lie against the big picture of the conversation – to see through our semantic forest of words to the stories we narrate. In tuning into a story by Listening with Fourteen Hearts, to help us connect with others, we can listen for timbre, volume, pitch, amplifier and shifter in conjunction with the informational language that's coming our way to get deep inside the structure of the truth or lie a person is telling. Activating our Credibility Listening to analyze the story a person is presenting gives us a window into their reality.

We'll begin by first reflecting on how we understand *truth* and counterbalance that with how we perceive *lies* to describe in simple terms what we're listening for. We'll work through a couple of lies in conversations to get a sense of how lies are often narrated as familiar stories, and then learn how to heighten our critical sensitivity in the talk we hear.

The Three Sides of Every Story

Film producer Robert Evans famously once said, 'There are three sides to every story: your side, my side and the truth. And no one is lying. Memories shared serve each differently.'[1]

Truth is a lofty concept that has been defined variously across disciplines as far-ranging as philosophy, literature, psychology, linguistics and mathematics. One simple way to see the concept of truth-telling in communication is through a perspective philosophers use called 'Correspondence Theory'. Correspondence Theory defines truth in language as an alignment between a statement and reality. In formal written communication secondary sources such as documents are evidence enough of the alignment between language and reality, but the substantiation of a statement and a reality is more difficult to obtain in real time, when someone is speaking.

That's where the British philosopher of language Paul Grice's Cooperative Principle of conversation and its four key maxims we perused in chapter two can be useful, since the top maxim of quality – say what you believe to be true – is the key on which the other maxims depend. Here are the maxims again:

- **Quality:** say what you believe to be true
- **Quantity:** say what you have to say in the right amount
- **Relevance:** keep to the topic in hand
- **Manner:** be clear and avoid ambiguity

For someone to be telling the truth, they need to believe they are telling the truth, and by contrast, if they believe something isn't true and they tell it anyway, then they are being untruthful. Since being untruthful undermines the maxim of quality, for the Cooperative Principle to work, a speaker should try to be as truthful as possible and avoid giving information they know to be false.

Although Grice's maxims place the onus on the speaker, the telling payoff of truth is ultimately resolved in the ears of the listener. As to whether the intentions of a speaker 'ring true', the listener has the final word. In other words, a speaker trusts their words will be well-received while at the same time a listener trusts what the speaker is saying is true. Trust is at the crux of the maxim of quality and this is literally spelled out in the Japanese characters that headline this chapter, 信頼性, where the characters for 'trust' 信頼, contains the components of 'person' 人, 'say' 言 , 'faith' 頼, and 'ability' 性, so that 'credibility' in Japanese means *the ability to place faith in what someone is saying*. The Japanese characters are a listener's interpretation of Grice's maxim of quality to say what is true.

In informal everyday conversation, listeners don't only judge what speakers say is true by the words they use, they also evaluate them by their tone of voice. Listeners tend to believe speakers who sound a bit like them, not just in their quality of talk but in their quantity, too. Grice's maxim of quantity states that to uphold the Cooperative Principle, we should generally try to convey just the right amount of information – to not be verbose, but not overly terse, either. Although listeners don't normally go around measuring conversations with Grice's verbosity yardstick, studies show that we generally like people who talk about things in the level of detail we want to hear.[2]

When we hear people talking in what we think is the right amount, we're more likely to think that what they are saying is true – they know what they're talking about. We have a Goldilocks's gauge for listening for the right amount of talk, and we hear those who achieve this as 'articulate', 'well-spoken' and 'smart', as well as speaking the truth. On the other hand, we judge people who talk more than the right amount as 'chatterboxes' or 'long-winded'. Hmm, do they really know what they're talking about and is it altogether true? We're not too positive about people on the other side of what we judge to be the appropriate 'quantity' either, since we call people who talk less 'a little quiet', and sometimes we might even call them 'sullen', 'insolent' or 'inscrutable'. Hmm, we now say, they must obviously not know what's what or be hiding something, which we'll see in a moment, is one way listeners judge someone as lying. The maxim of quantity is important to listeners because the idea we have about the ideal amount of talk shapes the way we positively or negatively evaluate people as truthful or untruthful.

Furthermore, our evaluation of the right amount of talk varies partly by how interested we are in a topic. For something to ring true, what someone is saying has to be relevant, on-topic and interesting to us. This accounts for why, in problem-solving meetings, word-counts are highest around the problem in which the meeting member in question is a stakeholder. In my study of business meetings, for example, I found that middle managers typically allocated the highest wordcounts to tasks for which they were individually responsible; their talk time was greatest when talking about the details in their own accounts.[3] Speakers tend to spend time talking about things they are invested in, and one way that listeners can hear what matters to a person is to listen to the amount of time they spend on a topic.

Verbiage and time spent talking about something, though, aren't just governed by personal interest but also by social expectation. Listeners expect speakers to abide by social rules like status and role by speaking in the right amount. For example, we generally expect those in higher positions to talk more than those in lower ones. We might also expect people in some occupations to talk more than others – we typically anticipate that a lecturer will speak for longer than an attendant taking orders at a fast-food chain and might be surprised if the lecturer's presentation consists of one or two comments or the attendant begins telling lengthy stories about the food on offer.

Finally, we are also generally more tolerant of people we like talking more, and less tolerant to hear them talking when we are not fond of them. When the likeability of source and content combine, we're all ears and are likely to believe in the credibility of both the speaker themselves and what they are saying. However, likeability can be a listener's Achilles heel, a manipulable factor that politicians, influencers and business leaders use to their advantage, talking more about the things they want us as listeners to endorse and less about things they're trying to draw away our attention from. In a press conference that lasted almost seven minutes, a politician denied an allegation in less than five seconds, showing perhaps how a lie doesn't take long to tell but, as we'll see in a moment, that defending one or covering one up does.

The Semantic Field of a Lie: When is a Lie a Lie?

Although we often think of lying as straightforward and distinguishable from the truth, the three truths of my truth, your truth and the truth, reminds us that the truth occurs in a big field of related concepts. A verdict of guilty or not guilty for those called to sit on a jury is not at all an easy process because of the moral consequences of inaccurately identifying, accusing and condemning a liar. Neither wrongful conviction nor acquittal is good for our common social health.

Thankfully, our day-to-day Credibility Listening is usually considerably less stressful than in the extreme example of the formalized setting of a courtroom. If we have a hunch that someone might be telling us a lie, social moderation will call for us to give our suspect the benefit of the doubt and let them talk as we listen slow and evaluate whether their offence is serious. While many of us prefer not to think of ourselves as judges of other people's credibility, we need to monitor the truth content of what others say to safeguard our own safety and well-being.

This was the case of Pinocchio, a puppet boy who gets into all sorts of trouble from lying. Although we often think of Pinocchio as the only liar in the story, there are many other devious characters who also tell lies. The Fox and the Cat, the puppet master Mangiafuoco, Candlewick, Lampwick and the coachman all con Pinocchio one after the other, until the puppet boy eventually resorts to lying himself, principally to cover up the fact that he sold the books the puppetmaker Geppetto bought him and then lost all the money to the scammer foxes and cats. Pinocchio commits what I call a 'cover-up lie', which can vary on our truth–lie gauge in degree and intentionality. Once we slide the marker further towards the truth side of the gauge, we arrive at what is commonly called a 'polite lie', used to protect listeners from feeling bad about something. Geppetto tells a version of the polite lie some call the 'compassionate lie' when he tells Pinocchio he sold his only winter coat because it was too warm to protect Pinocchio from feeling bad about the truth, which was that he sold the coat because he didn't have the money to buy the books Pinocchio would need for school.

We tell and listen to all kinds of polite lies that come in various intensities. The subtle polite lie is the most common of these because it is important in maintaining relationships. Like Geppetto's lie intended to save Pinocchio from feeling bad about having to sell his winter coat, polite lies like telling a friend they look great or that you like the present they gave you when you actually didn't, looks after others' feelings. A polite lie is both performative – meaning a speaker hopes to achieve the desired outcome of good relations – as well as regulatory, since listeners would prefer and even expect to hear a polite lie rather than the honest truth. In fact, most adult speakers with polite language as part of their repertoire probably wouldn't say, 'I really didn't like your present', but instead tell a lie. Indeed, Japanese comedy is filled with the kinds of things people say to try to extend this kind of polite-lie kindness in their listener relations. This variety of polite lie is not unlike the lies we tell to protect a child's innocence – tooth fairies exchange lost teeth for money, storks deliver babies, pets jump over a rainbow and go to a farm when they die.

Sometimes we tell a polite lie by pretending not to know about something and feigning ignorance. This is related to another polite lie, which is the silent lie. When my grandmother asked four-year-old me, 'I wonder what happened to that bear cub?' about the ceramic cub I had stolen from its mother's lap in the glass display case at the entrance to my grandmother's house, I replied by not answering her question or telling her of my real intention of taking it with me when we moved to New York City.

While I claim innocence about my silence in the case of the stolen bear-cub ornament, other silent lies might have more deceptive undertones. These are often referred to as a lie of omission and typically occur when someone deliberately withholds important information with the intention of deceit. An example is the potential business partner who does not disclose their past debt or financial liability. In communication, this may take the form of evasiveness, so that rather than leave a gaping hole in the conversation, a speaker might use ambiguous and general language to hide the truth. For example, a comment like, 'I think we've addressed everything we need to say about finances here,' lacks the specificity a listener needs to qualify its truthfulness. Circuitous talk generally takes longer, which brings us back to this idea of how a greater amount of talk is a potential red flag for a lie. If a person talks at length about matters that don't relate to the discussion at hand, breaking Grice's maxims of quantity and relevance, this could be as a decoy for a lie of omission or cover-up. When there is amplified talk volume, it's a good time for us to check in with our Credibility Listening.

One last kind of lie that tends to show up frequently in conversations, is the 'big-up lie' that exaggerates achievements, abilities or possessions. A listener can hear a big-up lie from someone who is trying to present themself with their best foot forward or from someone who is bragging. The big-up lie has a huge range and is highly sensitive to culture. Not surprisingly, in Japan, the land that is often caricatured as a place where people are overly polite, listeners don't consider relationally polite lies as lies at all, but consider even the smallest amount of self big-up a distasteful lie. Whereas Pinocchio's nose grows for cover-up lies, the folk-spirit Tengu's nose grows every time it brags. In short, Japanese listeners don't hear polite lies told not to hurt someone's feelings as lies, but do hear braggart lies told not to hurt one's own feelings as lies. Culture sets up the story frames around our forest of realities that speakers set up and present, and listeners interpret as true or false.

A Story Frame Set-up of a Lie

Your story, my story and the truth – a truth or a lie is most often told in the context of a story – like a photo that is framed. A frame is something a speaker uses to mark off their story, the way a camera's viewfinder outlines the boundaries of a picture. As you compose the shot, you as the storyteller decide what to include and what not to include in your frame. When you later show someone the photo, of a couple getting married, for example, they see what you put in the frame and not what you left out. They might, for instance, see the couple against the beautiful sunset on the horizon and not the rubbish that has washed up onto the beach. Similarly, if you shot a video, you might later edit it to include the wedding vows and geese honking as they take off into the sunset, and exclude the tourists having an argument, overlaying it with background music instead. Frames help photographers, videographers and storytellers guide their audience to see and hear what they want them to see and hear.

In communication, a speaker gives relevance to what they have to say by setting verbal and nonverbal language in a frame that guides what a listener hears. A frame in conversation is like the selective auditory attention we discussed in chapter one, except that whereas the listener selects the focus to their selective auditory attention – for example, choosing to hear your friend over the background noise in a café – a speaker controls what is in a frame, like the wedding couple in the photo. Framing gives the bias of power to the speaker, while selective auditory attention gives the bias of power to the listener. It's why in a situation in which the balance of power is greatly in favour of the speaker, for example in a political debate, listeners need to amp up their Credibility Listening and be highly selective about what they hear.

A frame in live, in-person interaction provides the context that shapes the information a speaker delivers and bounds the way a listener hears it.[4] One of the most effective frames we use in everyday conversations is what the cognitive linguist George Lakoff calls a 'conceptual metaphor' that uses words to present complex ideas in simple terms.[5] *Time is money. A good leader is a strong parent. Life is family.*

A conceptual metaphor can be highly useful for a speaker to fast-map an abstract or complex idea onto something familiar. For the listener, engagement with a conceptual metaphor is a little like going to watch the next film in a movie franchise. They don't have to be sold the story at all but can instead sit down with popcorn to follow along with the familiar theme. As a result of its simplicity and familiarity, listeners often don't recognize that they have been invited to listen in the frame of a particular conceptual metaphor.

The simplicity of a conceptual metaphor makes it both powerful and risky because its familiarity can frame any reality as potentially truthful and convince us to believe that whatever the person is talking about when using the metaphor is also true. Like hashing words when we're listening fast, we hash metaphors to 'get' the story so that we aren't actually listening for the credibility of the story and instead only going along with it. This is a potentially dangerous complacence, since a fast-mapped metaphor can become the place where truths are evaded, amplified and shifted in favour of the speaker. Credibility Listening is the sensitivity we can use to notice a speaker's persuasive strategies and consider the strength of truthfulness by the way they tell the story and the pictures they frame with persuasive devices like conceptual metaphors.

Time is Money

In an excerpt of a public recording,[6] a journalist who saw a British member of Parliament had received a hospitality gift raised the issue of transparency, by highlighting the lack of information an MP had provided about a gift entry in the Register of Members' Financial Interests. Although receiving gifts isn't illegal, in the case of a politician, it can take on the appearance of being improper and under the Bribery Act of 2010, accepting gifts with the expectation of repayment through improper behaviour is illegal in the UK. The inexact nature of a 'gift', even though there is no suggestion of wrong-doing and the MP had complied with all the relevant rules regarding the receipt of gifts, means it is open to question, however, and the MP can set up a conceptual frame to defend receiving the gift in his own terms.

The frame the MP sets up to tell his side of the story starts when he receives a phone call from a staff member. The staff member had been working long hours, the MP says, and telling the MP he had been sent a pair of complimentary football tickets, asked if he could have them. As the MP knew the staff member was a football fan, he explains that he gave them to the staff member to compensate him for his hard work. Compensating someone for time spent working, for example with money, is not only a legitimate transaction but a common one, so the MP sets up the conceptual metaphor *Time is money* to slip in his denial that he received the benefit of a hospitality gift himself: 'I never accept hospitality and I didn't.' In a tale of generous compensation for hard work, the MP shifts the frame from a story about receiving a gift to one about ordinary compensation for time at work: *Time is money.*

Next, the MP deepens his persuasion with an emotional appeal, asking the journalist-listener for their consultation. 'I'm going to seek your advice: what should my response have been to that hard-working member of staff, in your opinion?' By eliciting empathy in the crafted frame, the MP turns the tables on the journalist and puts them on the stand, *What would you have done in my shoes?* As the MP shifts into the role of the interviewer, he appeals to the journalist to answer the leading question: *Yes, I too would have done the same.*

Seeing through the conceptual frame the MP sets up and its shift of focus, the veteran journalist responds literally to the question to disagree: 'I would say you would refer him to the prime minister . . . all his staff are incredibly hard working and therefore deserve a drink at the end of the day. There's lots of people who are hard working. You might have thought, "Oh, this free ticket should go to the nurse in the ICU."'

By directly responding to the question and rejecting the invitation to align his reality with the MP's, the journalist uses Credibility Listening to challenge the MP's story and demonstrate that they have duly observed the MP's shift of frames from the written evidence of the gift entry found in the register to the conceptual metaphor *Time is Money.*

Credibility Listening can help listeners get closer to the truth in public content. Rather than accepting information we hear at face value, we can listen critically to the contents of the MP's narrative frame that perhaps fit a little too conveniently into the familiar conceptual metaphor.

Time is money is a catchphrase attributed to US Statesman Benjamin Franklin, who presented the concept as advice to young workers in an essay he wrote in 1748. *Time is money* spawned centuries of a belief in the idea that time, like money, is a limited resource, and just as we invest money to gain returns, we invest our time in activities that achieve the highly desirable and recognizable validation of success – money.

We use the *Time is money* metaphor frequently in everyday conversation to promote productivity and influence outcomes. This can be by direct instruction, such as, 'invest in your relationships and it'll pay off in the long run', or by indirect suggestion in a frame that works like a leading question. For example, by asking, 'Can you really afford to waste time going out tonight?' a speaker simultaneously states their own position while trying to convince their listener that their time is like money, a limited resource.

Time is money is a convincing conceptual metaphor that can remind listeners that it's important to put the limited resource of time to good use, which gains it an easy buy-in. From a listener's point of view, like hashing a train destination to obtain our platform number, we can tag onto a fast-mapped story frame without really listening to the details of what we're endorsing. *Time is money* is an example of how a listener can quickly latch on to a story they already know, creating and sustaining what the psychologist Daniel Kahneman called a 'confirmation bias'. A confirmation bias is when we keep on listening for things we already believe to be true and don't listen to things we believe are false.

Computer algorithms are experts at finding the stories you believe are true to feed your confirmation bias and gain traction. By tracking your clicks, likes, shares and search history to learn your preferences, algorithms can create personalized content that reinforces your existing beliefs, which, in turn, can put you into echo chambers that limit your exposure to other perspectives and keep showing you your preferences. Over time, confirmation bias can become the indomitable truth that drives us to further overlook any contradictory evidence that makes us feel uncomfortable. Our desire to seek comfort in the familiar makes the conceptual metaphor simultaneously effective and a potentially powerful deceptive device that can make a lie credible. Credibility Listening is essential to gain clarity on whether conceptual stories are created to share truthful information or cover up lies. Let's look at another example.

A Good Leader is a Strong Parent

With our popular love of youth culture, it's tempting to dismiss the image of a strong parent as outdated, particularly when we're speaking of a male role like a father. But, like confirmation biases, effective conceptual metaphors tend to stick around. The conceptual metaphor *A good leader is a strong parent* is alive and well today, in everything from political oratory and business talks to fiction, where it is replicated time and again. From the children's animation and live-action CGI adaption *The Lion King* (1994, 2019) to portrayals of former political leaders such as Winston Churchill in *The Darkest Hour* (2017), we see representations of strong parental figures who impart important lessons about life and the 'children' who learn from them. As one of the oldest and most effective conceptual metaphors, these framings signal to us that the parental figure in question can be trusted as a leader.

Credibility Listening

Many examples of *A good leader is a strong parent* are found in *A Few Good Men* (1992), a film based on a true story about a colonel tried for ordering an unauthorized disciplinary action that lead to a private's death. As the defence lawyer, Lieutenant Daniel Kaffee (played by Tom Cruise) questions Colonel Nathan Jessup (played by Jack Nicholson), the colonel denies the allegation that he ordered the 'code red' that authorized the disciplinary action. In one reply that sets up his position, the colonel invokes the conceptual metaphor *A good leader is a strong parent* by contrasting his role as the responsible adult to Kaffee, who he infantilizes by calling him 'son':*

> 'Son, we live in a world that has walls, and those walls have to be guarded by men with guns. Who's gonna do it? You? You, Lieutenant Weinberg? I have a greater responsibility than you can possibly fathom.'

Fast-mapping words like 'son' against 'men with guns' to concepts like *guarding walls* and *responsibility*, Colonel Jessup distinguishes grown adult men from children in the semantic field of family, instructing Lieutenant Kaffee to fall in line. Using words to populate the concept that a strong parent has both the power and the authority to command people like his 'son', the colonel puts his listener, Kaffee, in the subordinate position of a child, using not only nouns,

---

* Based on the story of the hazing of Private First Class William Alvarado at Guantanamo Bay. As a result of writing letters to request transfer for being forced to partake in illegal activity such as firing into Cuba, Alvarado was gagged with a cloth while having his head shaved as part of an illegal hazing and code red. Deborah Sorkin, who defended the lieutenants who carried out the code red, was the sister to Aaron Sorkin who wrote the original play that later became the film, *A Few Good Men*.

but also personal pronouns to reinforce the hierarchy of the powerful parental figure who commands the weaker child listener. Repeating the first personal pronoun 'I' to represent himself as the strong leader, Colonel Jessup subsequently repeats the second-person pronoun 'you' seventeen times in a lengthy exposition to further demean Lieutenant Kaffee as a weak child who 'rises and sleeps under the blanket of the very freedom that I provide', and someone who 'can't handle the truth'. Further relating the authoritative father figure 'I' as the head of the institution of the Marines to a family, the colonel uses words like 'honour, code and loyalty' to present himself as the leader of that upstanding family. In the end, though, despite repeated big-ups, six back-and-forth exchanges and 216 words, the colonel loses his cool and finally confesses he ordered the code red: 'You're damn right I did!' A truth or a lie takes a mere second to tell, but the excessive verbiage he needs to cover it up exposes the colonel.

Although we might not encounter language as strong as Colonel Jessup's every day, we often hear the sounds of the metaphor *A good leader is a strong parent* represented in speeches where a leader rallies their group forward as a team. We'll see in an example below that while most such speeches don't have the sinister undertone of Jessup's rant, recognizing such conceptual metaphors can help listeners hear the set-up of the story where someone might be trying to shift the truth. Conceptual metaphors offer the speaker one way to set up their reality and convey it to their listeners, while Credibility Listening for this fast-mapped story empowers the listener to gauge the quality and quantity of talk, noticing any amplifications or shifts in talk volume so that we can gain insight into the truthfulness of what someone is saying.

Developing Credibility Listening Sensitivity by Listening for Shifts

Since conceptual metaphors are an example of a story that can be a handy fast-map to information or a rabbit hole to misinformation, it's useful to be a highly tuned and versatile critical listener who practises Credibility Listening on a daily basis. Developing credibility sensitivity can help listeners not only navigate the negative energy that siloes us more deeply into highly polarized zones, but also deflect everyday scammers from asking us leading questions that eventually draw us to the conclusions they want us to reach within their narrative frame.

My auntie said her scammer began by telling her a story about how they were victimized by a ruthless system that took vast amounts of money to treat their mother who had suffered a stroke. The insurance the scammer was selling was supposed to protect against such debilitating costs. They also added that as it was the end of year, it would be wise to act expeditiously. As no one wants to get sick on the first three days of the year in Japan when everything is closed, a story about a sick, vulnerable person can be an effective con to deceive a victim.

Life is family is a conceptual metaphor that is often used as a motivational speech at work. In Japanese, too, the saying, *ikka ichimon* 一家一門 means 'one house, one gate' and serves as a unifying factor for any team. Speeches like the one below can quickly galvanize support for a team under the banner of the metaphor, *Life is family*.

We are a strong team that looks after the lives of each and every one of you. We see it as our responsibility not only to provide you with guidance, but also to support you to reach your full potential, because when one of us succeeds, we all succeed as a family. In heading towards a common goal, we want each of you to take ownership of your work and contribute to the success of our team. With hard work, you can all achieve the greatness you deserve. We have no doubt that every one of you will rise to the occasion and together continue to make our family proud.

In this rally, the leader uses the personal pronoun 'we' to frame the team as family to lend power to the unity of the group. Once the conceptual metaphor is set up, though, there's a shift in voice where the unity is split between the leaders and the rest of the team. The personal pronoun 'we' now belongs exclusively to the voice of the leader, hinting at their authority in the conceptual metaphor *A good leader is a strong parent* and sending the message that on the basis that what they are saying is a credible truth, the work they are asking everyone to do is achievable. Further on, with words like 'support' and 'pride', the speaker signals the compensation the team will get for 'the greatness you deserve', invoking the metaphor *Time is money*. By synthesizing and shifting amongst conceptual metaphors in carefully crafted language, leaders can motivate a team to unify under their authority and eventually win their support.

Unfortunately, scammers too can capitalize on listeners' reactions to fast-maps and manipulate victims into doing what they want. By encouraging us to listen slow, Credibility

Listening allows us to take a step back out of the listening space. Instead of minding the people as we do in the channels of Listening with Fourteen Hearts and Soft Listening, in Credibility Listening, like Informational Listening, we analyze the conversation before deciding whether to join in cooperation or walk away.

As Credibility Listening reminds us to listen slow, it gives us the time to reflect on *why* someone is saying the things they are – for example, why are they telling you a personal story about their mother when they are selling you insurance? Why does a person spend a long time talking about fathers and sons when they are discussing the death of a corporal? Or why does an MP swap positions with the interviewer and use irrelevant and emotional language? All these shifts in conversation towards evasiveness push the marker on the truth–lie credibility gauge over to the questionable side, putting our Credibility Listening on high alert and asking us to consider the details with further investigation. So while there are no sure-fire remedies to catch out a scammer or a liar, Credibility Listening increases your critical sensitivity and, to this end, can make you less likely to end up a victim.

To help my auntie avoid scammers, I asked my listener focus group what they normally said to walk away from them. The most common reply was not to respond to scamming lies at all – it's best to walk away as soon as you have identified the scam. The second most common strategy of walking away from a scammer was a polite-lie answer that ranged in registers from formal 'No, thank you' to informal 'I'm good'. Some indirectly told scammers they knew what they were up to, saying things like, 'Sorry, I'm not interested', while others were more direct. Here are my three favourite turn-downs you can consider in your next rejection of a scammer, though I doubt that either my auntie or I could use them:

1. Sorry, what's your company again? Thank you, I'll look you up.
2. What is your company's physical address?
3. Please send me your credit card number as well as your expiry date and the three numbers on the back so that I can charge you for my time. Also an address so that I can send you my invoice. Thank you.

Credibility Listening is necessary for detecting and turning away from malicious deception – a bad lie, like the ones we get from scammers – not the polite lies we hear from someone trying to protect a relationship. Like many grandmothers, mine told a lie to protect her granddaughter – pretending she had no idea it was me who stole the bear-cub ornament from the glass casing by the front door. 'Oh, I wonder what happened to the bear cub? The mother looks so sad,' was a little lie, though, and a crafty one at that because it did get the bear cub back.

Lying, like truth-telling, really does take shape in the ears of the beholder. A good lie, though, minds the relationship, whereas a bad lie doesn't. Exposed, a bad lie is weak and has a way of disappearing as soon as it is discovered. Perhaps it really is as the saying goes, 'A lie has speed, but truth has endurance.'

7 Credibility Listening Finds

- We need Credibility Listening to tell truth from lies but also to build trust and cooperation.

- Two truths we seek to advocate in communicating cooperatively are quantity and quality, so we can try to say both as much and as little as we need to be as truthful as possible.

- Our truths and lies occur in a range of the realities we perceive. We tend to believe things are true when we are interested in the topic and speaker and when they share communication patterns with us. A truth or a lie is so heard by a listener.

- A conceptual metaphor is a representation of reality, an effective way for a speaker to relate complex ideas in a simple way.

- A listener can accept a conceptual metaphor at face value when listening fast or spot it when they listen slow with Credibility Listening, which allows them to reflect on why someone is telling a particular story.

- A shift in the pattern of conversation, like making the interviewer reply to a question, gratuitous additions of emotional language and use of irrelevant conceptual metaphors and language are red flags to watch for to increase our sensitivity in Credibility Listening.

- Polite lies differ from deceptive lies in that the teller of a polite lie minds the relationship, whereas the teller of a deceptive lie exclusively protects themself. Credibility Listening can help us distinguish one from the other.

3 Credibility Listening Reflections to Try

- Practise Credibility Listening by listening for conceptual metaphors in media. Do you hear any conceptual metaphors at play? Do you notice any shifts in frame or tone of voice like verbosity?

- Next time you hear someone go off topic, listen for their volume of talk. What are they talking the most about? Why might this be?

- Practise Credibility Listening the next time you hear a scammer. How did they frame the scam? What did you say in your rejection of them? Have fun with it, but don't forget the goal is to turn away and block the scam, reporting it when you can and telling friends and family about it so they won't be caught up in a similar situation.

5

Nonverbal Listening

空気読む

Reading the Atmosphere

There's a pub cat two doors down from our house that regularly visits our tiny garden. Our cat, Blaze, hates her. For one, she's younger and much faster than him. But mostly it's because the cat leaves markings in the garden to try to claim the territory as hers. For Blaze, the pub cat is enemy number one. The pub cat is foe. The humans, though not always the timeliest when it comes to feedings, are her kin. We are friends.

Although as humans we strive to be more complex than Blaze and the pub cat, what we do have in common with the feline family is the speed at which we decide if someone is friend or foe. It turns out first impressions are formed much quicker than the general consensus of three seconds. Five replicated experiments by psychologists Janine Willis and Alexander Todorov showed that participants made judgments about new faces within 100 milliseconds of exposure.[1] We literally make decisions about people in the blink of an eye.

There's a good reason for making that flash first decision. Like a siren to our hearing, a first visual impression is the important initial alert that can keep us out of potential danger. *Is this stranger dangerous?* That was the key question for our hunter-gatherer ancestors 13,000 years ago that has more or less stayed in our consciousness.

We extend our safeguarding knowledge about first impressions to everyday practices, advising our children 'Don't talk to strangers' and performing safeguarding rituals at places we encounter strangers, like networking events. In situations that oblige interaction, human meeting rituals require us to check each other out and decide whether we actually want to meet. This mutual ritual observation has somewhat euphemistically come to be called 'reading the room', an exercise of sizing one another up that looks a bit like what peacocks do in their 'train-rattle' and response in mating. When a peacock first initiates interaction, it fans out its signature feathers that rattle on its way up, drawing the attention of the female peafowl. Having heard the rattle, the peafowl first observes and evaluates the peacock from a distance, deciding whether or not it should approach. If the peafowl does decide to get a closer look, it'll then approach the calling peacock, head bob, wing flick, circle and/or peck the ground around its caller. Alternatively, though, it might choose to ignore the peacock and walk away.

While human hairstyles don't possess quite the glamour of a peacock-train-rattle fan, people do have the ability to present themselves in what the sociologist Erving Goffman called 'self-presentations'. Goffman theorized that as every human creates and performs their own presentation, they manage the impression they make on others. Linguists call this unspoken part of interaction 'nonverbal communication', which includes not only the body language and facial expressions of the presenter, but also the demonstrated non-verbal feedback of the listener. While in the last chapter we talked about how we do credibility checks on informational language, in this chapter, we'll explore how we use Nonverbal Listening not only to read the atmosphere of the space we are in but to mutually meta listen to one another and read each other's moods.

Nonverbal Listening is expansive, limited not only to auditory listening but visual and tactile listening, too. As both self-presenting speaker and listening audience, we use and listen for vocal gestures of demonstrated listening, like the back-channel cues, 'yeah', 'uhuh' or head nods, that show we're following along, but we also use and listen for nonverbal communications like eye contact and intermittent eye-gazing patterns that continue throughout the conversation. Such visual listening of the face is extended to the body, which we use as a presenter and listen for as an audience. By supporting auditory information with other cues, Nonverbal Listening is a practice we use to heighten our overall sensitivity, which our Listening with Fourteen Hearts then synthesizes to gain insight on what we are experiencing so we can move on. In this sense, Nonverbal Listening not only grounds us in the current conversation, but also helps us navigate what to do next – for example, stay in the conversation or leave it.

We start our investigation of Nonverbal Listening by exploring what the face has to say when we pay close attention to three facial expressions. We then extend our listening receptors to include the tactile gesture of the ritual hand-shake, increasingly a universal symbol of demonstrated listening that shows the level of trust two people have in one another in a structured social meeting like a networking event. Whereas words, semantic fields and conceptual forests were at the centre of our selected attention in the previous chapter on Credibility Listening, it's people's faces and bodies that are at the centre here.

The Face Says it All

Our face is one of the most revealing parts of the human profile, and humans believe the face says things about a person. It's why audiences study presenters' eyes and mouths to read what they say, and why presenters practise grooming and aesthetics on and around their faces. Before face-to-face in-person and virtual self-presentations, we look after our face with daily hygiene but also through dentistry, facial and head grooming and potentially the application of various cosmetics and accessories as an expression of ourselves and also to ensure we look our best.

The presentation of our face is important to us because the face is a primary source of human identification. Increasingly used in biometric identification, our physical face represents our existential identity, so that when we say things in English like, 'I need to show my face,' it literally means, *I need to show up as myself.* As your identification, listeners look for your face when they meet you and notice its absence. A friend once shared that eleven of the fourteen attendees of a virtual residents meeting with their building's managing agent were off camera and continued that way even after the managing agent urged them to turn their computer cameras on. This friend read the off-camera gesture as discourteous. She said it was as if they were saying, 'I can't be bothered to show up.' Listeners like my friend visually 'hear' a show of someone's face online as attendance, like the student who responds to a roll call on camera by saying, 'Present!'

On-camera presence, though, can feel awkward, as it has for me when students calling into online classes with on-camera mandates feel obliged to dial in from private corners of the house like bathrooms to guard the privacy of other people sharing the house. Online classrooms helped me see that those who choose to go off-camera typically do so for privacy reasons rather than to mean any disrespect. To account for both respect and privacy, especially for students dialling in from abroad, institutions quickly adopted on- and off-camera guidelines.

On-Camera/Off-Camera Virtual Meeting Guidelines

One thing both on- and off-camera advocates agree on is that our eyes and ears are the two most important features on our physical face. An fMRI study of neural mechanisms in our visual cortex shows that eyes and mouths are the most recognized physical features of the face by visual listeners, and that of these two facial features, we pay the closest attention to the eyes.[2] This finding is not surprising since our eyes are truly remarkable human instruments of vision. When you detect objects, light refracts off your cornea and onto the retina, firing up some forty regions in the visual parts of your brain. Then when you look at someone's face, you process the image you see together with information your other receptors such as hearing have been collecting and synthesize it, which ultimately helps you to identify what the neuroscientist and biologist Doris Tsao calls 'face patches' – particular features of a face that help you identify people.[3]

Tsao's studies show how we identify others by their prominent features, filling in missing parts to clarify who they are, the way a photo editor does with blurry photos. It's a listening-fast ability that allows us to 'see' a person, identifying someone by a particular feature, a little like the way we identify someone by the timbre of their voice. It's also how we can recognize someone by their side-profile, or even with some of their face hidden, in the same way we can fill in missing information in Informational Listening. Nonverbal Listening is a testament to the power of Listening with Fourteen Hearts, the source from where we draw the energy to listen all ears, eyes and heart to find out what people are like.

Politeness Registers and Nonverbal Cultural Norms

My friends often roll their eyes when I try to convince them that the Japanese aren't any more polite than the next person. I tell them that what seems like politeness or even excessive politeness, such as bowing in greeting, is just the Japanese way of abiding by the norms of their own culture. Some of the nonverbal rituals the Japanese use in communication only seem polite because they are out of the 'normal' range of things you might do in your own culture by comparison. For example, bowing in English-speaking contexts are typically reserved for formal occasions and expressed towards people of a superior social standing such as royalty. The nonverbal gesture of bowing to anyone is noticeable if comical – as if you were treating everyone like royalty.

We notice nonverbal communication that is outside our own social and cultural norms. If you're not from a culture that uses ritual cheek-kissing, you would notice that, as I have experienced both as cheek-kisser and kissee. In France, where cultural pride can be fiercely regional, they'll notice someone outside their region by the way they cheek-kiss in a greeting. For example, a relative living in Grenoble told me, 'We start with the left and then go right. In Grenoble, go right then left. In the Ardèche, it's three times!' Then, on reflection, she said, 'No! Actually, it's the other way around! Right first in Paris. And in Belgium, I remember it's four times!' The Parisian right-left one-two is corroborated by many, but a Belgian told me that four times was excessive. While how many and which side to start seems absolutely key in distinguishing locals from outsiders, it turns out that what ultimately makes a cheek-kiss greeting feel right is what feels normal in each regional and generational sub-culture. For some time, I've been observing younger generations in France exchanging hugs with their local friends. When I asked them about it, they giggled and said, 'It's okay now. We do it, too, but only with special people.' Like on-camera and off-camera norms in virtual meetings, gestural norms need to respect privacy and boundaries so that they feel appropriate, polite and normal to their users.

One politeness gauge that underpins appropriate tone of verbal and nonverbal communication is the measure linguists call 'register'. 'Register' is our way of adapting verbal and nonverbal language to the formality of the encounter – for example, by using a more formal register in a networking event and a more informal register for a chat with friends in a café. In an event with a formal register like networking, you'll probably adjust your self-presentation by wearing business attire and using more formal spoken language, like introducing yourself with your full name and including your professional affiliation. You might also address others using their titles and surnames and avoid swearing or using slang, unless it's professional slang like the acronyms we'll talk about in a later chapter on business. Professional slang falls in between formal and informal registers to signal in-group professionalism, a little like abiding by the dress code 'smart casual'. Self-presentation in professional circles these days often requires striking a balance between formal and informal registers so we can present ourselves as smart but also friendly.

Contemporary listening today involves a level of self-awareness by which listeners are not only the audience to presenters but also to themselves. We listen for language and voice and watch for nonverbal language to understand others, but we also regulate ourselves to listen and watch for how others are reacting to us. We'll go deeper into this kind of reflective listening in the very last chapter, but as a primer for nonverbal communication, eye contact is the perfect example. When we establish eye contact, we don't just look the other person in the eye, but also engage with them to try to see what they think about us.

Eye Contact: I'm Interested, Too

Networking these days starts long before you even get to the event. By the time you arrive, you've probably already researched some of the people attending, worked on your elevator pitch and thought about a couple of topics to discuss. Background research helps you to feel ready, and being ready can help you get rid of any jitters you feel about meeting strangers at this kind of formal-register event.

At the top of the list of things experts highlight in regards to nonverbal communication at a networking event is to make eye contact with other participants. There's a physiological reason for this. Eye contact can trigger the release of oxytocin, the hormone associated with building social trust. Sometimes called the 'bonding hormone', some psychologists argue that mirror neurons are responsible for firing up and stimulating a reaction to replicate another person's intentions, creating a near-compulsive drive to reflect back the nonverbal gesture you just saw, like eye contact or a smile. Mirror neurons are a type of brain cell that activate both when an individual performs an action and when they observe someone else performing the same action. These neurons were first discovered in primates but are also thought to exist in humans. Although mirror neurons are still debated within the scientific community, what we know is that when the occipital lobe located at the back of the brain is activated by eye contact, it communicates that information to the amygdala, which is involved in managing emotions. Furthermore, if we are physically attracted to the object of our eye contact, our pupils dilate to physically show our interest.

If initial eye contact can signal interest, a second glance over can send the meta-message of an inclination for engagement. To gauge whether it's worthwhile meeting someone, you're likely to have already done a preliminary body scan of the other person, which researchers tell us involves a brief scan from toe to head rather than head to toe as is typically thought, because a ground-up scan allows you to take in a person's overall appearance before you look more closely at their face. What we visually listen for in a toe-to-head scan are things like a person's posture, clothing style and grooming, because our social cultures tell us that these are what can give us clues about someone's social status and personality. How are they standing? What's their hair like? Depending on the answers to your questions, you might decide to make a bee-line for the bar or move towards them with the intention of spending the next five to fifteen minutes that people typically end up engaging with a person at a networking event. Either way, you have made a decision as a nonverbal listener about what you are going to do next.

If you have decided to join someone or a group, now your Nonverbal Listening will be scanning for something the linguistic anthropologist Edward T. Hall called 'proxemics' – the comfortable distance between two people during in-person interaction. Proxemics is the ultimate example of how we personalize social distances in various registers. If you picture yourself in Hall's model of a typical socio-physical spacing between people in an English-speaking environment, as shown in the infograph opposite, you can gauge how you might feel when standing in each of the four proxemic zones of intimate, personal, social and public distances. Although the general distance between people in a networking event might be the one metre, four feet or arm's length away from another person, you might feel more comfortable with a little more or less. Hall's model is a typical social guideline for those in English-speaking interactions, though they vary by person and culture. You can observe them for yourself at your next networking or social event to gain insight into your own

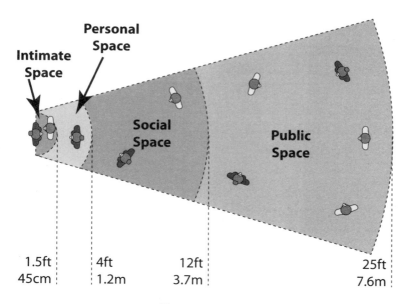

Hall's Proxemic Zones

nonverbal communication and the listening information you gain from others.

Once we decide on a group or individual to join and begin moving towards them, we often make eye contact with the person once again to communicate 'I'm on my way'. Although this is also the time in which some occupational psychologists suggest you 'eyebrow flash', expressing further interest in your imminent meeting by raising your eyebrows and widening your eyes, it's important to know that this nonverbal gesture can be misunderstood as in-your-face, flirtatious or even cringey in other cultures! Recall from the chapter on Informational Listening that 75 per cent of English-speakers worldwide are second-language speakers of English, so even at an event that is conducted in English, misunderstandings can occur, especially when we consider that first impressions are made in a fraction of a second. Since the eyebrow flash is a nonverbal gesture that generally signals a more informal register that can easily be misunderstood, first-language English listeners might be best to keep this eye contact gesture for networking events composed of uniquely first-language speakers of English (or more informal events), while second-language English listeners can likewise recognize this nonverbal gesture is generally intended as friendly and not condescending.

Nonverbal language, then, has an even greater possibility to be misunderstood by its listeners than verbal language, and not only between language cultures. Mismatches can occur between what a communicator meant and what a listener understands between gender, generational and work cultures, too. Knowledge of nonverbal sensitivity to culture can expand our Listening with Fourteen Hearts fitness and make us supple in our use and interpretation of nonverbal communication.

Gaze: In the Eyes of the Beholder

Now that you've engaged your interest with eye contact and you're an arm's distance away from other communicators in the listening space, you're pretty much committed to at least a couple of minutes – five minutes normatively – of talking and listening. Walking away now is risky as it might be visually heard as ghosting the person, sending the listening meta-message, 'I'm sorry, I'm not interested in you after all.'

Stay and you can read other people's proxemics and see if they match yours. If someone comes up too close and personal, you might not only feel crowded but also like they're talking down to you. But if they stand too far away, are they shy or aloof? Although online meetings eliminate this physical means for sizing people up, potentially saving you some social discomfort and awkwardness, they do also jettison a visual listener's ability to read proxemics. By doing away with many of the nonverbals we use and listen for in in-person interaction, virtual meetings take some of the pressure off social interaction, while at the same time eliminating a whole observational dimension.

Once you meet someone, you're likely to go on autopilot as you carry out your habitual gazing patterns. Although we sometimes think of eye contact as something that happens throughout a meeting, eye contact is a single point of meeting, which when sustained over a period becomes a gaze. Marketers study these gaze durations and use it to quantify interest in products, generally understanding a longer sustained gaze as indicating greater interest. Listeners too use gaze patterns to quantify attention but in a different manner where there is a qualitative 'right amount' of interested gaze in them. A gaze that is too long feels like you've been stared at, and one that isn't quite long enough feels like you've been slighted a little. Did they maybe think you weren't that interesting? Both speakers and listeners look to each other to get a sense of whether they are resonating with the other.

Although continued eye gaze displays interest in many cultures, research also shows that some vary in their demonstration of engagement by extended eye gaze. In Masuda et al's study of eye gaze, for example, North American participants found that their Japanese counterparts displayed a duration of eye gaze so short it was almost imperceptible.[4] Although a frame-by-frame analysis of eye gaze patterns revealed that the Japanese did engage in eye contact, the duration was so short that it was visually heard as no contact, perhaps explaining the common misunderstanding that Japanese don't engage in eye contact at all.

A colleague once told me about the time she tried to get a Japanese student to use 'more eye contact' with the audience in a rehearsal for a poster presentation. When the student tried to practise what he thought was an appropriately longer duration of eye gaze, it looked embarrassingly like he was ogling her. Eye gaze isn't just looking at someone for as long as you can keep your eyes open; ideally, it follows a pattern of looking and looking away, a little like the rhythm of words in speech.

English-language learners often ask, what then is the right duration of eye gaze in a place like a networking event? Tracking pupil dilation, UCL researchers studied 400 participants and found that dilated eye contact that lasted just a fraction over three seconds was the typical duration.[5] Once eyes are locked on for more than five seconds, participants reported that it started to feel like staring and even a little 'creepy'.[6] Like with pausing when speaking, listeners punctuate their eye contact and gaze language by blinking, nodding and/ or pausing, briefly moving their eyes away to the side before engaging again. The rhythm of a three-to-four-second eye-gaze period punctuated by blinks, nods, pauses and glances away is part of what gives a conversation in English rhythm, and makes it feel natural and agreeable.

When a communicator's sociocultural eye-gaze patterns are in line with yours, a nonverbal listener, you're more likely to feel that you have their attention and that they are co-operating with you in the conversation. Eye-gaze patterns in step with your own give conversations a feel of authenticity and familiarity, making us as Credibility Listeners gravitate towards those who behave in similar ways to ourselves. In the same way we are drawn towards circles of those with comparable education, career and work ethic in professional networking events, we also tend towards others who share a similar style of verbal and nonverbal communication. Researchers call this tendency to lean in towards those similar to ourselves 'homophily' – a Greek word that is composed of *homo* meaning 'same', and *philia* meaning 'love'.

Career advisors often cite eye contact as one of the top skills in improving professional interaction, but we also need to know eye-gaze patterns, such as the standard three-to-four-second eye-gaze duration, as well as situations in which we shouldn't use them. Competence in nonverbal interaction, like verbal interaction, is knowing when and where to engage in contact. For example, within English-speaking cultures, there are variations in the way visual listeners interpret eye gaze, with groups like the military advocating both short and long eye gazing to show respect. Get the duration of eye-gaze wrong and you are in trouble. Too long and it's, 'Don't you dare eyeball me!' Too short and it's, 'Look at me while I'm talking to you!'

Expectations of nonverbal gestures like eye-gaze vary according to cultural interpretations of hierarchy. While the global suggestion to establish eye contact is an important one, it's good visual soft listening practice to employ the novice mindset and exercise the flexibility that allows for different gaze patterns in various cultural contexts. In the chapter on Cultural Listening, we'll explore once again how a culture's sensitivity to hierarchical authority has a powerful impact on communication.

Macaca fuscatas are intelligent alpine snow monkeys who live, amongst other places, in my hometown in Japan. I love these monkeys even though they are hardcore traditionalists with a full-blown social order who will fight you if you disobey their gaze culture – for example, by engaging in extended eye gaze with the boss, even if it's through a camera lens. There's a story nearly every summer about an unknowing tourist in the Japanese Alps who has been chased down by an unhappy fuscata, having looked them in the eye a bit too long. For the short-tempered fuscata, human eye gaze can be visually heard as bellicosity rather than the agreeable engagement it is amongst humans in networking events.

Whether you're primate or human, eye contact and gaze are important features in nonverbal communication because they set the tone for the remaining conversation – whether you want to stay in or politely bow out. When someone makes eye contact and supports the initial engagement with an appropriate amount of sustained but intermittent gaze thereafter, listeners can be convinced to stay on to search for further confirmation of agreeableness and to discover more about their conversation partner.

Smiley Faces, Genuine and Polite

The facial feature we look to for signs of friendliness after the eyes is the mouth. In addition to talking, the mouth can physically shape-shift into many expressions for the listener to interpret, as a frown, pout, yawn, grimace, grin and, of course, a smile. When attending to a speaker, we aurally listen for what linguists call 'phonemes', which are the smallest units of sound that allow a listener to distinguish one word from another. An example of this is the sound difference between /p/ and /b/ in English that can help a listener distinguish between a word like 'pat' from 'bat'. The visual equivalent of a phoneme is a 'viseme', which listeners use to 'read' lips. We regularly use visemes even if we don't lip read as well as hearing-impaired persons do. In everyday conversation, the lip-reading ability of the hearing abled is reportedly only able to capture a maximum of 30 per cent of what is spoken,[7] primarily because they can afford to rely on language phonemes. Instead, hearing-abled listeners look to the lips as back-up, to visually qualify and support the information they are audially hearing.

One of the most common temperature readings of an ongoing relationship visual listeners rely on from the mouth is the smile, an upward movement of the lips that involves twelve of the forty-three muscles in our face. We believe the smile signals agreeability and approachability, and research corroborates this perception with findings that suggest that the presence or absence of a smile while someone is talking affects how listeners perceive and remember conversations. One study found that smiling made the speaker appear more likeable and trustworthy,[8] and another that listeners were more likely to remember a story when the narrator was smiling than when they weren't.[9] Although specific interpretations of the smile vary across cultures, alongside when and where to use them, smiles have been observed as occurring throughout the world.

In the western part of the world, we tend to class smiles in two categories – one that is spontaneous and 'genuine', and one that is constructed and 'polite'. The legacy of the distinction between these two types of smiles is owed to the nineteenth-century neurologist Guillaume Duchenne, who studied the muscle movements of his muscular dystrophy and psychiatric patients. Duchenne claimed that the recognizable difference between genuine and constructed smiles was biological – the authentic smile using the zygomaticus majoris muscles that stretch from the corner of the mouth upwards to the orbicularis oculi that surround the eyes, while the polite smile uses only the risorius muscles around the mouth.

In everyday language, we think of the real smile as the one where our whole face lights up and we smile with our eyes, too. This real smile complete with crow's feet contrasts to the polite smile where the lips are pulled across in a flat line. As visual lip-readers we think we can tell the difference. However, given Duchenne's highly questionable experimental conditions of probing patients with electrical shocks to the face, it's important to at least ask the question: is there an actual difference between a genuine smile and a polite one? Can we accurately read the lips of a smile?

Studies of babies as young as a few months seem to suggest that yes, even these young visual listeners can tell a spontaneous smile from a polite one, and that they themselves reserve their own eyes-inclusive Duchenne smiles for their primary caregivers.[10] Ironically, it's also the baby's primary caregiver who teaches them the deliberate risorius smile – how to do that 'pretty' polite smile for everyone else. Over the years, children learn that developing and crafting the polite smile can signal approachability and general friendliness while inviting appeasement, making the deliberate smile essential for their social survival, in both informal and formal settings.

Although it might seem as though we generally favour the genuine smile over the constructed risorius smile that we sometimes call 'fake', over time, adult lip-readers seem to develop an appreciation for both kinds of smiles. Of course, what's not to like about the all-round feel-good of a genuine smile? Most of us welcome and need the extended empathy and joy a genuine smile can bring about. However, it seems we have also acquired an appreciation for the niceness of playing by the social rules that a polite smile can display, particularly in events in formal registers.

Humans have been smiling for quite some time, but historically, smiles have had many meanings. Classicists believe archaic closed-lip smiles observed in paintings and statues merely signalled the contentment of a person in general good health, while the Roman smile carried the look of mockery. Thought to indicate the sense of a diminished or hidden form of laughter, the Roman smile is spelled out in the Latin word *subridere*, which literally translated comes out as 'under laugh'. The derisive concept of *subridere* lives on today in words like 'sneer', but the derivative modern French word *sourire*, which transliterates as *under smile*, where the word *rire* means 'to laugh' or 'laugh', took a turn for the better in the thirteenth century when the statue of the smiling angel of Reims was interpreted as displaying a smile of benevolence.[11]

As for the genuine smile, it's purported that a single portrait changed the negative perception of showing teeth in a smile. When Louis XIV's court painter's wife Elisabeth

Louise Vigée Le Brun displayed her self-portrait in the annual Salon of the Louvre in the eighteenth century, where it still is today, it didn't just launch a whole new generation of dentists and unregulated teeth-pullers, it introduced the idea that a show of teeth in a smile wasn't a failure of mind to control the body, as was preached in influential writings of the time. Some art historians have gone as far as saying that the portraitist originally commissioned to reverse the negative image of the government not only succeeded but also replaced it with the enduring image of a happy family person that can be represented in a smile.

Although the Swedish language gave the English language the word 'smile', it was English and American cultures that ultimately put the concept through its paces in the twentieth century. Not long after the public delighted in Mme Vigée Le Brun's toothful smile, the smile took a nosedive in political satires and cartoons once again as a fake, insincere or untrustworthy gesture, before it was restored as a positive image through the camera lens of 1920s Hollywood promotion. Fast forward to the digital world today, and it seems there's no turning back on the positive value many societies afford the smile, both genuine and polite. Whether in virtual meetings, social media or via the use of emojis in texting, there's hardly an interaction that goes by without the use of an impression-managing smile, toothful or toothless.

As physical smiling manages impressions in face-to-face interactions, emoji smiling manages impressions in texting, a hybrid language of spoken and written forms. Emojis, a word that transliterates to *picture symbols* in Japanese, and which were originally designed in the 1990s by mobile phone provider NTT DoCoMo's designer Shigetaka Kurita, are now widely accepted and used as spoken language in text form to help listeners understand the nuances of what people are saying by mimicking the way conversationalists use facial expressions in in-person encounters.* To demonstrate just how much emojis have been normalized as a nonverbal language alongside words, the Oxford English Dictionary chose the smiles-with-tears-of-joy emoji as 'word of the year' in 2015. The humble emoji, previously ridiculed as a fad of the younger generation, now enjoys the same status as older, traditional words in the world's most comprehensive dictionary.

Indeed, even before the emoji, the merchandizing brothers Murray and Bernard Spain sold products affixed with the smiley logo illustrator Harvey Ball originally designed for State Life Assurance Company to boost company morale in 1963. No sooner had the Spain Brothers popularized the expression 'Have a nice day!' and cemented the idea of service with a smile, sales people all over the US were employing the polite smile with the phrase at every turn. The service message implied in the polite smile was briefly called 'the Pan Am smile' because flight attendants were trained to wear the smile just as readily as they wore their uniform. Today, the absence of a broad service smile doesn't go unnoticed. However, professional smiles are highly cultural, and differ in degree, especially when combined with sales talk. I remember My French father-in-law was at first deeply flattered by

---

* Emoji grammar works in a similar way to Japanese verb inflections. In many languages like English, verbs are inflected by time. In other languages like Japanese, verbs are inflected by affect – how the action should be read emotionally.

the exuberance with which he was greeted in retail stores in the United States, until he discovered that the service smile was distributed to everyone.

Like other industry standards, though, a mandate to use a nonverbal gesture like a smile can be heard of as an expression of hierarchical subservience, especially if the requirement is not democratic across the board. This inequality is often visible in public encounters between leaders, for example when the former UK Prime Minister Theresa May observed a smile only to find then European Commissioner Jean-Claude Juncker didn't,[12] or when a journalist asked tennis player Serena Williams why she wasn't very 'smiley' after she had just lost a match, which sounded very much like the journalist was asking her to smile to pay professional lip service to gain increased public viewership.

Professional smiles can influence listeners' moods and shape social outcomes alongside words to rally feelings of cohesion and union. One study found that participants used more genuine smiles alongside words such as 'us' and 'together' to drive group cohesion, and the professional smile with words like 'others', 'them' or 'far away', to distinguish their own group from others.[13] While a genuine smile can create cohesion amongst those with close ties, engendering a feeling of closeness within a cultural group, the professional smile can create a sense of order through social respect. In this sense, we can see a genuine smile as an expression of personal value that honours cultural mores, whereas the professional smile is an exercise of social regulation. Either way, both smiles highlight once again that the smile itself has no moral meaning on its own, but that it's us, as actors and audiences, who, together, derive the meaning of a smile.

As nonverbal listeners, we lip-read the smiles and give them the meaning we need to bond within our own cultures while lubricating and moving through social conversations.

Feel Listening

Can professional smiles promote the same good feelings that genuine smiles can? Researchers who study mirror neurons believe they can, observing that when visual listeners see a smile, they often experience the smile and return the gesture. The idea that a smile could potentially win back a smile together with the favour of customers was an enticing one, especially as a way of sourcing keen customers. The thinking here is that a customer who smiles back at a sales person is more likely to be open to a sales suggestion than the customer who ghosts them.

Smiling and other nonverbal expressions are cues to a kind of 'feel listening' that listeners can use to get a sense of what the other person is like. Listening with feel is called *sasshi* 察し in Japanese, which roughly corresponds to the English words 'guess' or 'sense'. Just like the fast-mapping children use when they're listening for and learning new words, and the Credibility Listening we use to read a room, you use *sasshi* to read a nonverbal cue like a smile, to learn a little bit more about the person, not just about how they're relating to the content they're talking about, but also about how they're relating to you. *Sasshi* levels up from Nonverbal Listening in that it can go above visually listening for physically tangible cues. As a cultural concept, *sasshi* relies on the idea that you can intuit others' unspoken and undemonstrated feelings and intentions, and that the 'understanding' you derive isn't any less important than the interpretations you make from audible words or visible gestures. *Sasshi* puts the listener first and doesn't devalue what a listener understands as 'just a perception'.

In the context of networking or other more formal events involving meeting people who are strangers, one feel-listening gesture that has become important is the handshake. Thought to have Greek origins, a handshake was, according to some, originally used to show meeting partners that their hands were free of weapons. In the world of business, the customary handshake signals goodwill on meeting and a show of trust on departure. In some situations, deliberately eschewing the expected handshake can be understood as unfriendly, unsportsmanlike or assuming a position as the enemy. Today, the handshake has become so commonplace in politics and business that representatives from non-handshaking countries learn how to shake hands.

As a feel-listening gesture, the handshake is notoriously difficult to describe. The generally agreed-upon view of a handshake in a brief greeting or parting is a nonverbal action in which two people grasp one of each other's hands, then create a brief up-and-down movement. Internet advice on a good handshake typically offers guidance that involves shaking the right hand, even for left handers, ensuring clean nails and a dry hand, and using eye contact and a firm grip. The late Queen Elizabeth II of the United Kingdom was known for lowering her hand so the other person could initiate the handshake, and only after she felt the handshake, did she return the gesture. Perhaps this is an example of the Queen's ability to listen, for which she was well known, where for at least the duration of the handshake, she and the hand-shaker were equals.

The ideal execution of a handshake is something both handshakers feel as equals; although, in practice, a handshake often takes on the tone of sizing one another up. The main feel listeners search for in a handshake is confidence exhibited as firmness – neither a limp and clammy 'dead fish' handshake without eye contact, nor an overpowering 'bone-crushing' one. A dead-fish handshake may be taken by its recipient to indicate the other person's confidence status is low, or that they are untrustworthy and insincere, while a bone-crusher is interpreted as arrogant and aggressive. The 'correct' firmness of a handshake is somewhere between. The right duration is interestingly similar to that of a single gaze, lasting about three seconds, which perhaps explains why handshakers are typically advised to engage in eye contact while they shake hands.

If people shake hands to demonstrate their own confidence status, they also shake hands to extend trust and fairness to the person with whom they are shaking hands. In politics, business and sports, or any other competitive match-up that can be perceived as adversarial, handshakes signal fair play. 'Shaking on it,' means they agree to collaborate together going forward, despite the challenges they may experience together. A handshake is like a promise based on a risk assessment, a mutual demonstrated nonverbal listening that confirms in formal register that we are friends more than we are foe.

As the oldest kind of listening we do, our sense of physical feel or touch is the first sensor we develop as a human foetus to find out about the world. Sensory nerves begin developing as early as three weeks after conception. At ten weeks, the foetus develops tactile senses in their genitals, at eleven weeks, in their palms, and at twelve weeks, in the soles of their feet. Olfactory nerves of smell also begin to develop early, around six to seven weeks of gestation, but these senses aren't fully developed until ten to twelve weeks. Taste buds arrive at fifteen weeks, hearing at sixteen to twenty-six weeks, and light detection for our vision begins as late as twenty-five to thirty-three weeks. The feeling of physical touch we develop in utero further matures into a complex tactile system that scientists are still trying to understand. For example, we know that we have basic sensors of touch that help us assess our pain and comfort levels, but the jury is still out on when and how bodily pain turns into emotional pain and vice versa.

What we do know is that we can get a snapshot of someone in a first impression, then get a better read on them as we get a sense of how they influence their face and body language. Nonverbal signs like eye contact, gaze, smile and handshake are important tells in a short-term first encounter that complement important data points provided by language, voice and sociocultural context.

Listening for nonverbal language is as important as listening for voice and language. Not extending any nonverbal listening considerations, on the other hand, is what Japanese youth in the 1990s chastised as poor 'AirReading' – an inability to read the atmosphere of the room. Our capacity for AirReading, found in the characters that head this chapter 空気読む, is what we capitalize on in nonverbal listening where we read nonverbal cues such as eye contact, eye gaze, smiling and handshakes, and also the *sasshi* vibes we get from listening slow and evaluating further. Good AirReaders are those who actively listen for both verbal and nonverbal language to read a person and understand what they are like, using all the Listening with Fourteen Hearts channels we have talked about so far – Informational, Soft, Credibility and Nonverbal Listening – so we can tune in to get a temperature reading of the room and the people in it.

Nonverbal Listening is a highly sensitive instrument for picking up on nonverbal cues. However, before we leave this chapter, I want to underscore the idea that while body language is important, it is not 'most' of a communication event, as sometimes sold in popular literature. Credibility Listening tells us that is misinformation. Although nonverbal communication is vital in a first impression, a first impression is, as its name implies, only the inital part of getting to know someone.

As we have found in the first half of the book, we have an abundance of untapped energy in many different kinds of listening, and there are still more channels to discover in the second half, where we will look at how we use our listening in different contexts. Like many things, the more channels you discover, the more it seems there is to know, because Nonverbal Listening interacts with other channels of listening to shape and direct our experience. Our Soft Listening channel will remind us that there is much to learn, even from those we classify as foes in our first impression. At least, that's what I've been trying to tell Blaze about the pub cat.

7 Keys to Nonverbal Listening

- Our receptors are designed for safety first and we make snap decisions about faces we see within 100 milliseconds of exposure.

- Proxemics is the study of physical social distance. In formal register, in in-person meetings like an English-speaking networking event, we typically tend to stand about 1.2 metres or an arm's length apart.

- 'Face patches' help us to 'visually listen' for prominent features on faces that allow us to fill in the missing pieces of a picture or identify someone, even when we don't have a full profile of them.

- Humans tend to rely on the eyes as the most readable part of the human face. Mouths come next but the visually-abled are generally poor lip-viseme readers.

- We establish eye contact to signal interest but also engagement. The duration of eye contact and its subsequent rhythm of gaze in intermittent looking and looking away varies by culture. Some cultures' preferred eye contact duration is so short that it feels like no contact at all.

- We have popularized the categories of the genuine and professional smiles. Babies can distinguish between them, and as adults, we have come to learn to value and expect both kinds.

- We use feel listening like a handshake as a way to understand and enforce goodwill and trustworthiness.

3 Nonverbal Listening Reflections: Mirror Mirror

Although it might be more challenging to observe nonverbal expressions in virtual meetings than in person, there are some advantages to meeting online. For better or worse, a screen allows us to see our own faces the way others see us in the moment. In in-person meetings, we don't have this mirror. Because virtual meetings can increase our awareness as visual listeners of facial expressions, both those of others *and* of our own, here are three nonverbal listening reflections to help you use technology to your advantage.

- In on-camera interactions, explore your own and others' eye-gaze duration.

- Can you notice a difference between your own and others' genuine and polite smiles?

- Online interaction can heighten your audial and facial visual listening by limiting you to these two forms of listening. You can't physically touch someone in a virtual meeting, but you now have a select focus of attention from which to pick up on AirReading vibes. What other facial expressions do you notice? Have a little fun with visual listening and discover new things you haven't noticed before.

6

Cultural Listening

Culture

In the K-Drama series *Crash Landing on You*, a South Korean woman goes paragliding to celebrate her appointment as heir to her father's business, when inclement weather causes her to crash into a tree in North Korea. While the story is about the romance that blossoms between the South Korean heir and a North Korean officer, the drama depicts the challenges she faces lost in a totally unfamiliar place. Though sadly I didn't have a handsome North Korean officer to show me the way growing up, I did face that same baffling feeling of encountering unfamiliarity moving from one culture to another every three years following my father's career around the globe. To help me in the day-to-day acclimatization to culture were people anthropologists used to call 'natives' and the corporate world calls 'locals', but children my age at the time just called 'friends'. Although initially, my friends and I didn't have the advantage of a common language the parachuter and the officer had, we did have our voices and an overactive novice mindset that got us to learn about what the anthropologist Edward T. Hall calls the hidden language of culture.

Cultural Listening

'Culture' is expressed as language by the ties people have with one another, and by the changes people go through together in time. The word for 'culture' 文化 in Japanese that heads this chapter is composed of two characters where the first means 'text' 文 and the second means 'transformation' 化. The idea that 'culture' means 'text transformation' might seem nonsensical at first glance, until the word is put in the context of Japanese cultural history. The Japanese characters for 'culture' are the very embodiment of the hidden language of culture, since the Chinese characters brought over to Japan literally transformed the Japanese culture in the fourth century from a uniquely oral culture to one that had writing too. Almost as if to play on the idea that culture is hidden in language, in formal linguistics, 'transformation' is the process by which an element of the underlying logical deep structure of a sentence converts an element in the surface structure. Like the hidden elements of culture exposed in the analysis of Japanese characters, formal linguistics conceptualizes *culture* as something that not only lies hidden deeply within a structure, but also as something that has the power to influence and change the surface-level language we hear and listen for.

Cultural Listening is the deep dive we do to listen for cultural meanings in communication. Recognizing hidden cultural language is like recognizing voice in Listening with Fourteen Hearts. Hearing our own familiar cultural language can be as soothing as hearing family voices and as enjoyable as listening to our favourite music, but learning new cultural languages exercises the novice mindset and expands our listening scope to include much more of the world. Studies by sociologists and anthropologists have long shown the benefits of interacting with people from familiar cultures with whom we have strong ties, but also with whom we have weaker, more distant ties. The former helps to create a feeling of security within a community, but the latter exercises the ability to expand into new ones. In Cultural Listening, an awareness of both strong and weak ties are important for strengthening connections within a culture and building bridges to cross over into new ones.

Moving between different cultures is something each of us does every day, whether it's transitioning between family and work culture, from same to different generation interaction, one group style to another, and one geographical or language group to another. Although this chapter focuses on language cultures, we'll continue to explore culture in its other senses in the following chapters. In any given day, we listen to multiple cultures, playing a role as strong-tie members within familiar cultures, and as weak-tie learners and bridges across them.

Because Cultural Listening occurs on a cline from strong-tie familiar to weak-tie unfamiliar, outside our homes, we are continually engaging in a form of intercultural communication – in the learning and exploration of weak-tie cultures. This is particularly true in a language like English which has a landslide majority of second-language and multilingual listeners. It's how listening within the same language like English can be massively deceptive, lulling us into a complacence that allows us to think we're operating within the deep structure of one strong-tie culture when we're actually communicating across multiple weak-tie cultures.

In fact, because speaking and listening in the same language doesn't guarantee you won't communicate across cultures, we'll start this chapter by busting a couple of myths about English and intercultural communication. Then we'll look at an example of just how dangerous it is to assume we are communicating in the same cultural language. The assumption that we're all in a big melting pot speaking the same English can lead to communication breakdowns with tragic consequences or long-term misunderstanding of the kind we'll explore in the second half of the chapter.

Language and Culture Myth: Busted

A popular myth about intercultural communication is that it takes place between two monolingual people who come from different countries and speak different languages. Even a moment's reflection, though, shows how this can't be true. If two people don't speak the same language it's hard to even start a conversation until one person learns the other person's language. If you've been in a situation where you don't speak the other person's language, you'll know you can't misunderstand them because the 'mis' in misunderstanding implies that you initially understood something that turned out to be not quite right. Ironically, misunderstanding arises when you think you've understood the other person and you haven't, as I discovered many times while growing up in different cultures.

The next myth is nearly the opposite. It says that if you speak the same language, there won't be any confusion or misunderstanding because it isn't intercultural communication. But this myth too is easily busted by simply thinking about a monolingual first-language English-speaker from the United States meeting a monolingual first-language English-speaker from Great Britain. As soon as they meet, each would probably agree that when they talk and listen to each other, they are talking across cultures.

The same misunderstanding occurred between the South Korean heir and the North Korean officer. Both parties thought they were from the same culture because of a presumed common language, Korean, only to find out that actually, they were from such vastly different cultures that they might as well have been speaking different languages. Intercultural communication does occur between speakers and listeners of the same language, although those with different regional varieties of English might again argue that Americans, Australians, New Zealanders, South Africans, Singaporeans and the host of countries where English is the primary language of the population don't actually speak the same 'English'. But take a look at the list of countries where English is the predominant first-language.

List of countries where English is the official first language[1,2]

In these countries, English is an official first language – an official language meaning it is legally recognized. Many of these countries are multilingual, but only the countries that have a legally recognized official language are listed with their co-official languages alongside them.

Antigua and Barbuda
The Bahamas
Barbados
Belize (Spanish, Mayan)
Botswana
Burundi (Kirundi, French)

Cultural Listening

Cameroon (French)
Canada (French)
Curaçao (Papiamento, Dutch)
Dominica
Eswatini (Swati)
Fiji (Fijian, Fijian Hindi)
The Gambia
Ghana
Grenada
Guyana
India
Ireland (Irish)
Jamaica
Kenya (Swahili)
Kiribati (Gilbertese)
Lesotho (Sotho)
Liberia
Malawi (Chewa)
Malta
Marshall Islands (Marshallese)
Mauritius
Micronesia
Namibia
Nauru
Nigeria
Pakistan
Palau (Palauan)
Papua New Guinea (Tok Pisin, Hiri Motu, Papua Guinea
    Sign Language)
Puerto Rico (Spanish)
Philippines (Filipino)

Rwanda (French, Swahili)

Saint Kitts and Nevis

Saint Lucia (Saint Lucian French Creole)

Saint Vincent and the Grenadines

Samoa (Samoan)

Seychelles (French, Seychellois Creole)

Sierra Leone

Singapore (Mandarin Chinese, Malay, Tamil)

Solomon Islands

South Africa (Afrikaans, Ndebele, Northern Sotho, Sotho, Swazi, Tswana, Tsonga, Venda Xhosa, Zulu)

South Sudan

Sudan (Arabic)

Tanzania

Tonga (Tongan)

Trinidad and Tobago

Tuvalu (Tuvaluan)

Uganda (Swahili)

Vanuatu (Bislama, French)

Zambia (Bemba, Nyanja, Lozi, Tonga, Luvale, Lunda, Kaonde)

Zimbabwe (Chewa, Chibarwe, Kalanga, Koisan Nambya, Ndau, Ndebele, Shangani, Shona, sign language, Sotho, Tonga, Tswana, Venda, Xhosa)

In these countries, English is spoken de facto by both the government and the majority population even though it is not a legally recognized official language:

Australia

New Zealand

United Kingdom

United States

The prevalence of the English language can be explained through the charged history of political, economic and cultural power. Despite the many who fought the spread of the English language in the world, the language has, to the chagrin and protest of many, emerged victorious as the recognized global lingua franca, overshadowing the nineteenth-century linguistic designer Ludwik Lejzer Zemjonhof's constructed language, Esperanto, once advanced as a neutral language for the international community. Although Esperanto had a dedicated community of followers, it failed to gain the status that lived languages like French and English held as the languages of global powers.

Beginning in the nineteenth century and accelerated by the internet and the media, the English language began to gain the advantage as the most widely spoken language in the world. Like other languages, English shows its battle scars and victories, and has used them both to its advantage. Current statistics reveal some 1.456 billion speakers of English, with a whopping 1.087 billion speaking English as a second language or alongside other languages. Chinese, the world's second most widely spoken language, has a majority of first-language speakers, numbering 939 million of the total number of 1.138 billion Chinese speakers.

It's worth repeating that if you're an English-language listener, you're likely to be involved at some level in intercultural communication, which turns out to be good news in promoting the robustness of the language. Despite what we sometimes hear, cultural diversity promotes language health. Cultural diversity has expanded English with word and grammar borrowings, invigorating not only the language but also promoting the individual well-being of the people using it. In a study of adult health, 50,000 respondents across eight countries were found to demonstrate a positive correlation between well-being and interaction with people from different cultures.[3] More than the intensity with familiar strong-tie persons or a high number of interactions overall, the researchers discovered the surprising finding that it was cultural diversity that brought health to the everyday lives of individuals. Like trees that benefit from biodiversity, humans too benefit from the interaction we have with the people with whom we have the weakest ties. As the sociologist Mark Granovetter's research shows, weak ties are the ones that provide us with the access to information and opportunities we might not have otherwise had.[4] Forging new connections fosters openness and the desire to learn even more.

That said, we also want and need interaction with people we know. Hanging out with our strong-ties people brings us all the benefits of the homophily we discussed before, where bonds with people we know can bring us the feeling of comfort and restoration. Our wellness is threatened, though, if we bank exclusively on strong-tie relations to the exclusion of weak-tie cultural interactions. When we lean in too long and often, cultural blind spots that promote siloed echo chambers like the kind we sometimes find on social networking platforms can emerge.

In ideal Cultural Listening, what we want is a mix of both worlds, to have the recuperative feeling of like-mindedness but also the expansiveness to savour adventure and learning. When we have the ideal blend of Cultural Listening, we can enjoy culture in language the way we do culture in food, music and dance. And luckily for the tuned-in listener, because cultural language is everywhere to practise and enjoy, you can embark on a journey of listening in every new inter-cultural interaction with something familiar to rely on and something new to learn.

One final myth to bust is that misunderstandings in intercultural communication mostly occur because the second-language speaker has a foreign accent the first-language speaker can't understand. Of course, misunder-standing of language because of 'an accent' does happen, and misunderstandings from being unable to listen-for and understand national or regional language are pervasive. One such misunderstanding is caricatured in a *Saturday Night Live* comedic skit, in which an American passenger trying to do an emergency landing can't understand a single word the ground controller is saying in his 'thick' Scottish accent. Though our inability to understand each other's accents can be as silly as in the *SNL* skit, our ability to understand each other's cultures as represented in voice and language is often down to much more than a surface-level speaker's accent and a listener's ability for language comprehension.

Intercultural communication failures do occur because the second-language speaker is mispronouncing words. But miscommunication can also occur because of the deeper underlying structure of culture. Accents and words are the transparent features of language in intercultural commu-nication that are easy to identify and blame for the mis-understanding, but it's often rooted in the deeper cultural language, such as time and authority, as we'll explore in this chapter.

An Anatomy of an Airline Crash

Weather conditions were hampering Avianca Flight 052 from landing at John F. Kennedy International Airport. Although the investigation that followed the crash acknowledged that it was a general misunderstanding about fuel management between the air traffic controller and the crew, the ruling stated that the 'communication failure' occurred primarily because the Columbian crew failed to use the word 'emergency'. A forensic analysis of the transcript of the radio transmission (RDO), however, can reveal that there were deeply ingrained cultural notions about time and authority that may have contributed to the misunderstanding that ultimately led to the crash. In our chapter on Credibility Listening, we said that every story has at least two sides, and a third that is the potential truth. Let's see if we can get to the truth of what happened to Avianca 052 by Cultural Listening.

Cultural Language Sensitivity to Authority and Power

I often joke with my partner and tell him that when I want him to really listen, I'll preface whatever I have to say with the name of a respected friend, James. All I need to do is start off a sentence by saying, 'James said that . . .' and my partner is switched on to whatever I have to say. James is a successful and influential person in the financial world, who has status and the authority to wield it. In the English-speaking world, we tend to think of status as a resource and power as something that is earned and built over time, giving the person with status authority. When a listener feels that a speaker has authority, they are inclined to be more attentive, considerate and cooperative. In other words, when we're in interaction with a person of authority, we're highly primed to listen to them.

The authority bestowed upon a speaker by their listeners gives that person the right to give commands and instruction, enforce obedience and make decisions. Both speakers and listeners look to authority to help us make sense of our world and ultimately make good decisions moving forward. Furthermore, because those individuals are part of a wider culture that supports them, by listening to and affirming their instructions, we're also abiding by the larger social structures that enforce aspects of our familiar strong-tie culture. When my partner listens to James, he is also listening to the culture that echoes his own beliefs as well as James's.

A belief system that echoes our own reality has enormous benefits, as sharing beliefs not only validates them but also fosters connection with our community. Within the strong ties of our own culture, we look to authority to keep ourselves in check, relying on it especially in times of crisis. This was the case for both the air traffic controller on the ground and the crew members aboard Avianca Flight 052 en route from Bogotá, Columbia, to New York City, when foul weather forced multiple flights to remain in a holding pattern above the airport for over an hour. In the case of Flight 052, however, they were in a holding pattern for so long that they could no longer land at the alternative airport in Boston.

When asked how much longer they could wait, the first officer replied, 'about five minutes'. As the controller gave

Flight 052 clearance to land, the aircraft encountered wind shear at a different altitude than the one given by the controller and couldn't land. While the JFK approach controller addressed other flights, they sent Flight 052 back on a climb for another approach: 'I'm going to bring you about fifteen miles northeast and then turn you back.'

By then, Flight 052 was so critically low on fuel that they couldn't afford to climb for another approach. In the transmission of the flight recorder, we can hear the first officer reporting this, repeating they were 'running out of fuel' four times in a span of two minutes. The captain also stresses the urgency of the situation, asking the first officer if they have pointed out the level of emergency of the situation to the controller on three occasions. The first officer replies to each that they have – and indeed, from the point of view of the flight crew, it appeared that they had communicated the dire situation of the plane.

It would be an understatement to say the transmission of the flight recorder revealed stress in the ground crew's voices. The speech volume of the ground crew's voices isn't only elevated throughout, but the pitch in their voices also becomes noticeably higher as they try to juggle the landing of other planes alongside Avianca 052. We can even hear this in the controller's instructional voice and language for the approach, as they add, 'Is that fine with you and your fuel?', which the first engineer hears as anger. In response to the captain's question, 'What did he say?', instead of feeding back the controller's comment verbatim, the engineer responds by describing the controller's tone of voice: 'The guy is angry.'

From the cool chair of a first-language listener of English, a specific topic introduced with 'you and your' might also be heard as carrying a tone of frustration tinged with sarcasm. As the crew in the cockpit process what the engineer perceived as the controller's anger, an unidentified crew member is heard replying on the RDO to the earlier question about whether the landing was good for them by saying, 'I guess so. [Thank] you very much.' The captain next asks for the 'ILS' – the instrument landing system for the runway approach to land the plane – and the flight engineer, first officer and captain each observe the controller's instructions, obeying the command for the ILS in turn to land a plane they knew was going to crash: 'We must follow that ILS.' 'We must follow the identified ILS.' 'I'm going to follow this. To die.'

As armchair analysts with plenty of time, we can shake our heads and say you should listen to your gut in crisis situations, especially when there are lives at stake and you have suspicions that something isn't going to work. As an absolute philosophy, putting life ahead of authority sounds like a good universal, but the social psychologist Geert Hofstede has observed that humans often take the decision to listen to authority over their own sense of what they think is morally or rationally right in everything from friends taking sides with the popular group, to organizational cultures that ignore malpractice. Just last week, I got out of the lift on the wrong floor of the hospital on my way to a blood test just because a physician told me the directions on the referral letter were wrong. Overriding my own check of the wards in the hospital layout plan that showed the information was right, I listened to the physician tell me the wrong place to go. Authority expressed in words is a powerful cultural influencer that guides our decision making.

Hidden Meanings: Say What You Mean

Culture that is expressed in language and voice is blatantly obvious when analyzed with hindsight, but it's hard to listen fast for it in situ. In the heat of trying to land multiple planes in poor weather conditions, the controller would not have had the time to be able to recognize the way the Columbian crew decided to give them absolute authority to decide their fate, especially since they didn't find the crew's reading of the critical supply of fuel left in the tank credible. And even if they did believe them, they still might not have understood how the flight crew could have given them so much authority given the time limit on their lives. However, the anthropologist Edward T. Hall shows that the flight crew aren't alone in the way they prioritize authority over time, characterizing such a 'polychronic' culture as one that systematically privileges relationships over time. By contrast, a 'monochronic' culture prioritizes time over authority, seeing adherence to scheduling as the necessary and democratic way of equally distributing the limited resource of time.

Japan is a culture that is classed as 'bi-temporal' since they are highly sensitive to both time and authority. We can easily see how the Japanese privilege time by observing how they regard train regularity – when a train is late by over a minute, an employee has the right to a time pass that can excuse their tardiness to work. The tardiness pass looks after the relationship of employees and employers, explaining why workers were late for work. The pass informs employers that it wasn't personal oversight that led to their tardiness but a train system error. The tardiness pass is one way the Japanese express their polychronic and monochronic cultures that simultaneously mind both relationship and time.

In crisis situations, cultural tones are stressed and become acute. It's how an authoritative instruction can become the creed of a dictator in the minds of a polychronic flight crew, carried out at whatever cost, and how a monochronic ground crew might try to do their job within the impossible time frame with a mindset that dismisses the flight crew's plight as less than theirs: 'Is that fine for you and your fuel?'

The investigation that followed the crash of Avianca Flight 052 attributed the communication breakdown to a flight crew who did not create an adequate sense of urgency of the fuel situation by not explicitly using the word 'emergency'. Indeed, although the captain repeatedly asked the first officer whether they had instructed the tower of the 'emergency' and the first officer responded that he had, the actual word was not relayed to the control tower. The transcript of the RDO, though, does reveal the officers' heightened concerns in no uncertain terms. In fact, by the end of the first aborted landing, more than five minutes had elapsed since the first officer replied 'about five minutes' in response to the question about how much longer they could continue to hold. A monochronic controller who does calculations all the time would have been aware that Flight 052 was in an emergency – if the estimation the flight crew was giving them was accurate.

What 'you and your fuel' does show, then, is that the controller is doubtful about the crew's estimations because they have evidence to support their suspicion that the plane is actually not in immediate danger in the fact that it has already lasted longer than five minutes. Based on this data point, when the controller hears, 'We're running out of fuel,' they could easily wonder if the Columbian crew are lowballing their fuel availability. The grammar of the English language would certainly support this hypothesis, since the phrase 'running out of fuel' couches the aircraft's fuel situation in much broader temporal terms – it isn't out of fuel yet. The progressive tense 'running' is also ambiguous as it doesn't give a time limit or the absolute sense of 'emergency' that a straightforward present tense might: 'We're out of fuel!'

Each language has its own way of carving up time, and it is often grammar that's called on to communicate this. One critical difference between Spanish and English grammar is the way each time-stamps the progressive tense. While both languages use the progressive tense to describe ongoing activity, Spanish uses the progressive tense in a polychronic sense to make 'we're running out of fuel' include the idea that 'we have already run out of fuel'. In other words, the progressive tense in Spanish can carry the same sense of urgency found in the word 'emergency' and the simple tense that first-language speakers of English would probably use to say the same thing: 'we're out of fuel!'

Different orientations to time can explain why instead of urgency, the controller heard arrogance. Since pronouns are optional in Spanish, using them adds the same emphasis that first-language English speakers employ when they want to stress a word. In a situation where the ground crew are juggling the time constraints of many, one flight's emphasis on the personal pronoun 'we', in the absence of a listening understanding of urgency, can make the statement 'WE are running out of fuel' sound like a demand – *Hey, can't you see? We're the ones who need special treatment!*

In sum, the flight recorder showed that cultural notions of authority and time added to the miscommunication that ultimately resulted in the crash of Avianca 052 and the death of seventy-three passengers in Cove Neck, Long Island. Cultural language isn't just the omission of words like 'emergency', it's also embedded in the grammar. Following the investigation, recommendations were made to improve communication by standardizing aviation phraseology, for example, by enforcing the use of the word 'correction' to correct a misspoken word and using more restrictive language in the event of an emergency. In addition to these improvements, aviation personnel could take part in sensitivity training on the hidden features of cultural language to develop an awareness of cultural features that can inform critical conversation in situ.

Aviation personnel aren't the only people who make decisions with cultural language under stress – we regularly listen to varying conflicts of authority and time in our everyday conversations, particularly at work, where we make decisions about whether it's the person with authority or the person with expedience who should complete a task. One way we can overcome the dilemma of time and authority in a stressed situation where there are competing goals is to share the responsibility of time and make each other the authority of a collaborative effort. This can be achieved by the traditional means of division of labour or through the kinds of 'listening loops' we will discuss in our chapter on Work Listening. Either of these involves cooperative communication, but also an understanding of cultural language.

In the chapter on Credibility Listening, we talked about the conceptual metaphor *Time is money*, where time is seen as a limited resource that an individual 'spends' on something or another person. In this chapter, we saw that a culture that is sensitive to time will tend to privilege time, especially under pressure, and a culture that is sensitive to authority will privilege authority, even when they are stressed. The solution to the dilemma of two cultural languages meeting is demonstrated listening, through which we show that we are giving each other the authority to use time as a shared resource and a mutual goal for both.

The Japanese characters for 'time', 時間, illustrate this collaboration because they include the idea of time as a shared resource, where the first character features the concept of time as a single point 時 and the second features time as a duration 間 – the way we use the word 'time' in English when we say things like 'I'm giving it time'. The second character 間 is literally written to mean 'the space in between' and is the same second character that symbolizes 'humans', which is written as, 'people with in-between spaces' 人間. When we give each other authority, the way the Zen Master Dōgen Zenji advises in 'seeing others as ourselves', all of us are in the in-between space of time and authority together so we can resolve the problem in collaboration.

In communication, we need to make each other aware of this call to be 'on the same page' and demonstrate that we understand our mutual dilemma from the in-between space. Assuming that we will automatically understand each other's points of view is potentially dangerous in crisis situations and that's why it's helpful to demonstrate we have heard the other person's position. Even though we have ways of indirectly communicating our collaborative intentions in face-to-face, in-person conversations, voicing them confirms that everyone is speaking in the same semantic field of language and culture together. Like the ground and flight crew stressed by limited time and fuel and bad weather, we need language that actually tells the other person we're listening. In stressed circumstances where time is of the essence, we need to jump in the space in between to join forces towards collaborative goals of time and authority and demonstrate our mutual listening.

The Power of Demonstrated Listening

In the early part of the twentieth century, the anthropologists Edward Sapir and his student and linguist Benjamin Lee Whorf proposed the idea that language expresses culture but also shapes it. Called the Sapir–Whorf hypothesis, the theory that language dictates thought is debated, but ongoing research supports the idea that the language we speak and listen to influences cognition. The use of imperfect progressive 'we're running out of fuel', in Spanish and the English equivalent 'we're out of fuel' are examples of how speakers not only use grammar to structure our cultural conceptions of time, but also how words and amplifiers affect our understanding of a situation.

What the English and Spanish language cultures have in common is that both see cultural language as a powerful form of communication. The novelist and poet Rita Mae Brown once referred to cultural language as a 'roadmap' that tells people where they've come from and where they're going. Language carries our histories, and this deeply influences the way we think and talk. Nineteenth-century poet, literary critic and philosopher Samuel Taylor Coleridge thought of language as 'the armory of the human mind, and at once contains the trophies of its past and the weapons of its future conquests,' suggesting that language isn't just a tool for passing down history, but also a powerful call to arms for action in the future. In more contemporary terms, we see cultural language as empowering talk so that the squeaky wheel is the one that gets the grease. Ask and you shall receive because, as the novelist and social critic Thomas Mann believed: 'Speech is civilization itself.'

In monochronic cultures where the assumption that talk is power, talk-time is regulated by a governing body, particularly in a formal register like a public speaking event. In a TED Talk, for example, the recommended length of talk time is dictated to be something like eighteen minutes – an optimal cognitive-load time after which listeners start to get distracted. Elsewhere in talk culture, a fifteen-minute airtime is one of the justifications for cutting up shows with advertisements. News and entertainment like interviews or podcasts can go on for longer as our brains can handle conversations when it's not one person talking all the time.

Not all cultures promote talk as power, however. To the contrary, some cultures see talk as carrying the risk of attracting unwanted attention. The old Japanese adage says, 'The bird would not have been shot if it did not sing.' In cultures where talk is dialled down, listening is the preferred mode of communication. We saw in the chapter on Credibility Listening that in listening cultures, talking quickly becomes too much talk that is heard as self-promotion. Instead of fixing things by gaining attention, in these cultural languages, talking can even be heard as non-action. There's a Chinese saying, 'Talk doesn't cook rice', and a Native American one that advises, 'It's better to have less thunder in the mouth and more lightning in the hand.' These cultures generally tend to think of talk as not necessarily the best means for resolving issues, certainly when compared to action, the way the English parliamentarian, John Pym once suggested in 1628 when he said, 'Actions speak louder than words.' Today, though, as words become formalized in policy, words can become action, leading us back to the idea that words themselves are empty until they are filled with our culturally normative values as right words, in the right amount and manner.

Cultural language helps remind us in our groups what we consider 'normal' talk. Too little talk compromises the quality of our talk, making us sound 'vague' and 'unclear', while too much talk can interfere with relevance and manner, making us sound 'in your face', 'pushy' or even 'rude'. When we use our own cultural language to understand other cultural languages, we sometimes end up misinterpreting what others mean, which can, over time, make us buy into stereotypes about them.

This chapter finishes with an example of how misunderstanding can arise from the different ways in which cultures distribute talk time. Listeners of different language cultures apply their own conversational maxims of quality and quantity that impact the way they hear each other's conversational rhythm and pacing. Just like we can misunderstand the words of a language, we can also end up misinterpreting cultural language represented in quantity and overlap. When we evaluate the rhythms of other language cultures with our own expectations, they not only fail to meet our standards, but we also hear the other culture as 'off'.

Queue Talkers, Pacey Talkers, Listener-Talkers

I think of myself as having pretty average patience. On a scale of one to ten, from hating standing in line at one to the patience of a sloth at ten, I'm probably a boring five. To serious queue haters, I'm cattle, resigned to listen to authority and follow the crowd. To serious queuers at ten, on the other hand, I look like a reckless inconsiderate who jumps the queue. Every individual and every culture has its own Goldilocks gauge for the threshold of patience for queueing in communication – the duration of time a person must wait to take a turn at talk.

Part of the reason why I'm at the noncommittal number five position in queueing-style preference is because I operate in three queueing cultures on a daily basis. I was born in a culture that advocates group queuing to maximize efficiency in public spaces, moved through work cultures that formally distribute individual talk queueing into rounds to improve equality in diverse settings, and live with a partner who has strong anti-queuing convictions that come from the cultural belief that queuing sacrifices individuality and leadership. With three different cultural queueing styles under my nose, I've come to discover that the stereotypical talk-queueing styles of Japan, the US and France each has its own advantages and disadvantages.

Queueing in conversation resembles physical queuing, except that unlike queuing to post a parcel, we can't physically see who is queueing to speak. If we could, we'd be able to see all the talk-distribution styles. On one end of the spectrum there are the pacey talkers who don't hang around and wait to take a turn to talk. They're the kind of talkers who ask frequent questions and overlap their talk with others'. At the other end, there are the people I've called listener-talkers, people who use a highly self-regulated cultural pacing style of folding themselves into the ongoing talk. In the middle are the listeners who wait for their turn in organized settings.

Most of us know this middle style the best and promote it, as it seems a kind of working equitable talk distribution system that's easy to execute and enforce. Many of us have hybrid cultural queueing styles, which we express variously depending on the occasion or setting. For example, we might have one style for our work culture that's necessitated by weak ties and enforced in an organization, and another that's supported by strong-tie friends and family members at home. In the following, we explore the less familiar talk distributors then come back to our strong-tie, middle-of-the road cultural talk-distribution style to see how the talk pace we consider 'normal' can feel strange to other kinds of talk-distributors.

Pacey Talkers:
Shared Talk Creates Dynamic Inclusion

After a talk at a conference, a scholar once came over to ask me a question. As it turned out, it wasn't one question but two, no, three. In the end, it may have even been four or five questions, I don't remember. The questioner was using a serial line of questioning where she asked a second question before I had the chance to finish answering the first one. Her style of questioning was so rapid fire that, as a listener, I could barely keep up. I felt like Gromit in the Wallace and Gromit movie *The Wrong Trousers*, where Gromit is in a cargo train laying down the tracks as fast as he can while being chased by the evil penguin. In my answers, I ended up stop-starting over and over again. If there were a transcript of my repsonse, which thankfully there wasn't, it would have probably shown that I didn't really properly answer a single question.

That scholar in question isn't the evil penguin but sociolinguist Deborah Tannen, who has written about a fast-paced New York Jewish style of talk she called 'machine-gun questioning' in her book *Conversational Styles*.[5] Machine-gun questioning is a cultural style of speech where a questioner asks multiple questions to show their interest in a person or something the person is talking about. The cumulative effect of this highly fast-paced style of speech for queue-talkers is one where everyone seems to be talking all at once. If you're not a first-language speaker of this cultural style, your first instinct is to clam up.

For two machine-gun questioners who share the same style, though, asking multiple questions builds rapport and forms deep connection. 'How you doing? And the kids? You still working yourself to death? How's that paper?' Each question asks something different but is often graded in specificity from general to specific. Like a discerning physician trying to hear the finer details of your heart murmur, it doesn't take long for the questioner to gain a sense of your overall well-being via the snippets of replies.

By comparison, think of the British greeting 'You alright?' and the response 'Yeah, alright,' which might be abbreviated to a smile or a nod, but accomplishes a similar objective of momentary solidarity – this time, with little to no talk. Here's an example of people from two countries, the United States and Great Britain, who both speak the same first-language, English, and yet still have distinct cultural talk styles that are miles apart. A Londoner friend once told me that she put off getting together with a friend from New York because they kept gunning her down with questions. 'Now she wonders why I'm so shy,' said my friend.

Different talk-distribution styles are often lost in translation, but at home with the same talk-distribution style they work to bond, even if the talk-style isn't mainstream. I recently heard a podcast host claim that her Italian-British family never listened. She said that the family didn't wait to take turns the way normal people who listened do. As I've never sat at their dinner table, I wouldn't know for sure, but apart from those who wish their relatives were more like the queue talkers they know outside the home, I'd wager that the relatives felt satisfied by the pacey cultural style of talk whenever they got together.

Listener-Talkers:
When Shared Silence Creates Togetherness

There's a joke amongst expatriates living in Japan about waiting for a lift. Outside of Japan, if a lift takes a long time to arrive, you might think a child was playing around with the buttons. In Japan, though, a lift that takes a long time to arrive means the people on the other floors are playing out the cultural custom of 'after you'.

I coined the phrase 'listener talk' in my cross-cultural study of bankers[6] to try to capture a conversational queueing system where people vie to be the listener rather than the speaker. Listener talk describes people queueing to talk (get in the lift) where the goal is for the other person to go first. This conversational queueing style is a cultural custom like other customs that becomes habit in which queueing up to listen is the comfortable norm. While it's no more polite than other talk-queueing systems, many non-listener-talker friends say the cultural style of queueing makes those with that style appear excessively and almost comically polite. Ironically, this positive but inaccurate depiction of listener talk has a negative correlate where not-talking enough in the context of queue talkers and pacey talkers is heard as insolent and non-participatory in classrooms, meetings and boardrooms. Within the listener talk culture, however, not talking or even having bumbly talk is considered genuine, considerate and, most of all, normal.

Unlike pacey talk that places the responsibility of communication on the speaker, listener talk places the responsibility on the listener. The result is the presentation of longer listening spaces, like the long pauses I found in a Japanese meeting I studied to allow for topic closure before making the shift to new topics.[7] The longest pause in the study was an eight-second pause between topics. Asked what the bankers were thinking about in the long pause, they said they were checking no one else had anything to say and enjoying concluding the topic.

In intercultural training sessions, I found that listener talk natives are generally more comfortable with longer pausing. When I stopwatch an eight-second pause with an audience who do not share this style, fidgeting and nervous laughter begins at around four to five seconds, at which point the pause is typically cut short by talk. When a listener-talker meets someone outside their talk-distribution culture, what often ends up happening is that a non-listener-talker begins filling up the space with talk, which ends up exacerbating the existing imbalance. We'll talk more about these aggravated intercultural misunderstandings in the next chapter on Social Listening, but first we need to set straight another positive bias about listener talk.

Listener talk isn't altruism – it isn't 'letting someone talk' like it might be in other more fast-paced cultural queueing styles where the goal is to get to talk. Listener talk differs from the charity model of giving resources to those who don't have it, in the way that merit-making monks are not passive receivers of charity but rather active merit-givers who create the opportunity for community members. It's a way of creating equity through the context of people rather than through content, the way queue talkers do when they talk in rounds according to an agenda. In other words, listener-talkers don't really see themselves as giving something up. They aren't practising 'shut up and listen'; they're vying for the chance to listen.

Regular Queuing

At a bakery in France, a young American who was chatting with me got to the front of the queue. When the baker asked what kind of bread he wanted, he responded by saying he wanted 'regular bread'. You can imagine the fun the baker had with the poor chap whose idea of 'regular bread' was probably not the baker's.

What's regular or normal in conversation is whatever you are used to using and hearing. Fall outside it and you are judged. Speech speed is an example. In the US, if your speed isn't regular and you speak too slowly, you're accused of sounding less intelligent. But speak too quickly and now you might be accused of sounding neurotic. The aim is to have that just-right brisk pace of standard American English, a somewhat regionally unplaceable accent to be found in a café on a sitcom somewhere between Chicago and New York City.[8]

So what is this ideal just-right pace, you might ask. A study calculated that the average speaking rate of English varies from 110 words-per-minute (wpm) at the slow end and 180 wpm at the fast end. Auctioneers allegedly go up much higher still, but radio readers and podcasters are asked to aim for about 150 to 160 wpm. They say that the average listener processes comfortably in the 140–160 wpm range, a noticeably lower rate than the average reading speed of 200–400 words per minute. We don't know for sure if this is because our brains are better visual than audial processors, or whether it's because all our effort in school went into reading rather than listening. There's still much to discover for the talk-distribution, pacing and queueing practices, even within our own national and academic cultures.

Much to the delight of many a sociolinguist, there is great cultural diversity in the micro-cultures within a country. Even in a small country like the United Kingdom, where the majority language is English, there are many regional varieties of cultural language. Culture listeners in the UK can hear multiple indigenous languages, such as English, Welsh, Scots and Gaelic, and many more dialects, like those the language pundit Ryan Starkey identifies in their colourful maps you can enjoy by linking to their website marked in the endnotes.[9]

As Starkey points out, language and culture are ever evolving, and there are no real hard lines around the borders of dialects. In fact, the very idea of dialect itself is problematic, mostly because it's an outdated way of thinking about language. We informally think of different languages as mutually unintelligible and different dialects as intelligible with specific words and an 'accent' that make them unique. But on closer inspection, this distinction falls short, since languages like Spanish and Portuguese share more similarities than Mandarin Chinese and Cantonese, where Cantonese has historically been considered a dialect of the former. Conversely, we already talked about the *Saturday Night Live* clip[10] that showed how dialect pronunciation in the same language can vary so much that they are indecipherable to those who are unfamiliar with a regional variation like Scottish.

Cultural language is everywhere and in the following chapters, we'll see that we interpret it in the way we classify and organize our social structures in Social Listening, too. Seeing all cultural language as intercultural action is helpful in stepping into the relational space in between our own cultures and others so that we aren't blindsided by the biases of our own strong ties. Outside our protective borders, there is always a greater risk that we might end up misunderstanding someone. Awareness about the cultural language in our weak ties, though, can go some way into preventing us from becoming stuck in our increasingly polarized and siloed worlds, where, despite the global expansion of communication, we still propagate misinterpretations of new and old normals, and unintentionally fan stereotypes that incite conflict. By stepping outside our world of strong ties with a novice mindset, we can enjoy Cultural Listening to learn about others from their perspectives and promote healthy relationships that can enrich our own multicultural lives. Cultural Listening might not help us fall in love with an officer in enemy territory, but it can help us know what to listen for in the eventuality that we meet a host of other people in our culturally diverse world.

7 Keys to Cultural Listening

- Intercultural communication is more than talking and listening to people from different countries, racial or ethnic backgrounds; it is talking and listening to people from any different language culture.

- Miscommunication between people of different language cultures is more likely to occur because of misunderstandings of culture expressed in language rather than mishearing words because of foreign accents.

- Two interconnected features of language cultures are different sensitivities to authority and time. Serious miscommunication, misunderstanding and long-term stereotyping can occur between people of different language cultures speaking English when one person privileges time and the other authority.

- Language cultures vary in the way they value, distribute and pace talk. For example, by taking turns to talk in conversation or distributing it in rounds in formal settings.

- Not all language cultures have the same sensitivity to talk and this difference can create misunderstanding. In listening for rhythm in conversation, for example, pacey talkers who demonstrate their interest with a rapid, high-overlap questioning style are often misunderstood as pushy and aggressive, while listener-talkers who vie to listen rather than talk are often misunderstood as people who don't take initiative.

- Many of us live in multiple language cultures that vary not only by geographical region but also by social organization, occupation and generation.

- Awareness in Cultural Listening helps us to prepare for conversations with people from different language cultures.

3 Cultural Language Reflections: Cultural Gauge Tune-Ups

■ Thinking of culture as more than countries, but also regions, social groups, occupations and generations, how many cultures do you see yourself a part of?

■ Thinking of time and authority sensitivities, which one are you more sensitive to? Are you equally sensitive to both? Does it depend on the time and place? Have you ever noticed a mismatch of these cultural language features in conversation?

■ Are you a pacey talker, a listener-talker, a queue talker or a mix of all three? What kind of talk-distribution culture did you grow up in? Do you practice different talk-pacing in different cultures – for example, at work and at home? Are you more comfortable with one than the other? Have you ever noticed the mismatch of these talk-distribution features in conversation?

7

Social Listening

Social Exchange

At a launch for a new joint venture, CEO Tak Watanabe was walking by the bar in his black tie when an employee asked him to make a drink. A first-language speaker of Japanese and a second-language speaker of English, Tak recounts the hilarious story about how he tried to reject the request without actually saying the word 'no' because he didn't want to embarrass the employee. 'Ugh,' said Tak, who had lived long enough in the United States to be familiar with their more direct communication style, 'you know what I said? "Uh, actually, I don't know how to make a Mojito".'

Unable to understand why a barman would not be able to fix a common drink, the employee asked, 'You don't?' This was Tak's second opportunity to back out of making a drink but in the spirit of building good relations with his future employees, Tak explained why he couldn't: 'Yeah, sorry, I only know how to make a Singapore Sling.' At this point, Tak said he was sure that the employee would come to his senses and that would be the end of that. But as he glanced over at the stage where he was going to be making a speech momentarily, he heard a voice behind him say, 'Okay, a Singapore Sling then.' Now under time pressure, Tak joked that he looked the part, making small talk while mixing the cocktail and recounting how he had learned to make a Singapore Sling when he was living there. 'You were a barman in Singapore?' the employee asked, but luckily by then, the actual barman had returned. Smiling as he handed the employee the drink, Tak was finally able to make his exit to give his speech for the launch.

Even though the ending of this true story is a happy one, I often tell it as an example of what the anthropologist Gregory Bateson called 'complementary schismogenesis', the aggravating situation in which trying to fix a problem by doing what you know best only makes it worse. By trying to be agreeable, Tak didn't achieve his goal of backing out of the situation until he was saved by the barman, and it took many back-and-forths for the employee to finally get his drink.

Other instances of complementary schismogenesis in communication aren't as comical, as we know from the interaction that took place on Avianca 052 between the Columbian flight crew and the New York air traffic controller, where the flight crew's priority for authority conflicted with the ground controller's goal of timing the landing of three planes. In trying to resolve the situation, each focused harder on their own fix that reflected their cultural values, only for it to end in disaster. A difference of cultural values can end in complementary schismogenesis, but so can a difference in communication style, like the direct and indirect styles of communication between Robert and Tak.

In fact, complementary schismogenesis that reflects direct and indirect communication styles frequently occurs between a seller and a buyer, as it did between a male vendor selling artifacts and a female tourist trying to back out of purchasing them. Like the CEO, the more the woman tried to appease the vendor, the harder the vendor came on with the next sales pitch. In the end, the woman ended up purchasing three artifacts, including one which turned out to be a national treasure, and for which she was arrested.[1]

When communication researchers observe the indirect style Tak used in relation to gender, they frequently frame it as a demonstration of feminine powerlessness. However, as the Japanese version of the CEO's indirect refusal shows, the style is not an inherent feature of powerlessness in a cultural language, whether national or gender, but a choice of a social listening tool for sending meta-messages about relationship. When an indirect style of communication is in play, its creator crafts a message about something like 'a drink', 'an artifact' or 'an event', but also provides a meta-message about the relationship. *Don't be embarrassed but I'm actually not the barman. Don't feel bad but I don't want to buy your artifacts.* When someone uses indirectness, whether a Japanese CEO or a female US tourist, it's a demonstration of Social Listening that helps the listener hear those meta-messages, live, in-person, in interaction in progress. Social Listening helps us to identify and analyze both the content and the context of actual cultural episodes so that we can have a shot at improving our conversations, in situ here and now, or in our next encounter.

In this chapter, we'll explore the echoes of the previous chapter on Cultural Listening that can help us hear a group's cultural values in social interaction. Deepening our understanding of a person's culture, Social Listening helps us to focus on how we actually play out our values and understand them in the immediate interaction. We'll look more closely at some features of conversational play, comparing the style of communication US and Australian researchers characterize as typically feminine with those of Japanese conversational style. Specifically, we'll observe how indirect conversational style includes features like no-saying avoidance, high-rising intonation (HRT) and nonverbal immediacy – all ways of sending meta-messages of relationship, but ones that have been historically viewed as feminine and portrayed as lacking in confidence in the English language. We'll then reflect on bantering styles in English that have traditionally been seen as gendered and ask if we still hear them as so. Finally, we'll also ask if the English language itself is gendered and take a look at how Social Listeners auditorily determine gender in the English language. Although Social Listening isn't just for gendered cultures, it's a good place to practise and grow your listening practice. As we work our way through different kinds of Social Listening, a great way to reconnect with your own Social Listening is to ask where you fit into the picture.

Just Say 'No'?

'Just Say No' was a 1980s and 90s US marketing campaign as part of the war against drugs that received mixed reviews, amongst which was the criticism it trivialized the health crisis of drug use in the USA. Today, mental health experts frequently advise saying no to set boundaries, but many people find turning other people down hard to do. Psychologists believe this is because of the social pressure to be agreeable. The fear of saying no, affectionately called FOSNO, sometimes causes listeners to unwillingly say yes and accept things they don't want, as it did for the US tourist and Tak. Researchers note that in daily interaction, indirect communicators have a tendency to say yes to an event we don't want to go to or accept extra work we don't think we should do.

Some things are harder to say no to than others, especially if cultural values are at the root of the response. If an authority figure asks you to perform a task, whether it's the ground controller asking you to follow a particular landing pattern or your boss telling you to complete a project by the deadline, it's harder to disagree than if it's a co-worker asking you the same. Cultural family values enforced by social regulation, like attendance at a birthday or anniversary dinner, might also make it difficult to say no and turn the invitation down. In these cases, we most often use indirection – a socially polite way of saying no.

In fact, we rarely say no in this context by literally using the word unless we're joking or angry, and the fact that every language has a repertoire of ways for saying no without actually using the word is enough to show how regularly we use indirect communication. Ways of saying no in English range from the direct 'No, thank you' and formal 'I'm afraid I can't', to the indirect 'I'm going to have to pass' and casual 'I'm good'. Sometimes we say no by apologizing for being unable to accept an invitation, with something like, 'Sorry, I need to finish something.' At other times we offer an alternative – such as 'Can I take a raincheck?' or 'Maybe next time?' Take a look at the ten ways of saying 'No', and see if you use or could use any of these.

10 Ways of Saying No in English

1. No, thank you.
2. I'm afraid I can't.
3. I would love to but I can't make it.
4. I wish I could, but unfortunately, I can't.
5. I've got a work commitment.
6. That sounds amazing but I can't.
7. Oh no, can I take a rain check?
8. I think I'll pass.
9. Not really.
10. I'm good.

Part of language competence is being able to socially listen for these highly indirect ways of saying no and infer from them an actual refusal, based on the Cooperative Principle we talked about in the chapter on Informational Listening. A socially competent listener who hears any of these ways of saying no would understand the meta-message that the speaker was trying to be cooperative and polite. Because indirect communication looks after the relationship in both formal and informal registers, socially listening for and evaluating the indirect no as the preferred choice is a way of acknowledging that the conversation doesn't need to end in conflict.

Japanese is a really handy language for saying no because it allows speakers to put the verb at the end of the sentence and pile on as many subsequent negations. Because there aren't any grammatical rules against making double or multiple negatives, an indirect no consisting of many no's are a staple in Japanese conversation even for those with authority, and for men and women alike. So here is an example of how language can enable cultural preferences that can be exercised in social interaction.

The Japanese listener-turned-speaker systematically privileges relationship over task, as was the case with the Japanese CEO at the San Francisco joint venture launch. In my study of the Japanese bankers' meeting in the US, I noted that one manager said no with three indirect nonverbal cues, then added six verbal negations at the back of a sentence to indirectly communicate the idea that he was against the idea of collaborating with a broker. Here's the translated excerpt from the meeting conducted in Japanese that shows the manager's explanation for why he is refusing:

> Well, uhhm, (I) would **not** say (I) would**n't** say that it's **not** that you know, it's definitely **not** out of the question. So, in other words, (I) want to say that it is **not** that it would**n't** happen. (I) could**n't** say that.

Even though the rejection of the idea is hyper indirect, the other middle managers are able to understand the manager's no, in part because it was preceded by three clear nonverbal signals of sucking in air, lowering his eyes and vocal doubt expressed as 'uhhm'. As the listening bankers laughed to appreciate the play of indirect communication style at its extreme, one of the managers teased how he would be poorly received by his US counterparts: 'That's terrible. It's in the recording. And it's going to be a huge minus in your performance review.' Extreme indirection, played out socially in a culture that values indirection, can be heard and welcomed as positive bonding.

Nonverbal Immediacy as Positive Bonding

Research shows that social bonding occurs amongst women in US communities through indirect nonverbal communication. The psychologist Albert Mehrabian, who studied nonverbal behaviour as a practice of likeability, advanced the idea that women more than men use 'nonverbal immediacy' to create and communicate psychological closeness. Other researchers have since agreed that nonverbal immediacies like physical proximity, sustained and extended eye contact and gaze, smiles and a rising intonation were all observed as a way in which women influence an interaction to create the atmosphere of informality, closeness and affection.[2, 3]

While some research suggests that competence in verbal and nonverbal immediacy enhances relationships, others disagree that nonverbal immediacy, especially when used solely to be likeable, can have negative implications for the relationship. For example, some social psychologists who study gender inequality argue that a woman's agreeability and no-avoidance can further encourage the social order in which women are socialized into being likeable. In communication, likeability can be understood as a socially learned trait that is both self-regulatory and performative, so that nonverbal immediacy such as indirection becomes a way for a speaker to manage the impressions they make on a listener.

One example of an indirect nonverbal immediacy that has been stigmatized is what Australian researchers call 'high-rising intonation' (HRT). We talked about listening for HRT in the first chapter on Listening with Fourteen Hearts, when listeners can hear a meta-message by listening for a shift in the standard English pattern of using a falling intonation at the end of a functional statement to the rising intonation typically used in questions. When a listener hears this shift in tone of voice, they can hear a meta-message about relationship. For example, if I say to a co-worker something like, 'I think I'll go to the launch today?' about a launch event after work, you can hear at least three additional meta-messages beyond the literal message that *I'm going to the launch event*:

1. *I haven't 100 per cent made up my mind about going to the launch event.*
2. *I'm not sure the event will be interesting.*
3. *I'm asking my co-worker if they are going, too.*

While HRT can be heard as a performative impression-management strategy for likeability, it can also be heard as an invitation to connect in the relational space between speaker and listener. When HRT is authenticated in close-tie social relations, its use can signal inclusive connection – *shall we spend time together?*

As a practice of bonding, likeability is easy to misinterpret, as it was by the media who negatively portrayed the HRT spoken by a group of teens in Southern California. Branding the variety of HRT as 'Valley Girl Speak', Australian researchers had long identified HRT as a communication style more prevalent amongst young people than older people and women more than men,[4] but it came to represent an image of loopy, vacant young women. From the media attention it received, the HRT, newly branded as 'uptalk', came to be perceived as a sign of insecurity and lack of confidence.

A style of communication, though, like a single word, has no intrinsic meaning of its own. People supply meaning and socially formalize a style by regulating and enforcing it. More recent studies show that young men also use uptalk in their speech,[5] suggesting what sociolinguists have known for some time – if ever uptalk was a feminine communication style, it could quickly change its demographics over time.[6] A communication style reflects the social environment of its time, so that as the context changes, so too do its users.

Social environment affects how a style is heard. The same study also found that the young men who used uptalk were generally not negatively evaluated as insecure,[7] suggesting that uptalk is not intrinsically a sign of insecurity or powerlessness, but so viewed only when the sociocultural climate so perceives it. If women are part of the sociodemographic perceived as powerless, it would follow that women using uptalk would be perceived as powerless.

In psychologist Anne Miller's study of communications styles typically associated with 'relatability', she found that demonstrations of nonverbal immediacy diminished with high-power roles at work, suggesting that social status can alter communication style. The study of uptalk also found that men used the communication style more frequently in the company of women,[8] suggesting not only that the men varied their style, but that they did this to accommodate their style to meet the listener's. So a style of communication doesn't only change in relation to the larger social climate of the time, but in relation to the gender of its listeners as well as the speaker's status.

Miller's study also found that although US American women used persuasive nonverbal immediacy more than men did, no such difference was reported between the women and men in their study from Brazil and Kenya.[9] This suggests that national culture also intersects with gender to influence a person's use of communication style, like indirectness and nonverbal immediacy. In my own study of Japanese business meetings, I discovered that there were expressions of intimate nonverbal immediacy in informal same-gender male inter-action. This finding came as a surprise, since the traditional view of male interaction at work is one that is void of such intimacy.

One example of nonverbal immediacy I observed took place in a branch office in San Francisco, where the Japanese middle bank managers were meeting for a weekly review. When a male manager lit up a cigarette, another male middle manager pushed over an ashtray then teased that the build-ing had a no-smoking policy. 'This policy was instituted by none other than you yourself,' he joked. As the other meeting participants joined in on the chuckle, the manager stubbed out the cigarette before tapping his accuser's hand and con-tinuing on with the meeting.

Demonstrations of all-male same-gender nonverbal imme-diacy that identifies and regulates each other's behaviour have also been observed in many countries outside of North America and Northern Europe, including South America and Mediterranean regions, Europe, the Middle East, East Asia, South- and Southeast Asia and Africa, suggesting that at least in these global regions, nonverbal immediacy isn't exclusively a feature of feminine communication.

Likeability is practised in the overlapping streams of cultural, social and personal relations, so that when we are socially listening for it, we can hear it play out in an episode of interaction. As we tune in to the dynamics of same- or intergender communication, Social Listening allows us to eavesdrop on these live episodes of conversational cultures at play, enabling us to listen in on others' cultural values and the social regulations they abide by. As social perceptions change, social listeners need to take the time and listen slow so they can hear both the echoes of traditional cultures and the changing social realities of the current time.

A communication style is evaluated in the mind of a social listener as good or bad, powerful or powerless. But language also influences culture and the new generation is innovating new hybrid communication styles, as we'll explore in the chapter on Generational Listening. With an active novice mindset, we can push the boundaries on the Cooperative Principle of communication for the social purpose of relating to and minding other listeners in the conversation. By exercising such demonstrated listening sensitivity, Social Listening can not only help young learners but also novice-minded older learners to actively engage in diverse expressions of communication styles in episodes that change with the times.

Listening for Informational Task and Relationship

In 1915, the psychologist Edgar Rubin wrote a doctoral thesis that has been immortalized as the Rubin's Vase, a picture that is remembered as a visual choice between a vase and two heads. The image was originally designed to explain how human vision could not cognitively process both images at once because visualizing one excludes the other – as the border of what you are looking at makes you see a vase, the two heads disappear, and vice versa. Although we can see both images, we can't see them both in a single point and time. If we mash the idea of Rubin's Vase with social interaction, we can say that while humans have the ability to focus on both the task at hand and the relationship of the people in the conversation together, it's hard to do both at the same. And if we mash Rubin's Vase with listening, we can say that while we can listen to a person and information at the same time, we often tend to emphasize one more than the other.

Like a selective auditory or visual focus, we have a conversational focus, too. In the throes of it, our focus can be on the immediate situation of the vase itself, or it can be on the context of two heads talking and listening, and the relationship of the people in the conversation. In the heat of the moment, especially in stressful or confusing situations like the one between Robert and the CEO, we often tend to focus on the conversational style we know best and use one listening strategy to try to resolve the problem.

Organizational psychologist Karen Jehn, who studies conflict in human relations, depicts a version of the Rubin's Vase where some conflict focuses on the task at hand (vase), while other conflict focuses on relationship (two faces in the background). Jehn argues that task conflict over ideas can be healthy, while relationship conflict tends to become filled with animosity and personal accusations.[10] Conflict resolution counsellors therefore often suggest minimizing relationship conflict and managing task conflict.

Some gender researchers who study differences in communication styles have posited that when there is conflict, men tend to focus on the task at hand while women tend to focus on the relationship. While not all researchers agree on the idea that men and women have exclusive communication styles, they tend to agree with the central idea that communication-style differences can give rise to conflict, or at least create confusion over what the conflict is about. Here's an example of such a confusion between flatmates Anna and David, where David has just bought tickets to a music festival.

> Anna: Did you already buy the tickets?
> David: Well, the festival is on Saturday when you aren't working, so . . .
> Anna: So you thought I'd come anyway?
> David: It's the only day they're on and the tickets could run out and—

When Anna first discovers that David already bought the tickets, she is surprised he hadn't thought about her schedule and asked her first. In her surprise, David can hear a voice of accusation, and he justifies his action by explaining that he bought the ticket because the festival was on a non-workday weekend. From what we know now, we can see it's a complementary schismogenesis in the making, where one person is talking about the task of purchasing the ticket, while the other person is talking about how the purchase should have involved thinking about their relationship.

Researchers disagree whether task-focus is masculine and relationship-focus is feminine, but converge on the idea that the distinction of a task-centred communication versus a relationship-centred one can help clarify potential misunderstandings in communication. In my study of communication amongst Japanese managers, I found multiple instances of what organizational experts call 'non-task sounding', which takes the form of long preludes designed to sound out the other meeting executives. Rather than being task-oriented, non-task sounding performed in the all-male group was relationship-oriented, confusing non-Japanese speaking business executives who believed such small talk was nonessential and a waste of time. We'll talk more about how non-task sounding can create an atmosphere where everyone feels like they're in the know in the next chapter on Work Listening, but for here, the insight is the idea that applying the task–relationship tool in Social Listening can play a role in discovering differences in communication styles, whether male or female, Japanese or non-Japanese. Gaining acuity on communication styles helps us listen slow, which in turn can help divert the flow of conversation so that it doesn't get personal and end in conflict or spin out of control in complementary schismogenesis, but instead, moves on towards more cooperative play.

Play as a Tool in Social Listening

In her research into gender and communication, sociolinguist Deborah Tannen distinguishes men's and women's conversational styles with a distinct social goal for each: competition for men and intimacy for women. This view of gendered bonding complements Jehn's gender-neutral description of task and relationship focuses of conflict, which can also be matched with the listening streams we possess to understand verbal and nonverbal interaction. Social Listening is the artful mixing of all the different listening practices we have talked about so far and more in daily interaction.

One way we create intimacy in everyday communication is through conversational play like banter. Studies show that play can help us frame and reframe everyday experiences as fun and entertaining, but also intellectually challenging.[11] Thought to have come from 1670s London street slang that privileges relationship and group membership, playful banter is a subverted intimacy that sends the meta-message *Even in the face of conflict, we're going to play as if we know each other well enough to tease each other.* Banter is a strong bonding communication ritual that exploits the energies of listening channels for the purpose of bolstering cooperation and fostering empathy through play. At its best in everyday conversation, banter is a subverted way to take the heat off stressful situations – when the phlebotomist I encountered following my scooter accident bantered, 'You can't stay here on holiday forever,' it was a playful but powerful way to conceptually reframe the ICU as a safe place and meant, *You're in safe hands here. We'll get you home.*

Although some research characterizes banter as a typically male form of social interaction, all genders banter in a range of styles that vary in intensity from lighthearted teasing to harder, more competitive exchanges. Like voice, banter can also range in frequency, from self-deprecation where the joke hinges on the banterer themselves, to irony or sarcasm that ribs the listener. Either way, it's the listener that 'gets' the banter or doesn't, meaning a speaker may initiate banter, but the outcome of the banter depends on the listener. Banterers need like-minded listeners, which is why many banterers feel safer in the hands of someone from the same culture or gender, and arguably in a couples relationship.

We perceive intergender banter as potentially more risky and dangerous, and we can see this perspective materialize in the kind of banter fiction likes to use to spice up the relationship of ordinary couples. Here's an exchange between Mr and Mrs Bennet in Jane Austen's *Pride and Prejudice*, where banter is used to let off steam:

Mrs Bennet: You have no compassion for my poor nerves.

Mr Bennet: You mistake me, my dear. I have a high respect for your nerves. They are my old friends. I have heard you mention them with consideration these last twenty years at least.

Mrs Bennet begins the banter by challenging Mr Bennet's lack of compassion; he ups the stakes by objectifying her 'nerves', disconnecting them from her and treating them as content in the third person, as he says, 'I have heard you mention them.' As the couple focus their attention on the disconnected nerves of their relationship, they walk a risky line between competitive sparring and playful entertainment. Which one it turns out to be depends on the listeners, but the success of a banter depends on both banterers walking away feeling challenged from the conflict but not ruined.

As commoners, my partner and I also engage in banter to let off steam, though not in a Regency ballroom with nineteenth-century concerns. Our conversation often centres around the most plebeian of all tasks, food and meal preparation, with the relationship background being who will make and serve the meal and when, and when the other person will eat it.

What time are you done?
I'm done when I finish.
Ha ha! That doesn't answer my question.
I know, but my answer is still the same.

This conversation between my partner and me demonstrates a situation in which one person overtly demonstrates they won't be attending to the other's needs by answering their question. This subverted Cooperative Principle incites the first person to retort back in irony, 'That doesn't answer my question,' in what could be characterized as the beginning of a common complementary schismogenesis – only, we know the schism is happening and we're doing it on purpose. By being intentionally inconsiderate and not answering my partner's question when he asks, 'What time are you done?' I signal the start of the play by literally answering the on-task question but not the social question, which is not actually a question at all, but the disguised command: *I finished cooking. Come eat.* Rather than debate what he actually meant when he asked, 'What time are you done?' though, I use banter to diffuse the tension involved in answering a question he already knows the answer to but doesn't like.

Don't worry, he gets me back all the time. Recently, when I asked him, 'What time does your plane land?' he answered, 'In time for dinner!' This time, he used a literal answer to be unhelpful. Instead of telling me what time his plane lands and helping me work out how to use the interim time before it became relationship time, my partner focused on the task that interests him – the dinner. As partners who have observed each other for a long time, our banter typically conforms to the traditionally gendered stereotypes of conversational style.

Although your own focus might be task or relationship or the hybridized use of both, understanding the focus of our own banter can help us recognize and benefit from the payoff in diffusing everyday tension by play.

Trash Talk Heard as Motivators

Many think of 'trash talk' as a competitive and masculine form of banter because historically it was typically observed in male interactions preceding and during a competitive sport.[12] As a kind of verbal jousting, trash talk is traditionally used as a face-off to unsettle opponents, mostly with intentionally inappropriate language. There is, though, a lighter version of trash talk, like Mohammed Ali's iconic declaration, 'I'm so mean, I make medicine sick.' In boxing arenas and on football pitches, banter in the form of trash talk has also been used with the intention of instigating a fighting spirit in both the trash talker themselves and their listeners. Trash talk has been used in locker room pep talks as a way of inspiring players to perform their best.

Today, this lighter version of trash talk also occurs outside of sports, especially in business, for competitive but also motivational ends. In their study of full-time office workers, for example, organizational behaviour researchers from Georgetown University's McDonough School of Business and the University of Pennsylvania's Wharton School of Business found that trash talk is a common workplace behaviour that impacted listeners in both surprisingly constructive and destructive ways. According to the researchers, trash talk has the power to lift team spirit and foster friendly competition, thereby motivating listeners to increase their effort and consequently perform better, benefitting the entire group.[13] That said, the same study found that trash talk can negatively affect listeners, not only distracting them from some tasks but also leading them to pursue their goal at all costs through illegal means.

As bantering styles change, there is evidence that trash talk is neither purely aggressive and insulting, nor uniquely male gendered. In competitive sports today, it's common to hear a melee of remarks, like this one articulated by a female tennis player: 'You're such a competitor. But don't worry, I'm bringing my A game.' Or the comments of MMA wrestler Ronda Rousey: 'I fear no woman. You can say anything you want about me, and it doesn't put a dime in your pocket or take a dime out of mine.' Today, conversational styles are mixes of traditionally gendered styles that build on rivalry and competition but also playful connection of the kind we see in flirting. 'Hey, heard you're a great cook. Want to make me a dinner?' – 'Not sure you heard right. I don't make dinners.'

Banter today is synthesized in the ears of the social listener who uses many modes of listening to create a space in which we can be challenged to social play but also be at home in each other's company. Banter is a way of potentially diffusing the conflict that can sometimes arise when language, like the gendered language we explore next, is misaligned with social inequality. Humour sometimes provides a relational safe haven where we can explore social challenges. But as trash talk researchers Yip and Schweitzer found in their research,[14] like all motivated conversation, it can go pear-shaped. Bantering speakers and listeners, tread lightly and gently!

Is Language Gendered?

Not all languages have gender identity, but the English language does – for example, in titles, names and pronouns. The fact that English has a long history of gendered language is important because words like titles that precede names such as 'Mister', 'Missus' and 'Miss' explicitly reveal not only a person's gender, but in the case of women, their marital status, too, in a way that the unisex Japanese title *–san* or the honorific *–sama* used at the end of someone's name don't. This does not mean there is no sexism in Japan but rather that the Japanese language does not openly expose a person's gender or marital status through language. The Japanese language also does not typically use gendered pronouns because of the habit of dropping pronouns. This means that the responsibility of distinguishing gender rests with the Japanese auditory listener, unless gender isn't relevant to the conversation at all.

One maxim in Paul Grice's Cooperative Principle is 'be relevant'. Whereas titles preceding family names were once considered to be relevant, they are becoming less so today. In fact, while the Old English word 'Master' was important to the society of the time in identifying educated young boys of higher gentry, it became less relevant by the middle of the twentieth century and has mostly fallen into disuse. Formal titles before names in general have become less common in the United States and the United Kingdom, as movements emphasizing equality, such as the civil rights movement in the US and the class-equality movements in the UK that have increasingly pushed these countries towards informality.

However, as we will see in the chapter on Generational Listening, vestiges of old inequalities can sometimes linger in language. For example, there appears to be variation in the way male and female researchers are addressed, with some students addressing female professors by their first name and male researchers by their title and last name,[15] thus illustrating that there is still a residue of social gender inequality as reflected in language. In the US, it's still common to add 'ma'am' and 'miss' at the end of sentences, but not 'mister', unless you are being sarcastic or trying to challenge the person. Instead of 'ma'am' and 'miss', a man might be tagged at the end of a sentence with 'sir'. If a woman is referred to at the end of a comment with 'lady', the equivalent to 'sir', this is often heard as rude. Even though language can influence social behaviour, language change can be slow.

Despite this, social engineers and policy makers have pushed to accelerate change towards more neutral language. Social Listeners will have noticed at least three ways in which the English language has become more gender neutral. The first is by making everyday words more language neutral, for example, in occupational names. Exclusionary gendered occupational names have given way to gender-neutral names, like meteorologist and firefighter – you might be amused by the list below of the sampling of occupational name changes in recent years in the English language, and you'll probably be able to add many more.

A Sampling of Gendered Occupational Name Changes

Previous	*Contemporary*
chairman, chairwoman	chair
mail/postman, mail/postwoman	postal worker
policeman, policewoman	police officer
salesman, saleswoman	sales executive/person
steward, stewardess, air hostess	flight attendant
waiter, waitress	server, table attendant, waiter
fireman, firewoman	firefighter
barman, barwoman	bartender
headmaster, headmistress	head teacher

A second way the English language has become more gender neutral in the twenty-first century is that people may now choose to indicate their preferred personal pronouns, such as masculine 'he, him, his', feminine 'she, her, hers', or gender-neutral 'they, them, their'. This third-person pronoun identification has the benefit of helping both first- and second-language listeners and readers appropriately identify someone, ultimately enabling all communicators of a gendered language like English to expand their social language competence and put everyone in the conversation at ease. While the articulation of gender language identification is less required in a language like Japanese that typically doesn't have to use a sentence subject, gender self-identification for a language like English that does require personal pronouns in grammatical sentences is useful.

Finally, a third way of using language to influence social change is by reclaiming words that previously had negative connotations. An example of this is a word like 'chick' that was used in slang to describe women as less intelligent. Today, the word 'chick' has been used to discard outmoded attitudes and instead signal camaraderie within the group. 'Chick lit' is a genre in women's literature, as is 'chick flick' in films. The word 'queer' is another example of a word where its sense of *oddity* or *weirdness* was once used pejoratively, but is now used by people with a non-heteronormative or non-binary understanding of gender to self-refer. Interestingly, the word 'queer' itself is a kind of banter that invites the listener to get comfortable with the idea of ambiguity in gender.

Social Listening is a channel in which we can use our Soft Listening to learn about new ways of conceiving identities. By connecting across genders and cultures, we can build a positive framework for conversations that can stamp out the pejorative language associated with outdated modes and even challenge prejudicial behaviour through dialogue.

Not all traditionally gendered language is negative, though, and nothing articulates this better than first names. Gendered first names were once a way of distinguishing between boys and girls and are still popular in many languages as one nonvisual way of identifying a person's gender.

Another traditional way listeners infer a person's gender is by listening to their physical voice. To distinguish the sex assigned at birth, listeners usually hear a male voice range as typically falling between 85 and 180 Hertz and a female voice range as falling between 165 and 255 Hertz. The lower pitch of voices born male compared to those born female is primarily due to the larger size of the larynx in males, which arise as a result of hormonal changes that occur during puberty. These anatomical differences lead to slower vocal cord vibrations and deeper vocal resonance in males, producing a lower pitch. This said about biological differences, we know from our own circle of friends and family, though, that these ranges can vary greatly. Voice quality of a person born male or female can vary physically by a person's age, health, stress and hydration levels and be influenced by air quality in the surrounding environment and also by their social identity.

In a training session on equality and diversity, a blind person, Mike Lambert, sits down next to a media psychologist and strikes up a chat.[16] 'I've never heard of media psychology and would like to ask a few questions about it,' he says. 'The man's halfway through telling me about his work, when the trainer interrupts.' As it turns out, as part of an ice-breaker, the participants in the training session must now find out something about the other person and introduce them to the group. Having thought he was slightly ahead of the game, Mike asks the media psychologist their name and they respond, 'Nina'. Now confused about the person's gender and therefore how to introduce them, Mike asks, 'Which pronoun do you prefer?' To which Nina replies, 'She.'

Later, as they walk to the tube station, Nina tells Mike she liked the way he politely asked for her gender, and that confusion about her gender often arises over a voice call. In turn, Mike writes how much he is comforted by the sound of Nina's demonstrated appreciation, illustrating how listening slow for gender in our contemporary gender-neutral and fluid generation can make for a positive soft learning experience. Gender identification is just one way a listener can relate to a speaker and be on the same wavelength. Streaming all our listening abilities through our Social Listening in the here and now is how we do this.

It's Coming Home

In a photoshoot session for the Paris Olympics 2024, American tennis player Chris Eubanks presented his teammate Coco Gauff with the news: 'You have the honour of wearing this jacket during the opening ceremony and being the flagbearer with LeBron James.' Although LeBron James, a professional basketball player, and Coco Gauff don't play the same sport, for the duration of the boat ride along the River Seine in the opening ceremony, the two joined together as American flagbearers.

We are each flagbearers of our different cultural groups, and while Cultural Listening helps us express and listen for the overall values that are important to a group, Social Listening helps us use and monitor them in each encounter we have. Big or small, at the Olympics or at a café near work or even at home, Social Listening allows us to identify members of a group to interact with and to get to know them better. Like verbal and nonverbal language, conversational styles provide social information that works like a flag – as a buoy in the sea of things we don't know about the other person.

While the Cultural Listening we explored in the last chapter is for interpreting an array of diverse values, Social Listening is for learning the boundaries of those values as practised in our daily encounters with others. We need Social Listening to listen for, use and sometimes enforce the social codes of the groups in which we participate. If you're in a work culture that values inclusivity, they might ask you to use language that reflects this – for example, to address everyone by name without titles. While social codes can be expressed in formal register as a policy, they can also be mandated informally through social pressure. If everyone around you is on a first-name basis, you are probably more likely to do so yourself. Social Listening helps you get a temperature reading of how culture is applied in conversations, and we use this information to regulate our own and others' behaviour, like the things we do and say in conversation.

We started this chapter by talking about how complementary schismogenesis can create a spiral of misunderstanding between cultures when we don't understand each other's conversational styles. When we do have an idea of others' styles, Social Listening can guide us to be more at ease and have enjoyable conversations where we feel at home. Feeling relaxed, we can play in conversation with banter that synthesizes previously gendered styles. As we learn about each other's conversational styles, we can not only learn and practise different styles, but also incorporate humour in our existing style to play and even potentially reframe conversations to dissipate tension.

Our gendered world is made up of subtle differences we need to understand, not only to recognize how conflicts like complementary schismogenesis can arise, but also to develop a diverse palate of social sensitivity. Though some would argue that empowering women, especially at work, means adopting a fully task-based style of communication, that would be a loss, not only of a relationship focus in communication style, but of the streams of listening to which we currently have access. Homogenizing styles would make communication a rigid tool of transactionally sending and receiving informational tasks without the freedom of conversational play. Social Listening encourages us to take risks – to reach out from our strongholds to the areas that are less familiar, to work and play and listen in on the richly varied communication styles and contexts we encounter every day.

7 Keys to Social Listening

■ Language evolves to reflect a changing society and Social Listening helps us hear it. Whereas Cultural Listening enables us to hear the currency of a group's values, Social Listening helps us to focus on the exchange in the immediate interaction.

■ Social misunderstanding sometimes gets worse even as communicators try to fix it, as each keeps applying the same focus that caused the problem in the first place. This phenomenon of spiralling miscommunication is called complementary schismogenesis.

■ Indirectness and nonverbal immediacy, such as high-rising sentence-final intonation (HRT), have been historically viewed as a feminine conversational style in the US, and portrayed as a sign of a lack of confidence and insecurity.

■ Both men and women use nonverbal immediacy and indirectness in conversational styles in Japan, where the practice of no-saying avoidance is a way of extending empathy in relationships, including in more formal relations at work.

■ Using the Rubin's Vase, we can see some communication styles as task focused and others as relationship focused. Not all researchers agree that task relationship communication styles are gendered, but most agree that recognizing the difference between them is useful in resolving conflict. Some suggest that task-conflict is healthy but relationship-conflict is risky.

■ Banter is a playful and teasing communication style used by all genders that subverts the cooperative principle of communication and allows us to reframe a conversation in a playful way. Typically used in an informal register with strong ties, banter can be useful for diffusing tension in communication. Trash talk, traditionally portrayed as a masculine communicative style, has recently taken on some stereotypically feminine features that show attention to the listener.

■ Not all languages are equally gendered, but the English language mandates grammatical subjects which are gendered. English-language listeners auditorily identify gender by physical voice, social language intonation, first names and titles. Social language regulation changes with the times.

3 Reflections on Social Listening

- Do you use indirect speech? What about uptalk/ high-rising intonation (HRT)? Do you say no often? Do you consider no-saying avoidance a flaw?

- In conflict, do you tend to focus on the task at hand, the context of the relationship, or both?

- Do you banter? What's your banter style? Is it competitive or playful? A hybrid of both?

8
Work Listening

協力

Cooperation

Workers at PEP, a personal protective equipment (PPE) factory, gave the new manager Bruce the ultimatum: 'Come listen to us or we'll shut down the plant.' Bruce was beside himself. He couldn't believe that after multiple informational sessions with the employees, they were still unhappy. The external consultant hired to settle the conflict, Greg, suggested they go back to talk to the workers, and Bruce reluctantly agreed.

On the factory floor where the workers had gathered, Bruce tapped on the microphone and thanked everyone for coming. He then introduced Greg and handed the mic to him, but Greg gave the mic to the nearest employee on the floor, saying, 'Talk to us.' For the next twenty minutes, that's what the workers did, overwhelmingly expressing their worries about the changeover.

With the mic in hand, one worker said, 'Until the morning meeting yesterday, we hadn't even heard about the company buyout until it was happening.' A murmur of agreement followed. 'In the afternoon meeting, they STILL hadn't explained anything.' Bruce later told Greg he was about to take the mic back because this simply wasn't true, but instead, he just continued listening to what seemed like an endless supply of complaints. 'Old management or new management, we don't know who's talking to us.' 'We don't know who we should talk to and anyway, they don't listen to us.'

In a follow-up interview, Greg told Bruce that his company wasn't unique – more than a third of the personnel surveyed in a recent study reported that they were dissatisfied with how their managers communicate.[1] Bruce then shared that he thought he was a pretty good communicator, which made Greg chuckle and report the findings of another study that most managers think they are better listeners than they actually are – as many as 94 per cent of managers who rated themselves as good or very good listeners were rated by their employees as the very worst.[2]

When Bruce asked what could be done about it, Greg replied that PEP needed to put listening first. He said that while it was the employees' job to manufacture PPE, it was Bruce's job to manufacture trust. To create a culture of trust, management and the workforce were going to have to work together to build and maintain listening relationships from the ground up.[3]

In a progress meeting three months on, Bruce said he could tangibly feel a healthier and happier workforce. When asked whether he had instituted any of the practical Work Listening tools Greg had suggested he use, he said he had rigorously instituted open-ended monthly briefing sessions that ensured all employees became part of what Greg originally called the 'listening loop'. Greg's listening loop was based on the Japanese decision-making practice called *ringiseido*, that requires everyone in the organization to air and discuss the opinions and insights of others, and the communication practice of *ho-ren-so*, that involves reporting, updating and consulting. The critical listening component of the *ringiseido* is the *gi* which means 'deliberate and discuss'. Combined with *so* 'consulting' of all employees in the *ho-ren-so* reporting system, co-workers carefully consider the perspectives of their colleagues, which 'loops' back around to create a dynamic where listening is for everyone. This system is effective because once decisions are made collectively there is relatively little resistance to go forward with them. A listening loop is the ongoing cycle of gathering information from employees, listening slow to the aired concerns and acting upon them. In the second cycle of a listening loop and thereafter, the first information-gathering phase would also include a report back to the group on the outcome of the actions.

This listening loop proved particularly beneficial at PEP when tension arose again, this time between the production team, who prioritized speed and efficiency, and the quality control team, who prioritized delivering a quality product. Rather than impose the traditional top-down command from management to quell the conflict, PEP used their listening loops to facilitate further dialogue so that each side could gain a deeper understanding of the other. In the end, sharing in the listening loop helped previously conflicted groups collaborate to work out how to deliver to deadlines without sacrificing quality. Listening helped co-workers problem solve collaboratively, which ultimately made for happier teams.

Open-ended listening loops where everyone feels involved fosters the willingness for people to cooperate, the coming together of 'many energies', as the Japanese characters that head this chapter explain.* In this chapter, we will explore the five important energies that create the Work Listening loop of cooperation – mutual respect, trust, innovation, recognition and demonstrated listening, all of which require a speaking and listening workforce. Former CEO and chair of Xerox Corporation, Anne M. Mulcahy said, 'Employees are your greatest asset – they're your competitive advantage. You want to attract and retain the best; provide them with encouragement and stimulus, and make them feel they are an integral part of the company's mission.' This chapter looks at the kind of listening we need to help build a healthy work culture where people don't stay because they have to, but because they want to.

Work Listening Loop of Cooperation 1: Mutual Respect

A photo came through on my social media of fellow alumni and Japanese Minister of Digital Transformation KONO Taro[†] sitting at the end of the stage talking at eye-level to students at Rikkyo University. When asked if he'd taken that position at the end of the Q&A, he responded that he'd sat on stage pretty much the whole way through his conversation with the students because the invitation to speak at the university was spontaneous and he felt that sitting like that was more conducive to dialogue between him and the students.

---

* The four Japanese characters for 'strength' 力 placed alongside the character for 'heart/energy' compose the character for cooperation 協力.

† Japanese names are spoken and written family name first then first name. There has been a movement to use this order in other languages, which KONO Taro himself has spearheaded, saying writing the family name in all caps brings attention to this authenticity.

Japanese Minister for Digital Transformation KONO Taro talking and listening to students at Rikkyo University

A pillar of Work Listening is mutual respect. Research shows that an atmosphere of respect fosters personal and collaborative learning and motivates a workforce to develop the product, brand and, most importantly, themselves. Mutual respect, regardless of status or authority, kickstarts the Work Listening loop of cooperation in daily interaction for the ultimate purpose of not only helping a business grow but also for creating a generally healthy work culture. Listening is an important part of generating mutual respect. By learning work colleagues' names and listening to stories of their backgrounds and interests, we contribute to our co-workers' well-being but also the health of the workplace. Professor of Communication Brigitta Brunner, who interviews business communication professionals, has observed that listening is the key to building and maintaining good business relationships.[4]

Work Listening Loop of Cooperation 2: Trust

Warren Buffett is regarded by many as one of the greatest investors of all time, having invested in big name companies like Apple and Japanese trading houses like Mitsubishi. He is also known for his folksy demeanour and ability to make people feel deeply heard and trusted. Pledging to give away the majority of his wealth to charitable causes, Buffett has been a strong advocate of building trust in business: 'Trust is like the air we breathe,' he says, 'when it's present, nobody really notices; when it's absent, everyone notices.'

When trust is at risk, the workforce, customers, investors – everyone – pays the price. Like at PEP, trust at Boeing began to fail as the workforce saw management as not listening to their concerns, prioritizing speed of production over safety.[5] Within five months of each other, in 2018 and 2019, two Boeing 737 MAX airplanes crashed, resulting in the deaths of 346 people. The crashes were linked to a faulty flight control system and an investigation later revealed that in addition to the absence of a safety culture and the exclusion of pilot input in aircraft design and operation, there was a disconnect between senior management and other members of the organization, such as the engineers, that ultimately created an atmosphere that hindered free discussion and challenged management to practise listening. Based on the recommendations of safety experts, Boeing have subsequently agreed to several changes to their corporate culture, including opening up channels of communication so that engineers can report directly to the chief engineer rather than the financial division head as they had previously done.[6] This improvement could then be further enhanced with a flight crew that is fully trained in the new design system so that communication is well integrated in a listening loop where everyone feels heard and informed.

As the second pillar of cooperation, listening for trust, can build loyalty within a company but it can also expand to reach its customers. The LEGO Group, famous for its interlocking plastic bricks, had enjoyed a loyal following, but in the 2000s suffered mounting losses and declining sales. With the company on the brink of collapse, the new CEO, Jørgen Vig Knudstorp, implemented a series of bold strategies that encouraged staff to reconnect with the loyal customer base by listening to them through online communities, forums and events. The result was an all-round success that ultimately returned LEGO to its former profitable glory, allowing them to achieve sustained growth in the following years. Listening to customers can help a company build trust and rebuild a fan base, not only making a company profitable once again but also gaining greater customer satisfaction. Just like trusted employees, when customers feel heard, they feel valued and are then more likely to develop loyalty to the organization.[7]

Listening and trust go hand in hand. They're mutually beneficial and without either one, a business culture can often be recognized by its low morale, high turnover of staff and diminished productivity. A Gallup study in the US showed that a disconnect at work is on the rise, reaching its highest level in a decade post-pandemic.[8] What's worse, disengaged employee behaviour has a negative snowball effect, where employees with poor engagement demonstrate low cooperation that translates into absenteeism and reduced innovation. Furthermore, undervalued employees often end up resorting to micromanagement or even bullying, creating a vicious spread of disengagement in a work culture. Accounts of managers who micromanage their subordinate by doing things like forcing them to produce multiple spreadsheets under their watchful eye are not uncommon, and nor are the reports that show how the micromanaged subordinate ends up creating another disengaged employee. Unfortunately, like trust and listening, disengagement in a work culture is also highly infectious.

Once trust is broken, it's challenging to regain it again, though not impossible. A regression analysis on data collected from participants of independent financial institutions demonstrates not only that work cultures with good listening correlate positively with improved sales and net income, but also that reaching out to employees to listen and reconnect with them can help them feel more committed to their organizations.[9] When trust is restored through listening, organizations can also improve financial outcomes.

Work Listening Loop of Cooperation 3: Innovation and Creativity

Listening doesn't just restore and promote trust at work, it also encourages innovation and creativity within an organization. In LEGO's comeback, they not only reached out to customers and listened to them, but also to their designers, encouraging them to explore new ideas that aligned with the reestablished fan base. Employees who feel empowered to share their ideas and perspectives are more likely to contribute innovative solutions to challenges and drive positive change. By fostering a culture of innovation through listening, organizations can harness the collective creativity of their workforce, simultaneously leading to a competitive advantage outside the company and a healthy employee engagement within.

One of my favourite examples that illustrates how listening encourages innovation is the origin story of Post-it notes. Post-it notes are the result of a mistake by a chemist at 3M, Dr Spencer Silver, who failed to develop a strong adhesive for aircraft construction, with which he was tasked. When Dr Silver shared his failure with his colleagues, and one of them joked that the non-tacky adhesive would make a useful replacement for the bookmark that kept falling out of his hymnal, he used the information he acquired in the listening loop to develop and commercialize the Post-it note. The invention of the Post-it note is a story about turning a mistake into a viable commercial product, but also about how listening creates

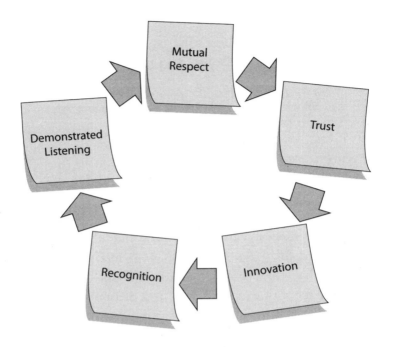

Work Listening Loop of Cooperation

the trust that sparks innovation, which, when heard and recognized, fosters even more listening. It shows us how many
benefits can circulate through a listening loop.

Work Listening Loop of Cooperation 4: Recognition

Listening begets trust at work, especially when it is demonstrated with recognition. A friend and CEO Darren Edwards
at Pomelo, a small tech startup, had the habit of practising
listening in an 'open-door policy' where colleagues 'hung
out' in the middle of a bullpen office to encourage one-on-
one sharing of ideas, concerns and feedback. When junior

developer Emma Kim approached Edwards with an innovative idea for streamlining the company's coding process, the CEO not only listened to Kim's explanation of a simplified user application but also implemented the idea and publicly credited Kim for their contribution on social media.* This action of demonstrated public listening not only improved the coding process at Pomelo in general, but also showed the entire team that their voices mattered at the startup, thereby fostering trust between employees and leadership and spurring on more innovation. Demonstrated listening to employee voices at work publicly displays respect and shares appreciation for the team's collaborative effort.

Rewarded effort can change the dynamics of a workplace from one that exclusively focuses on productivity to one that listens for more than results. By recognizing the effort of an individual and a workforce, a company culture can foster a feeling of satisfaction within the community and knowledge that efforts are valued. As the workforce feels fulfilled, this generates more motivational efforts to help the company.

Recognition is a huge motivator. A survey by McKinsey & Company found that non-financial incentives can be greater motivators than financial incentives like cash bonuses, increased base pay and stock options. These bigger motivators were things like a chance to lead projects or task forces, but also one-on-one mentorship conversations.[10] As well as its potential benefits to career development, mentorship offers a great listening space for navigating the workday with someone who has experience in something you are trying to learn.

---

* This event actually happened at a tech startup, but the name of the company and its staff are pseudonyms.

Mentoring is a cultural practice in Japan that begins at home in an environment of *amae* interdependence and Soft Listening. Although hierarchical relationships at work aren't typically associated with intimacy, mentoring relationships can be. For example, mentoring exists between older and younger students at school in Japan, where the older students look out for the younger ones like sister and brother in senior–junior *senpai-kōhai* relationships to mutually benefit from sharing knowledge and experience in an interdependent relationship. As mentors soundboard their mentees, over time mentees also soundboard their mentors, providing a fantastic Soft Listening and learning experience for all involved. Mentoring is an archetypical example of demonstrated listening, the final pillar in our Work Listening loop of cooperation.

Work Listening Loop of Cooperation 5: Demonstrated Listening

When we give evidence to our listening through tangible demonstrations, we not only cement mutual respect and trust, but we can also catapult and spread positivity towards work engagement, sometimes in unique ways. Former PepsiCo CEO Indra Nooyi not only grew the company's revenue from $35 billion in 2006 to $63.5 billion in 2017 to increase total shareholder return to 162 per cent,[11] but also developed a highly personalized style of recognizing employees who she called her 'other family'. In one podcast interview, Nooyi talks about how recognition in her other family was one of the surest ways to improve the bottom line at work because this can be a potentially greater motivating power than more traditional monetary rewards. Nooyi's recognition at PepsiCo took the unique and highly recognizable form of writing letters to the parents of her mentees because she remembers nothing made her day as much as knowing how proud her parents were of her. Later, her mentees would provide the feedback that Nooyi's appreciation letters were a particularly rewarding form of demonstrated listening that made them engage with work with an even greater aspiration.

There are potentially many forms of demonstrated recognition. It can materialize in a formal form such as an award or certificate, or more informally as a social media shout-out. Recognition can be presented publicly in a team event or in a private letter, like Nooyi's to her mentees' parents. Demonstrated listening enables recognition. By saying, 'I'm listening to what you're saying', it sends the meta-message that what that person has to share with the world is interesting.

Demonstrated Listening in a Diverse Workforce

Whereas traditional corporate structures involved unidirectional styles of communication that relied on top-down instruction, the workforce orchestrated today is increasingly composed of engaged employees who, when listened to and recognized through both financial and nonfinancial benefits, become more engaged and productive. Cooperative productivity is infectious and has the potential to influence the entire brand of a company. This unifying, collaborative influence is important in a digital age, where diversity has the double-edged influence of shaping a richly textured work culture or polarizing it divisively.

Listening is a key moderator in a diverse workforce. The

most famous tech story that exemplifies how listening to a variety of perspectives promoted innovation belongs to the development of the iPhone in the rapidly evolving mobile phone market then dominated by players like Nokia, Motorola and BlackBerry. When the CEO of Apple, Steve Jobs, recognized that despite its success with the iPod and Mac computers, Apple needed a revolutionary product in order to stay competitive, he chose to handpick individuals from various backgrounds, assembling a diverse team that included engineers with an expertise in hardware, software, user experience and industrial design, but also designers, artists and marketers. A key difference from their competitors was that Apple's teams were not siloed into separate departments but instead placed in open communication hubs that operated with the principle that anyone could innovate. Focus groups met in a highly collaborative environment where the cross-pollination of novice mindsets led to unexpected and creative solutions.

Central to Apple's success was not only listening to its diverse task force but also customer feedback from diverse sources to further study market trends. This differentiated Apple from its competitors, and contributed to the creation of a simple and intuitive device that would resonate with many different users. In the Apple iPhone, which launched in 2007, the company had created an entirely new product aimed at all kinds of users and not just tech enthusiasts, as was the case with many other devices of the time.

Apple differentiated their product from those of its competitors by integrating hardware and software to create the effect of a seamless user experience. As a product that was at once aesthetic and user friendly, the iPhone gave the consumer greater control over both the design and the performance of the phone. Because the task force listened to diverse consumer feedback, they understood that attention to a variety of design features was important. It's how Apple was able to launch a game-changing product that not only revolutionized how people interacted with technology, but also a product that 'had something for everybody'.

Listening Loops in the Everyday Workplace

Although the Japanese workplace is known in popular culture for hierarchy, in some ways, its structure is democratic. The cultural value of seeing others as oneself is played out in everything from office layout to the kinds of organized listening loops that have been in practice from the early postwar days of the Japanese company. While a manager might sit at the head of a department in a bullpen layout, they don't typically take 'the corner office' with the great view. Japanese leaders characteristically try to dress in the same inconspicuous manner as their subordinates and practise camaraderie with shared food and drink with the staff. While most such get-togethers are identified as informal gatherings, they're also often an excuse to have impromptu sound-outs, called *uchiawase*, written in Japanese characters as 打ち合わせ, which literally means 'strike up a meeting'.

Indeed, part of the manager's job is to create an environment of listening loops where employees perceive themselves as working together for a common goal. In section meetings, a manager will ensure they draw the focus away from competitive and individualized aspects of the team, refocusing the group instead on shared ventures such as programme planning, project management and joint comments on proposals in circulation. The series of sound-out listening loops that take place both in and out of the office in both informally spoken and formally written registers form part of an old tradition of consensus-building efforts formally called *ringiseido*, where all stakeholders deliberate the task or proposal and discuss how to move forward. A precursor to the formal *ringiseido* is the preparatory step of *nemawashi*, which literally means 'root-binding', conceptually borrowing from the age-old arboricultural practice of moving trees by protecting their roots. *Nemawashi* in communication refers to the custom of laying the groundwork of interdependence we discussed in chapter three before the processes of discussions that ultimately lead to decision-making.

The different loci of US and Japanese decision-making means misunderstandings between communicators from these cultures can be common. The US managers in my study said they had been both intrigued and frustrated to find that instead of negotiated outcomes in meetings, the Japanese managers had discussions 'behind the scenes' that only seemed approbated in the formal meeting where they met interculturally. The Japanese managers on the other hand, felt that the US managers seemed impatient and unwilling to do the groundwork that could lead to consensus decision-making.

In short, first-timers in Japan often find Japanese due diligence meetings exasperatingly 'formal' and pro-forma, as to them, nothing seems to happen. By contrast, Japanese first-timers in the US often report feeling hurried and overwhelmed by their words. By incorporating Cultural and Social

Listening into their due diligence, both national groups can learn the other's work culture – principally, that much of Japanese decision-making tends to be done in listening loops that take place outside formal business meetings, whereas US American ones take place at the negotiating table. This contrast can be explained in terms of a difference in selective auditory focuses and listening channels: while the Japanese managers tend to focus on 聴く Listening with Fourteen Hearts and Soft Listening, US American managers tend to focus on 聞く Informational and Credibility Listening.

Work Listening and Professional Development

One way in which companies have been helping employees to improve the quality of listening in their work culture is through employee development programmes. Although previously trivialized as 'perks' or 'benefits', employee development programmes are now fully recognized as not only helping in enhancing employee competencies – for example, by bumping up tech skills – but also in making each employee's communication more effective. Professional development helps cultivate listening in the workforce, particularly with regards to the collaboration of teams.

There are now numerous development programmes on offer in many different types of organizations, such as leadership development, mentorship and coaching programmes, tuition reimbursement and educational assistance. For example, aiming to create development training programmes that foster learning and open communication, and take into account career aspirations, skills gaps and areas of interest,

Google has developed '20 per cent time', a concept that encourages employees to spend 20 per cent of their work-week on projects of their choosing. The 20 per cent policy is a direct result of listening to employees' desires for creative freedom and autonomy, and provides a good rule of thumb for the rest of the workforce to pursue passion projects and innovate in areas of interest.

Another listening forum that serves to expand a Google employee's initial interest is the 'Googler-to-Googler' (g2g) initiative aimed at providing a series of internal workshops, seminars and training sessions that cover a wide range of topics, including technical skills, leadership development, diversity and inclusion, mindfulness and more. By recreating the listening space of a conversation in a work context, employees can informally seek mentorship and tap into the expertise and knowledge of colleagues. This employee benefit can be explored alongside more formal learning opportunities like GoogleEDU, where employees can learn about more traditional topics such as coding, data analytics, project management and digital marketing. Ultimately, development programmes such as these help both employees and leaders commit to listening to learn about topics but also the people, which in turn helps to grow the company in competition with others while fostering the work culture within.

Listening While Working from Home

A silver lining of the pandemic was what we now abbreviate to 'wfh' and verbally articulate as 'work from home'. As someone from a generation that didn't have this option, I confess that I am green with envy that the many more caregivers in the workforce today have the flexibility and the choice to work from home. Being obliged to go to a physical workplace used to mean that caregivers either had to forego work or find work-hours care for their children. Although this is still true, a more prevalent culture of working from home has not only introduced more flexibility into our lives, but also the opportunity to access jobs we couldn't before the concept of working remotely.

Greater flexibility in work structures has changed the way we communicate in numerous ways. For one, it has significantly reduced the level of formality, an impact we will explore in greater depth in the following chapter on how listening in digital times has come of age. The loss of a physical boundary between work and home has made our language in the home and work cultures less distinct than it used to be for the commuting generations that touted 'keeping work and personal life separate' as the gold standard. Instead, many work cultures now favour personalized interactions, particularly on social media, where the traditional social divisions between 'work' and 'life' we hear about are articulated more in terms of *balance* than *separation*. Time previously spent commuting can be used relaxing with family and friends, and also provides the opportunity for more frequent, smaller, more personal meetings. Team collaborations and one-on-one meetings are positive byproducts of working from home that can afford us extra time to soundboard and listen more fully to each other at work. However, young people in shared accommodation, parents with young children and those who live alone may have more complicated experiences with the new work from home dynamic.

As smaller discussion groups take on the vibe of informal *uchiawase* meetups, working from home has democratized the distribution of talk- and listening-time through online communication platforms. Providing access to a wider audience and reducing exclusivity, online communication opens up the possibility of talk and listening in, regardless of physical location or time zone. But with all the benefits of work-from-home arrangements, this has also created challenges that have taxed both our productivity and personal well-being.

Productivity issues that impact our Informational Listening range from technical failures that disrupt hearing alongside other physical distractions to impede the flow of remote communication, such as local building works or a neighbour's music. Physically but also relationally, giving up home space to work can make it difficult to keep up momentum and focus. At the office, it's often easy to engage in personal activities like internet shopping or non-work social media, but working from home mixes Work and Social Listening on another level, as employees can engage in personal activities even while attending a meeting. Instead of a highly visible, old-school office watercooler conversation with a colleague after a tea break, work-from-home now makes it easy to engage with work friends in digital communication without being able to see them.

As remote communication increasingly becomes a camera-off listening interaction, as listeners, we sometimes end up automatically accepting the informational task the presenter selects. Without people to mind in the conversation, a speaker presenting to an absent audience also disengages, giving rise to a presentation with task content at its centre, virtually void of presenters and listeners. If you've ever wondered why the meeting couldn't just have been documents attached to an email, that was probably what was happening. When remote communication has the negative outcome of mutually disengaged meeting presenter and attendees, listeners not only feel bored by the impersonal presentation but also isolated. Ironically, exactly what made working from home attractive in the first place – the idea that you didn't have to be there – can also be what hinders the benefits of listening.

As broadband speeds increase and we're ever more connected to devices around the world, we're paradoxically more disconnected than ever. Taking on the challenge of digital isolation, industry leaders survey company health and have begun putting in place a range of measures that aim to make remote work less isolating and reconnect with employees who feel unheard. Amongst these are one-to-one and group listening loops, which provide the first antidote to isolation. Small group meetings to stay connected with bosses and workmates is essential for Work Listening health, whatever the medium or form. Virtual team meetings, brainstorming sessions, check-ins through video calls, phone calls, online messaging platforms, text messaging or emails – ultimately what seems to matter the most in any listening loop is small size and regularity.

In staying connected, size and frequency matter. Regular listening check-ins are a prescription that can't be oversold. Scheduled short one-on-one chats with a mentor, co-worker meetups in video break-out rooms, in-person lunch-and-learn collaborations, impromptu corridor or street meetings – the form doesn't matter as much as developing a regular practice of intimate and demonstrated listening. As work-yourself-to-the-bone or stay-until-the-boss-leaves habits increasingly become work trends of the past, balancing work and rest has become a goal for companies who understand that employee retention is best maintained when a workforce is not only satisfied but healthy in body and spirit. More than ever in a world of work cultures that are connected twenty-four-seven, companies need the sustainable energy of a healthy workforce.

Work–Life Balance: Leaving Work Behind to Listen to Yourself

Leaving work behind is a modern problem, first sparked by the telephone that made it potentially possible to communicate with co-workers and bosses at any waking hour even when we weren't physically together. Since Alexander Graham Bell won the patent to the first telephone in 1876 and Thomas Edison secured the English-language listener's reply to a phone call as 'Hello?', listeners all over the world have fast-forwarded from the analogue to digital era of communication. In saying goodbye to mechanical typewriters in favour of computers connected in the worldwide web, humans breathed new life into the idea of 'being in touch'.

Through vastly reduced wait times and real-time collaboration of documents and projects, automation and digitization brought on much faster communication, which led to faster decision-making and increased productivity. In a work culture that saw speed as both intelligent and cost-cutting, digitization was a godsend. Digitization was like a magic pill to productivity – we were never going to be lazy ever again.

Only, as productivity gained status, the expectation of constant availability and quick responses became increasingly normalized, too. Employees started to feel the pinch of pressure to be 'on' all the time. Whereas working hard was once admirable, now it seemed increasingly necessary. In fact, organizational psychologists William A. Gentry and Claire M. Harbour, surveying 763 managers in 2018, found that 74 per cent of the respondents reported that they found it difficult to leave work behind, mainly because of the worry that their career progression would suffer as a result of not being constantly available around the clock.[12]

For many of us, the nine-to-five workday originally envisaged by the Welsh social reformer Robert Owen – divided into the three orderly segments of eight hours' labour, eight hours' recreation, eight hours' rest – now feels like a quaint template imposed on us in the distant past. Henry Ford's eight-hour day, forty-hour week now also seems infeasible, as it can't be taken too literally with networking and after-hour socials that all seem to contribute to career advancement. As technology expands, our worldwide visibility and our 'on' hours seem to be expanding not only in time, but in our existential virtual space, too.

The demands of being present physically or virtually, to keep our listening 'on' twenty-four-seven, can have a significant impact on listening and relational health, both for the individual and the organizational culture as a whole. Constant availability leads to work fatigue that reduces our attention span, increasing stress levels to unhealthy limits. A reduction in attention directly impacts Informational Language comprehension, and an increase in stress influences our ability to comprehensively use Listening with Fourteen Hearts to empathize and listen on all of our listening channels. A workplace culture that emphasizes constant availability can create a listening atmosphere of hurried conversations, rushed decisions and an all-round lack of consideration for others.

Fortunately, although there is no panacea for overwork or twenty-four-seven listening-on mode, we have become more aware of the need to manage our time to try to balance work and life. We can, for example, do things like set our own limits on checking our phones outside of work and be disciplined about not responding to work-related correspondence during non-work or relaxation hours. We'll see in the last chapter that good listening means setting boundaries, and that limiting reactivity to emails and texts isn't ghosting a person, especially if you've made your nonavailability transparent. As listeners come of age, we need to remind ourselves that we're the boss of whatever technology we choose to use.

If setting boundaries can help improve both listening health and work–life balance, setting realistic goals can ensure that achieving a goal in one context doesn't have to cost us in another. Goals are important in helping us to focus on what we want to achieve and holding us accountable, but they can become stressful if we're firing full blast on all cylinders in multiple contexts 100 per cent of the time. A young caregiver once told me the heart-breaking story of how she needed to mute herself in a work call because she wanted to listen to her child's concert 'live' in an online school event.

There are two strategies to try when you feel like you're being pulled in all directions. The first is based on the 'Pareto Principle' also known as the '80–20 Rule'. The Pareto Principle was named after the economist Vilfredo Pareto, who noticed that roughly 80 per cent of the land in Italy was owned by 20 per cent of the population. Outside of economics and notably in business, social science researchers observed that roughly 80 per cent of a company's revenue comes from 20 per cent of its customers, which, when translated into a percentage of productivity, meant that results come from focusing on the top 20 per cent of business tasks and activities. In everyday work applications, the Pareto Principle has come to mean prioritization.

The Pareto Principle is a kind of selective auditory attention as applied to Work Listening. By identifying 20 per cent of the most urgent matters and echoing it back to the group, a Pareto listener helps incorporate work–life balance by actively ensuring they aren't spreading themselves across everything that comes into their inbox, but allocating their time to the most important. Procedurally, Pareto listening might involve annotated note-taking with ranking distribution and consensus feedback that resembles the kind of feedback support Japanese work listeners obtain in consensus-building listening loops. Global CEO coach Sabina Nawaz notes that good listeners in business settings are those who can capture important information.[13]

The second strategy for prioritizing tasks is Nawaz's note-taking system which lists the informational task items in the left column with reflections on the right, including questions flagged to ask at the end of the meeting or privately in their own time. Interestingly, in Japanese, the character for 'ask' 聞く is the same character as 'listening for information'. Questioning helps further clarify topics and their urgency which, in turn, helps to lay the groundwork necessary to build consensus on the topics of importance. Note-taking can be a form of demonstrated listening, a recording that illustrates how Informational and Listening with Fourteen

Hearts are included in the process of building consensus from the ground up.

Nawaz's note-taking system also resembles the Japanese aesthetics of continual refinement. As a part of soft power used to improve a product, continual refinement has been recently popularized in the word *kaizen*. Rather than set the boundary at the macro-level of the 80–20 Pareto Principle, continual refinement is based on the idea that small amounts of effort exerted every day can prevent a big pileup of overwhelm. Like Listening with Fourteen Hearts and Soft Listening, the idea of continual refinement starts with a preventive approach to the problem of having multiple tasks.

Working to Listen

Just like listening at home, listening in business conversations isn't just about understanding the work-related content but about listening to customers, co-workers, bosses, employees and other stakeholders associated with the organization. A friend and CEO at an investment company said, 'You should always listen to the people who work for you because you never know what capacity you'll interact with them again.' Five years after the CEO hired an employee, the tables were turned and the employee became a customer who hired the CEO as consultant to their company. A communicator who was once your boss can become a co-worker and vice versa. Work Listening is democratic – employees and bosses, sellers and customers, all need to be heard and listen for information about tasks but also people. Doing so can help us not only to make informed decisions, but also to adapt to changing market conditions to stay ahead of the curve, which in turn will help us build the kinds of work environments we prefer and long-term relationships that can evolve with us in changing contexts.

In this chapter, we talked about the value of mutual respect and trust promoted by listening, not only within a company but also with customers. Mutual respect and trust create engagement which can reap the benefits of recognition that inspires innovation and efficient systems. Without mutual respect or trust, there is no transparency, no conflict resolution and often poor work–life balance. These two vitally important constructs of social capital can create collaborative environments and strengthen listening loops at work.

One way in which companies increase employee engagement is through development programmes that not only help enhance employees' competencies in technology and make communication more effective, but also help companies to be more productive and innovative. When formal structures aren't in place, we can build our own engagement by combating isolation and working to achieve work–life balance. In the end, we proposed Pareto Listening as one way of identifying work priorities, so we aren't overextending and becoming disenchanted with life at work.

Work Listening helps build and maintain trust long term, creating a strong foundation of well-being in a professional environment. By prioritizing listening, leaders, employees and customers can all demonstrate their mutual respect and commitment to foster open communication and professional development so that every voice is heard and everyone can feel fulfilled. Business consultant and professor Laura Janusik notes that we spend up to a quarter of our waking hours listening.[14] If we assume social reformer Robert Owen's 'eight hours' labour, eight hours' recreation, eight hours' rest', that means we spend four to eight of our sixteen waking hours listening. For most of us, that means more hours spent on listening than eating, and probably many more hours than what we spend on looking after ourselves in other ways. While of course it's great that we put in as many hours as we can into that in-between space of listening to others at work and at home, we need to balance the space we share with others while meeting our own needs. This means that as we create a work culture that is home to trustworthy communication, we need to listen to collaborate with our co-workers but also to ourselves, an idea we'll explore further in the final chapter on Adaptive Listening.

For now, though, you can try carving out good listening time from your demanding work schedule by prioritizing tasks or, equally, chip away every day through continuous refinement as you regularly check in and out of requested conversations and share the responsibility of regular talk with other listeners. Whichever you do, take a moment to listen slow before getting back to your tasks at work with the mindset of your pocket Zen teaching that work will always get done: a journey of a thousand miles begins with a single step.*

---

* 千里の道も一歩から, *senri no michi mo ippo kara*, or 'even a journey of a thousand miles starts with a step' is a saying typically attributed to the Chinese philosopher Laozi and popularized through Zen Buddhism, heavily influenced by Chinese philosophy.

7 Keys to Listening at Work

- The Work Listening loop of cooperation is composed of mutual respect, trust, innovation, recognition and demonstrated listening.

- Establishing mutual respect and trust is key to listening at work and we build these work values through recognition.

- Recognition is an expression of demonstrated listening. There are many ways of recognizing someone and non-financial recognition – for example, through a listening loop like one-to-one mentor listening – is sometimes more memorable than a financial reward.

- Listening loops have long existed in Japan as *uchiawase* chats and laying the groundwork *nemawashi* sound-outs.

- Formal demonstrated listening loops like employee development programmes can also foster innovation and creativity.

- We need to prioritize our tasks at work to create work–life balance and make sure our Work Listening isn't always on twenty-four-seven.

- We can apply the Pareto 80–20 rule to optimize listening in order to create work–life balance. We can nominate or self-nominate to become Pareto listeners and prioritize what listening is important at work. We can also apply the concept of continual refinement so we can use the listening loop as a preventative measure.

3 Listening at Work Reflections

- Do you use listening loops at work? What are they like and can you share the benefits in and across other listening loops?

- Are you in a mentorship relationship? Discuss mentoring benefits with co-workers and innovate creative ways to buddy up. Discard outdated ideas about age and authority – you don't have to be the older or more senior person to be a mentor – for example, the next chapter encourages those born in the digital era to mentor the older generation.

- What do you think about the 80–20 rule, Pareto listening and continuous refinement? Is it worth volunteering or nominating a Pareto listener at work or taking on the mindset of continuous refinement to gain better work–life balance?

9

Generational Listening

Generation

In a time before the internet, travelling back to Japan gave me the privilege of seeing a physical world I hadn't seen in a long time. Some things didn't change. The mind-bending neon lights in the Shibuya Scramble contrasted with the makeshift foodstand down the road a generation or two away. The signature subway jingles in every station in Tokyo stayed just the way I had remembered them. In many ways, travelling back then was a time-travel back to the same generation I had left behind and I loved these familiar old things that identify Japan to tourists even today.

Television deepened my return to the old world and, even as technology advanced, the same shows ran on TV. Junky reality shows and reaction videos of celebrities commenting on things of the kind that are popular all over the world today have been around in Japan since the seventies, and I'd return to watch them as comic relief from the news. Even when the boring news came on one of the four stations we could watch, I could quickly reacquaint myself with the familiar newscasters, happily remembering them and their voices and styles.

Then something strange would happen. You might know this feeling. Following the thrill of initial rediscovery, I'd be watching the news and something I had absolutely no idea about a moment ago would pop up. A fisherman crabfishing off the northern coast shot dead for straying into territorial waters. What? Once I heard one piece of news about a reality I didn't know, it was like a whole other universe opened up. I'd even hear different news about the US, where I had just come from, like this was a parallel world I didn't know either. That's when I'd start to be filled with that unsettling feeling of groundlessness that many of us experience today when we're exposed to different views on the internet all at once.

The internet, digital messaging and social media define us as humans today. When people ask why there is overtourism in Japan today, there are the easy answers, like the weak yen. But I also wonder whether it is about people wanting to go to check that the place that appears so easily on their phone, and imagined in Japanese manga, anime and the plethora of games, is real. A physical visit to Japan is a kind of self-enforced reality check that all the landscapes imagined in the digital and virtual worlds exist. The even weirder phenomenon, though, is that once tourists arrive there, a must-do is to capture an image of the physical places they visit on their phone cameras, making it seem as if the places are real only after they have been digitized. Digital technology validates our reality but also puts it in constant jeopardy.

Media technology today evokes this same sense of insecurity. Back in the day, the generation that controlled the media used to broadcast the news to the masses, presenting it as a single truth. We called this kind of news reporting 'mass media', where listeners were a monolithic mass. Today, media broadcasting has been fragmented and is delivered through the many channels of social media, giving every listener the opportunity to broadcast to many others. To the extent that anyone can hear a marginalized voice that couldn't have been heard before, in theory, the contemporary form of news dissemination is more democratic. Ironically, however, multiple possibilities of reality become overwhelming, and algorithms help us choose amongst them as our selected reality by delivering content we like to see. Over time, our selected channels become all we see so that we're pared back to a few individualized channels that we may be tempted to take as gospel.

The upshot is the vague and uncomfortable idea that there exists a number of alternative worlds that we're called to move between on a daily basis, knowing something of each world, but not really, and not with the security we once had when we were listening to news that felt more certain and critically shared by everyone. The Japanese characters for 'generation', 世代, encapsulate this idea of 'alternative worlds', as the first character, 世, means 'world' and the second, 代, 'alternative'. In today's digital world, we aren't only different people who manage a host of different cultures but also different generations with different world views. Every day, we're called to move in and out of an explosive number of generational cultures as we speak, text and listen.

This chapter scans the generations living together in the digital age by listening for generational touchpoints and suggests how the generations that are often juxtaposed by media as antagonistic might instead collaborate moving forward.

Along the way, we'll explore the language that has described the generations of the last century, and how the later generations that have taken on the challenges of communicating in the era of online learning, e-commerce markets, social media and texting can not only innovate new ways of listening for both language and voice, but can also encourage Soft Listening and help other generations to learn from them.

Listening for Generational Touchpoints

The sociologist Karl Mannheim observed how individuals of a generation tend to have a shared awareness of cultural touchpoints that mark their generation, including such things as natural and manmade disasters, historical events like wars, social movements and political upheavals, economic recessions and booms, job markets, trends in music, fashion, popular media and technology. A traditional way of describing generational cultures is along a timeline that cascades one generation to the next using such iconic touchpoints as its representation. The US hippy culture is a typical example of a touchpoint in the Baby Boomer generation that comes complete with a host of icons we can listen for, like anti-war music, slogans and the nonverbal gesture of a peace sign that stood for the activism against the Vietnam War draft. The extent of the view into alternative worlds back then was a cross-cultural trainer who would warn those using the peace sign hand gesture, because it could mean something offensive in other cultures. Today, we call the generations like Boomers who were born before virtual worlds 'digital immigrants' to contrast them from the 'digital natives' who were born with those worlds in their smart phones.

Since the late nineteenth and twentieth centuries, Western sociologists have defined a 'generation' as a group of individuals who are born around the same time, typically spanning fifteen to twenty years. Marking a generation is its music, fashion, entertainment and, with much more emphasis recently, its technology, but also its language and voice, especially from a listener's perspective. There's nothing that describes a generation better than the language of the time.

Hearing words like 'groovy' and 'far out' will likely time-travel a US Baby Boomer back to the generation that protested against the protracted Vietnam War that spanned two decades from 1955 to 1975, at once inflating the economy and draining government funding away from domestic priorities such as infrastructure and social programmes. The media of the time portrayed the hippy generation with its peace signs and flower crowns as a somewhat trivialized challenger generation to the status quo. Marked by the undertone of a revolution that inspired music like the John Lennon–Yoko Ono anthem 'Give Peace a Chance', the hippy generation rebelled against the establishment by protesting the war. To the previous generation and establishment who funded the news, the hippies of the counterculture were 'draft-dodgers', while the Baby Boomers who protested the war were 'conscientious objectors' who offered their time in what they saw as peaceful community service in place of a draft to go fight a war they didn't believe in. When US Boomer generation listeners heard the references of 'draft-dodger' or 'conscientious objector', they knew exactly which side of the sociopolitical spectrum the speakers were on.

Language represents cultures but also generations. Although we don't always fit neatly into the classification of a sociocultural group like a generation, the language we use sends signals to listeners about which one represents us most. Listeners can hear whether speakers are part of the defending status quo or whether they are one of the new challengers. Every generation has a voice expressed in language, and as listeners we can hear what is important to each one.

To each generation, the previous generation represents the status quo, regardless of their touchpoints. The word 'status quo' is Latin for 'the existing state of affairs'. As the Baby Boomer generation moved into power, the next generation, Generation X, born mid-1960s to early 1980s saw the existing state of affairs as not revolutionary at all but more conventional than they were. In turn, as the groovy and far-out Baby Boomer generation became the establishment, they characterized the next generation as lazy 'slackers'. While they said all the kinds of things older generations say about younger generations, the 'Millennials', born early 1980s to 2000, were puzzled because they saw their predecessors as the hard-working establishment.

A bridge generation that is easily forgotten and often left out, Generation X is notable for being on the cusp of technological change when Boomer language was disappearing as quickly as their touchpoint products of the time. Although cassette recorders, floppy discs and typewriters persisted for the good part of the Boomer generation, they were quickly replaced by technological advancements and hardware, notably, the mouse. The computer mouse itself had actually been introduced by the computer engineer Douglas Engelbart in the Boomer era, when, in a historic presentation in 1968 called 'The Mother of All Demos', they demonstrated not only the computer mouse, but also video conferencing, hypertext, word processing and collaborative real-time editing. However, in addition to contributing to developing the precursor to the modern internet, Engelbart can also be credited for starting the trend of calling tech hardware by cute memorable names, like 'the mouse', rather than what the other engineers were calling it at the time, which was 'X-Y Position Indicator for a Display System'! Gen X can be remembered for the age when tech hardware began its rule, and also for the introduction of iconic words, which not only popularized the mouse but also democratized technology. By branding technology with cute names that were easy to remember, Gen X can be credited for leading the tech language change that very much became the tone of the Millennial generation.

Words of a generation are its semantic field, and touchpoints, the headline to the conceptual forests that conjure our realities the way conceptual metaphors do. When we listen to iconic words and touchpoints of a generation, we are hearing history in the present and what that may mean for their future. Listening to words and touchpoints gives us the historic landmarks through which we can listen in on a generation, a kind of ambitious plan to see others as yourself in the way Zen Master Dōgen Zenji describes.

'Easy' words have staying power in the ears of listeners, and are often born in the intersection of generations, allowing the most clichéd of intergenerational words – like 'cool' – to live on. These on-trend 'cusper' words are an example of how words influence our listening behaviour so that we'll continue to promote it into the next generation. As the anthropologists Edward Sapir and Benjamin Whorf observed, a generational culture can influence language but that language can influence the following generational culture, too. Every time we use a word, we actively broadcast it, so that every time we listen, we are presented with the opportunity to advocate the word for potential future use.

It's not just conceptually easy words that live on from one generation to the next, either. Cognitively easy grammar is taken up by the next generation, too. While the expressed tones of Gen X's 'totally', that shows agreement intended to be heard as, *I absolutely agree with you*, may have faded away, its effect of adding emphasis has stayed on in popular conversation, keeping what linguists call the 'pragmatic force' of the word intact. Pragmatic force is the impact spoken language has on the listener. Today, we use 'totally' as an intensifier that emphasizes what we're talking about: 'The band was totally on fire.' Words that have the pragmatic force of an amplifier that are still used are 'actually' and 'literally', and these words make for an emphatic tone of voice which listeners in the cusp of generations have since reinterpreted to acquire new tones and meanings.

In the same manner, some generational expressions fade away completely but live on in relational meta-meaning. For example, even though the Gen X standalone fad words 'totally' and 'whatever' have waned in use, the generation's use of the words to convey relational meta-meaning in addition to literal meaning remain in Millennial language with new expressions like '100 per cent' to emphatically agree with something, or to give reassurance or encouragement and mean, *I agree wholeheartedly. You can totally do it.* 'I'm good' is another Millennial expression to decline something that minds the other person in a relationally sensitive manner. Meaning can metamorphose in words and grammar from one generation to the next.

Sometimes, changes in meaning can take a couple of generations to evolve. The newer meaning of 'I'm good' is an example. With roots in the practice of making words mean the opposite, it has an ironic tone-of-voice play that has been around from an earlier time. Back in the time of Boomers, the word 'uptight' used to mean 'excellent' in jazz slang and not 'not-relaxed'. Words can be the secret codes of an era designed to include insiders but keep outsiders at bay. As generations subvert words and use them as a kind of password, listeners learn to hear 'bad' as 'good' and 'I'm good' as 'No, thanks'. Like the shift in intonation that can send a meta-message about the relationship hidden within, words can sound out membership to a generation.

When you're part of a generation, you know about generational words that are on the cusp before they enter popular language and become a normalized 'thing'. At the start, these 'things' are intentionally ambiguous – like a code word – providing exclusivity for its members. In-group members are privy to the nuance of the word, so that if you hear a word like 'lit', you can understand its public meaning that describes something exciting in the sense of 'intellectually brilliant', but also the meta in-meaning of the word to the group. Because the word 'lit' originally meant 'drunk' or 'high', and still carries the sense of risk and attraction to potentially dangerous substances associated with being high or drunk, using the word 'lit' can send the meta-message about user appreciation for risk – something that has high value in the challenger generation. Being able to listen for a word the way the speaker in your particular group, generational or otherwise, intended it, means that you're not only able to understand the meaning of a word as appropriate to your generation, but also in the voice of the speaker and their identity to that generational group. Like the secret knocks to your childhood clubs, hearing words in the way a speaker intended them means that you're able to decipher the particular code of inclusion that is exclusive to that generation.

While a generation's words and cultural touchpoints serve to create intimacy within a generation, they can create distinctions between generations, exacerbating preconceptions about each other. Younger generations may see older generations as rigid and uncompromising, while older generations may see younger generations as lazy and irresponsible. Language has no inherent meaning on its own, but because we use it to bond with in-group social groups like a generation, it can serve to include or exclude people from the group.

Listening for Abbreviations that Create a Generation

Abbreviations serve as one kind of generational language that acts as a membership code we can listen for and hash. Initialisms are one form of abbreviation that facilitate using multiple complex words by shortening them to their first letter. Historically, medical initialisms were most common – 'ICU', 'MRI' and 'DNA' were easier to say and recognize than 'intensive care unit', 'magnetic resonance imaging' or 'deoxy-ribonucleic acid'. Over time, initialisms replaced the words in long form, and we can become so habituated to the abbreviation that we forget the original words. Because listening for the initialisms gives us access to the group, knowing what they mean doesn't just help us understand buzzwords, it also provides us with the access code to a generational culture, and the ability to keep words and social touchpoints alive for use in future generations.

Acronyms can similarly provide listeners with access to younger generations and the future. While there was a period when internet acronyms like 'FOMO' were taken as trite youth buzzwords in comparison to older, more established acronyms with political or commercial weight, like 'NATO' for North Atlantic Treaty Organization or 'PIN' for Personal Identification Number, this is no longer the case. Acronym use in any generation becomes important as the generation not only challenges the status quo but comes of age and becomes the relevant power. As digital communication increasingly gained clout, the digital native born with the internet at their fingertips has become the new holder of power.

When we listen for initialisms and acronyms to sound out generational membership, we listen for a variety of cultural information to determine whether the other person fits our criteria, but also for the social skills we might need for cooperative interaction and collaborative work together. Generational fit might stack up differently for different generations, making each generational listener tune in to the specific sense of the acronym that makes sense to them. For example, while both generations might listen to acronyms that signal technological adeptness, commercial knowledge and business savvy, Boomers might dial in to listen for business-savvy, while Millennials might tune in to hear lifestyle vibes and trends through tech adeptness. As Generational Listening also incorporates Cultural Listening, we need the flexibility to be able to shift between our channels, a skill we'll explore further in our last chapter on Adaptive Listening.

As cultural values and social codes shift along with technology, so too do acronyms, which can go out fast as trends and culture move on and become obsolete. 'NIMBY' was an acronym for 'not in my backyard' that was used to protest real estate development, like the highly controversial tower that was half-erected in a residential neighbourhood in Washington, DC, USA before the NIMBY residents halted the works and eventually got it torn down. It became a mocking term for people who only protest things when they feel it negatively impacts them, whether or not it contributes to a wider good, and is currently mostly used in this way. While some millennial acronyms have died out, others like the internet acronym 'YOLO' have transformed. 'You only live once' has fallen out of fashion as the original sense of the word but lives on in irony. 'OG' for 'original gangster' is another example of a modified meaning, used to compliment someone who is cool in an old-school way. As one abbreviated form survives and shape-shifts from one generation to the next, it builds the momentum to potentially mark the next generation who will normalize its use in everyday language.

A primary difference in acronym usage between the telephone generation of Boomers and the digital generation of the Millennials is that while Boomers were using acronyms as a way of establishing in-group membership in conversations prior to instant messaging, Millennials were using abbreviations in the early years of texting as a way of exchanging information quickly in the new medium of SMS. As such, Boomers primarily use abbreviations to express status information for things and people to know. Millennials, on the other hand, are more likely to use abbreviations to communicate what a person is immediately experiencing or doing. For example, the letters OMWB stand for 'on my way back', telling the listener about an action that is about to take place rather than pointing out an object. An initialism like OMWB is informative while also mindful of its recipient. For example, a texter might add, 'Start dinner without me' as a follow-up message to further look after the relationship. In short, whereas the purpose of abbreviations born in the Boomer generation tend to be to point out nominal referential content like 'CEO', those born in the Millennial generation and later point out relational actions that can impact the people in the conversation. This emphasis on minding the others in the conversation has influenced all generations in the digital age, but especially the new challenger generation, Gen Z, for whom minding listeners in texting is the norm.

Reading Texts is Listening in the Digital Native Generation

If listening for internet acronyms is an important part of understanding the language that defines the digital generation, so is knowledge of the communication medium of texting. For a majority of Generation Z, the hybrid mode of texting that combines written and spoken modes is the preferred mode of communication. In a UK survey, nearly three-quarters of eighteen to twenty-four year olds – who were born from the mid-1990s onwards – said they would rather hear from someone by text than a call, with over a quarter saying they actively ignored calls and more than half saying they regularly ghosted their parents.[1] Caregivers, mobile networks and marketers have come to terms with the fact that if you want to talk to a digital native, you probably have the best chance of reaching them by text. Indeed, leaving out texting would make it hard to have any relevant discussion in the digital native generations at all.

Texting has the benefits of both spoken and written forms of communication: it is like speaking because it has the same informal immediacy that voice in spoken language has, but it also has the clear benefit of writing insofar as it remains available for later retrospection. As such, listeners of texting have the benefit that readers of written language have. To go back to the idea we borrowed from Daniel Kahneman's fast and slow thinking systems, text listeners can listen slow, choosing to take time to respond and reflect, in a way that is not possible in spoken communication.

Furthermore, whereas an email takes the form of a monologue in written form, a text is an interactive dialogue predicated on the conversational assumption that the listener will respond promptly. To give texts this easy feel of on-the-fly immediacy, texters chat in a conversational voice that doesn't always capitalize words at the start of sentences or use full stops at the ends as they might in writing. It's this immediacy and dialogic quality that leads communication researchers who study digital communication to think of texting as chatting and reading texts as listening.

Not using punctuation caused a stir at the beginning of texting use in communication as many of the early finger-waggers thought of texting as a form of writing. Gradually, though, as texting became normalized as an everyday mode of communication, users began to appreciate its informal conversational qualities that not only democratizes interaction the way conversation does, but also opens up a dialogue so that texter and listener can share the load of communication the way they do in conversation.

In addition, the meta-messages in texting punctuation ensures that a listener is playing their part. Punctuation in texting functions in the way that voice and tone of voice do in conversation. For example, using ALLCAPS turns up the volume of voice, adding emphasis to the overall tone of voice. A friend told me texts sent in capital letters prompted her to respond 'Stop shouting at me!'

Intonation shifts are indicated by using question marks and full stops where they normally wouldn't be, so that adding a question to the statement 'You are going?' signals a positive surprised tone and attention to the relationship to send the meta-message *I thought you weren't coming*. A full stop at the end of a grammatical question creates the effect of the same sarcastic tone found in a descending intonation of speech. For example, you might text, 'Are you going.' when you are asking a friend a question for the third time and they haven't responded, perhaps softening the message with irony by supplying an emoji. As texters, we manage our relationships the way speakers do, with nonverbal communication so we can convey what we think is the right dose of tone – a little annoyed but still polite enough? Texting has become popular for its convenience as it redistributes communicational

privileges between chatters and text-listeners, giving communicators the benefit of an informal flexibility, and the benefit
of time to listen slow and respond, having considered what
they want to say.

Listening in Asynchronous Communication

One of the great gifts of the digital age is asynchronous communication – that is, interaction that doesn't require speakers
and listeners to be engaged simultaneously at a single point
in time. Asynchronous communication in the digital age goes
far beyond personal relationships, extending to schools and
workplaces, where the advantages are many. Asynchronous
communication in online education, for example, offers the
student the opportunity to listen to a pre-recorded lecture
and review course material on an as-needed basis at their
own pace. Afforded the time to develop deeper reflection and
thoughtful answers, self-paced learning not only builds better
learning opportunities for the students themselves, but also
helps the faculty provide more personalized and meaningful
feedback. Asynchronous listening combined with traditional
learning empowers students to take control over their own
learning experiences, promoting greater accessibility and
engagement.

In business, too, asynchronous communication not only
helps teams in different time zones to collaborate more effectively across projects, but also affords them the time to fully
understand the tasks at-hand before responding. Researchers
who study online listening behaviours confirm that students become not only more time efficient in asynchronous

discussions,[2] but also post better-quality assignments and comments on forums[3] because asynchronous listeners can revisit discussions and update their contributions, coming back to read and listen to them multiple times. Furthermore, asynchronous communication can decrease time pressure, promoting the knock-on effect of focus, which can then improve the quality of decision-making and, potentially, productivity.

Back to the Future in Digital Communication

Neil Papworth, the British software programmer known as the person to send the very first text message, 'Merry Christmas', in December 1992, could not have known how text messages would forever change the way the world listens, where text-listeners would be listening to some forty-six messages a day.[4] With more than 5 billion device owners, worldwide texting statistics show that texting is the medium of communication that is most likely to be actually listened to by its listeners. Much to the delight of marketers, a whopping 98 per cent of texts sent are actually opened, while 95 per cent are read within three minutes of having been sent, compared to a mere 20 per cent of form-emails.

As consumers, we like the conversation-like one-to-one personal quality texting can provide. It's like a phone call but less intrusive to the listener and a lot less costly – digital natives are sometimes surprised to hear the lengths digital immigrants used to go through just to make an expensive telephone call only to be disappointed to discover the person they called wasn't there and the call had gone through to answerphone: a form of asynchronous telephone voice recording in the pre-digital age, whereby an analogue machine would record a message from a caller on a cassette. More alarming still for the digital native, though, is the fact that voice messaging back in the day had zero privacy because the voice of the caller could be heard by anyone in the physical room at the time or at any point after that, as anyone with access to the machine could play the messages back. If ever you're experiencing tech privacy issues, go ask your favourite Boomer for a story or two about a cringe moment in a voicemail leak. It might not help your privacy issue, but it could provide a moment of comic relief.

Privacy has become much more of a pressing matter today. Text messaging, together with the proliferation of digital technologies and online platforms, has changed the way we view privacy. In light of high-profile data breaches, surveillance scandals and debates about online privacy, privacy-enhancing technologies have been developed and marketed, empowering listeners to take control of who hears them in the form of encrypted messaging apps, virtual private networks (VPNs) and privacy-focused browsers. Yet, stolen and faked digital identities mirror the misinformation that comes through social and news media, while online harassment and doxxing, the intentional public sharing of an individual's private or personal information without their consent, still loom large. Despite all the benefits of the digital revolution, there remains the challenge of regulating and monitoring potential misinformation using AI technology. With its exponential possibilities, listeners need to be vigilant in guarding against misinformation. Critical listening on public platforms is more important now than ever before.

Technology-Assisted Listening

Technology is here to stay and it's in our interest to harness it and use it to our advantage in technology-assisted listening, the way we do with the other types of listening available to us. The impact that social media has had on the way we communicate does not need explaining. Millions of people across all generations post images, videos, memes and text to social media platforms, amplifying voices and narratives that were previously largely unheard in mainstream media. Businesses too have joined in the mix – the vast majority of companies today have a social media account and an army of employees to manage them.[5]

The advantage of social media isn't just its ability to connect people who wish to speak and listen, but its ability to do so in both private and public domains at once. With digital devices available to many all over the world, almost anyone can open a social media account to share content and ideas, and any individual can join or build a community with people even in the most geographically remote places. Furthermore, social media's chatty feel gives a public platform the feel of personal engagement, making it significantly more immediate and interactive than more formal modes of public communication. A study of online users found that the participants listened more readily on social networking sites than other ways of listening.[6] Because social media listening is at once personal and private as well as networked and public, it gives us the feeling that we've been heard and validated in the larger community.[7] Like the complaints department that listens to customers, social media has the dexterity to reach both private and public concerns, explaining why many companies today use their social media channels to respond to individual customer complaints.

Today, some 30 per cent of top companies have a dedicated social media account just for listening to customer complaints,[8] turning the negative impact of customer complaints into customer engagement. Listening tools such as tracking brand mentions are now common practice, in which human listening and artificial intelligence actively monitor online conversations side by side. Online listening isn't just a way to identify emerging trends and gain a sense of how customers feel about a brand – the information can also be used to personalize and tailor products. As customers share both positive and negative feedback through photos, stories and experiences, they beta-test new products and become part of the process of branding. Social listening can be a positive experience for all as it can build a sense of community and increase brand awareness.

If social media listening is one way we use technology to listen to humans, search listening is another. Many of us know the convenience and the utility of asking a search engine a question and listening for a response as an informational answer to a simple question: 'What's the weather today?' will usually return the straight-up answer a listener wants on the outside temperature and a forecast of how wet or dry it will be, and not the kind of reply you get from a human, like, 'It looks like it'll clear up. Just throw on a jacket.' We use machine-assisted listening searches when we're just looking for a direct answer.

Human listeners ask machines trillions of questions through search engines every year, averaging more than three to four searches per person on any given day. From weather forecasts to the news to what TV series to watch, search engines look through the archive of data to provide us with functional answers and shortlisted recommendations to help their listeners make decisions. With a machine, we don't have to manage any part of our relationship, which is probably why the most searched answer the British workforce listened for following former Prime Minister Boris Johnson's announcement of the government's plans for a staged easing of the lockdown during the pandemic was, 'Should I go to work tomorrow?'[9]

We like the perceived certitude with which a machine can supply an answer. A no-nonsense and definitive 'yes' answer is as welcome for tech troubleshooting as it is for how to lose weight or the answer to 'Why aren't they talking to me?' Listeners ask questions they often don't even ask their most intimate partners because in asking a machine a question we feel we can get an answer with certitude – or at least the illusion of it.

Our uncertainty avoidance not only leads us to ask search engines for easy answers, it makes us more inclined to do so even at the expense of our privacy. Even though we know the search engine stores our questions, and we can see this in the way that other people's questions come out as suggestions when we begin to type our own question, we still go ahead and ask the search engine and might even feel comforted on seeing that we're not alone in asking our question. Ironically, perhaps, part of our feel-good in search listening comes from listening to the public content message as if it contained the contextual meta-message, *Don't worry, all these other people asked the question you want to hear the response for, too.*

We are masters in anthropomorphizing machines. Programming machines in voice and face recognition as well as tone and sentiment interpretation is a good start to making machines behave like us. Between human creativity and machine intelligence, it's likely a question of time before machines will be able to do most things that we can do – at least nearly. This scares many humans, particularly the digital immigrant, and, for sure, with machine listening intelligence on a par with or better than a human's, we need robust regulatory frameworks that safeguard privacy and promote ethical use of technology. We also need to develop our own personal digital literacy, with listening intelligence that can critically discern between credible sources and the trolled-up ones.

Limitless in its expansiveness, listening on social media can be challenging for the same reasons it is advantageous. With all their power, social media algorithms can bias content curation, spreading false or misleading content that fits smartly into fast-mapped metaphors which explain complex ideas in terms of a disarmingly easy equivalent of the kinds we talked about in chapter six. The proliferation of unchecked misinformation can not only perpetuate systemic inequalities and discrimination, but can also further fan public confusion and fuel distrust, polarizing groups into silos where cyber trolls bully and harass. If machines learn to convincingly simulate the human voice, much critical listening care will be needed to filter out the inappropriate language that humans use in their everyday language.

Some scaremongers suggest turning away from technology altogether, but to optimize communication in the digital age, we need to learn the benefits of tech-assisted listening and mitigate its danger so we can encourage responsible digital listening and citizenship. Through content moderation, algorithm design and community management, organizations can combat misinformation and listeners can be part of the process by enforcing privacy at ground level. To navigate online listening spaces responsibly, we need everyone, all the generations – the generation born into the digitized community, but also those who were born outside it.

Digital Age Humans in the In-Between Space Between Generations

The digital native generation composed of Gen Z and younger Millennials, and the older generations of digital immigrants, represent two cohorts with different experiences and skill sets but their collaboration can lead to mutual benefits. The most obvious way that digital natives can help digital immigrants is by assisting them to acquire technological literacy, which might mean updating their digital media competencies at the task level, but also conceptually about the mindset of the new technological order. It's this mindset that has benefited me the most and, for lack of a better name, I'll call it, 'Being okay in beta'.

When apps were first coming onto the market, a language app designer enlisted me as their consultant. The app was already in full-throttle development when I joined and was released not long after – to my horror, though, in beta. As a novice to apps and the way they worked, I couldn't understand why it had been released in what looked like an uncompleted form. But when the lead programmer explained the process to me in language I could understand, it made so much sense.

Faisal explained that developing an app is just like the Soft Listening we use in learning our operational languages. In the beginning, you make mistakes and you use those mistakes to intuitively understand when and how rules apply. Testing the new rules out next time, you learn if your hypothetical rule was a good one. Just like speakers and listeners work in collaboration to learn a new language, app users find mistakes so developers can debug the app and update the programme. While they are offered free use of the app in beta, the users can help improve the app in return. I learned that app development, like language learning, requires the cooperation of at least two people communicating, so we can mutually improve our Soft Listening practices and continue to learn even more.

A strong feature of the technological digital native generation is their orientation to uncertainty and their adaptability to it, right down to a nonchalance about 'glitches' and changes in platform layouts. When classes first went online during the pandemic, I remember video platform developers kept moving around the record button as they developed other parts of the platform. This drove me mad until I remembered to use Faisal's being-okay-in-beta mindset. As I tested my own threshold for uncertainty, I realized that I had already practised a version of this in moving from country to country and learning new languages. I remember always starting at the bottom of the learning curve where nothing seemed to make sense and everything is hard. The grammar felt nonsensical, with irregularities changing on a whim. I'd make a ton of mistakes until, at some point, usually around three months in, things began to fall in to place. It's then I'd somehow learn to listen for a complex idea fast-mapped onto a metaphorical image to conjure an image and 'get' what someone was saying. Being okay with beta means there will be uncertainty for a while but eventually there will be a resolution. That's one of the most instructive lessons the digital generation has taught me.

Digital natives can in turn benefit from digital immigrants, too, and potentially to a greater extent than a programmed search engine might tell you. When I first looked up 'How can digital immigrants help digital natives?' the search engine came back with a list that had sewing, DIY and the rather cryptic 'meeting people in person'. Gen Zers point out that this last entry, face-to-face in-person communication, more than digital interaction, is what they find most challenging in contemporary contact because many things are left unresolved in live interaction whereas in digital interaction, you can wait and see how the other person interacts. One Gen Zer explained that not having an idea about outcomes is disconcerting because 'it's more challenging to get a read on how the interaction went'. What digital natives can learn from digital immigrants then, is that it's okay to be in beta and 'not know' outcomes before they happen in interactions unassisted by technology. By sharing their experiences, digital immigrants can assure digital natives that sometimes the best outcomes and the biggest learning experiences are the ones stumbled upon in listening slow without the predictive maps.

Moving Forward with Generational Listening

In my visits to pre-internet Japan, despite the intense feeling of discomfort and incomprehension about the substantially different worlds presented in the news broadcasts, with time on my side, in listening slow, I'd somehow always come around to a new level of understanding that I can only explain as a palpable respect for different worlds. This renewed awareness that humans can operate in such drastically different realities and still cooperate to mutual benefit, made me realize that by engaging in open-minded conversations we can spend our time learning from one another instead of guarding our own corners.

Digital communication brings many complex challenges we've only just begun to tackle, but it's a powerful tool for personal self-expression and a community bridge that's here to stay. Learning from a human of any age might not be as fast or immediate or mistake-free as the information you can obtain from a search engine, but learning to listen to humans in beta will always be valuable, not least because it can help you navigate not only your digital listening but also the messier, slower and textured listening you do when you're exercising the energies of Listening with Fourteen Hearts.

7 Keys to Generational Listening

■ Touchpoints help us characterize generations when listening for and capturing iconic language in Baby Boomer, Generation X, Millennial and Generation Z groups.

■ Words and acronyms are examples of cultural touchpoints we listen for in intergenerational communication.

■ Some words and acronyms have staying power while others fade away.

■ The concepts of some words and acronyms are reinvented in the next generation.

■ The types of acronyms have changed across generations. Boomers tend to use acronyms to express a status. Digital native generations tend to use acronyms and initialisms as a shorthand to action that also reflects lifestyle membership within the group.

■ We have normalized asking for and listening for replies to technology-assisted searches. Organizations need to regulate for privacy and online safety; individual listeners also need to amp up critical listening in tech-assisted listening.

■ Digital natives and digital immigrants need to fortify our intergenerational listening and learn from each other so we can be okay in beta online and in-person.

3 Listening Reflections across Generations

- What generation do you identify with?
- What words can you think of that typify your generation?
- Make a vow to learn something from another generation, selecting from the digital immigrant or native lists below, or come up with your own.

If you're a digital immigrant, ask a digital native:

- How to create, manage and critically understand social media accounts.
- How to understand privacy settings, spot clickbait and navigate online safety.
- Which app stores to use, how to download and use apps.
- Messaging app protocol ☺
- How to store, share and collaborate on documents on different video conferencing platforms.

If you're a digital native, ask a digital immigrant:

- How to spot misinformation in traditional media sources and transfer the critical listening to online media.
- How to spend time away from online interaction – there's more than sewing and DIY!
- How to use in-person stories in digital storytelling.
- Share funny and challenging stories about in-person interaction.

Generational Listening

■ How to learn from mistakes. As the former first lady of the United States Eleanor Roosevelt once said, in keeping with the Zen Master Dōgen Zenji's suggestion to see others as yourself: 'Learn from the mistakes of others. You can't live long enough to make them all yourself.'

10

Adaptive Listening

Match, Adjust, Adapt

In my last year of primary school in Tokyo, my mother declared Tuesdays and Thursdays were language dinners. Tuesdays was all-Japanese language at the table. Thursdays was all-English. No mixing. We would speak and listen to one language only. It was a policy instituted by a mother who, while advocating for our family's multilingualism by, for example, registering us in local schools around the globe, was also terrified – alongside other caregivers of the time – that her children would turn into hybrid babblers who couldn't speak one language untainted by another.

Although there is the little fact that you usually don't speak in a language unless you think the person listening to you understands it, the fear in the multilingual community of developing hybrid babblers was intense and arguably not altogether unwarranted. At the table on 'free-talk' days, my siblings and I would happily jumble languages, mixing words and grammar, sometimes even in the middle of a word. The day my mother brought in the one-language-only policy was probably the day after my sister pointed at something on the table and called it 'futotning' to mean 'fattening', mixing the Japanese verb *futoru*, which means 'become fat', with the present participle '–ing' to make the verb an adjective. All this because the English language is equipped with a way of turning a verb into an adjective while the Japanese language isn't – although that wasn't why we jumbled our languages. We spoke and listened the way most people speak and listen – because it sounded right, matching the way we talked with others, using similar registers and style. We work harder at minding our Ps and Qs in public but at home we do whatever comes naturally, including mixing languages, which much later I'd learn is called 'code-switching'.

Although code-switching is an interesting focus of academic research, there weren't a lot of people who used it in countries which were predominantly monolingual. In fact, my mother's fear of being caught mixing languages was echoed in the larger communities around the world where code-switching has had a long history of being forbidden. My partner's grandfather, for example, was asked to check his native Provençal at the school gates in the south of France, and bilingual children in Californian public schools faced an English-only language policy until 2016. In these states and others, operating in more than one governing code has traditionally signalled split loyalties, spawning a preference for a one-language-only selective focus and the mindset that you can't do more than one thing at once.

And yet we often do more than one thing at once. We multitask all the time. In the digital age, we multitask a lot, in fact. For example, a study by global professional service company Accenture that surveyed 3,600 professionals from thirty countries found that 80 per cent of the respondents said they multitask on conference calls. While they are on a conference call, 66 per cent of the respondents said they multitask with work emails, 35 per cent multitask with instant messaging, 34 per cent with personal emails, 22 per cent with social media and 21 per cent reading news and entertainment. The research that compared responses across three generations found that there was an important amount of multitasking in every generation, with Millennials reporting that they spent more than half their day multitasking.[1] So it seems that the vast majority of our workforce multitasks at some point in the day.

Such research is often cited to underline how our lack of focus can potentially hurt us, leading to lowered performance and increasing the number of errors we make when we multitask. Advocates of single focus further argue that multitasking reduces our ability to recall information accurately and that we pay a 'switching cost' in moving from one task to the next. The prescription from such research is to restrict multitasking to simple and routine tasks only and use single focus for complex ones.

Proponents of multitasking on the other hand observe that while multitasking isn't easy, we are called to multitask all the time. At work, we are often multitasking, not necessarily because we want to, but because we need to – we aren't always multitasking to slack off on work making party plans as management might fear, but because we actually need to keep up with our communication network. So rather than trying to avoid multitasking, like my family tried to avoid code-switching at home, we can use the idea of 'being okay in beta' to optimize multitasking, too. Optimizing multitasking is adaptation and that's the premise for this final chapter on

Adaptive Listening. Adaptive Listening is important because it can enhance each of the listening streams we have talked about and keep us flexible, ready to navigate less-than-perfect days. Adaptive Listening can make our curious mindset even more open, sharpen our credibility check-ins and help us navigate through a number of sociocultural listening experiences we're presented with on a daily basis.

Multitasking in Communication

In communication, we listen as we talk and we talk as we listen. Although we might think of our conversations as neatly packaged into a queueing culture of taking turns in an I-go-you-go pattern, we actually do them both together all the time. For the pacey talkers we identified in the chapter on Cultural Listening, this is a given. Pacey talkers think out loud, talking about what they are thinking about while listening. But while pacey talkers make their multitasking explicit, queue talkers and listener-talkers do the talking inside their heads, coding the answer to a question while someone else is talking. If you're a queue talker who waits your turn to talk, or a listener-talker who leads by listening, you're multitasking not once but many times over the course of a conversation that requires we fit what we have to say into the back-and-forth of listening and speaking, thinking about what we're going to say next. So, communication is a multitasking cooperative effort between individuals, but also within ourselves as we multitask to follow the conversation and adapt what we are going to say to the conversation in progress. If we don't do this, we can end up becoming that no-filter person that 1990s Japanese youth called out as poor AirReaders. And, if we don't think about what we could potentially say and adapt it to the ongoing conversation, we could end up forgetting what we were going to say.

One of my favourite listening stories is about a boy at a Sunday church service, who, sitting amongst other children, became so deeply immersed in what the other children were saying, he forgot his own answer to the question of what he wanted for Christmas. When his turn finally came, he was at a loss for words and stood up red-faced, not knowing what to say until he plunged his hands deep into his pockets and pulled out a coin. Suddenly, there was the answer. Overjoyed, he raised his hand with the coin and replied, 'Money!'

Common advice we hear about listening is that we should do it wholeheartedly without thinking about speaking. Research backs up this kind of no-holds-barred listening, arguing that thinking about what you're going to say next compromises the quality of listening and sacrifices our listening comprehension, critically producing an effect psychologists call 'response planning interference'. To combat response planning interference, they say we should stop whatever we're doing and just listen 100 per cent. Putting away your phone and selecting the person as the focus of your auditory and visual attention is indisputably good advice, principally because it reassures the speaker and slows down the conversation. Studies show that even pacey talkers who habitually overlap their speech with others' when they ask in serial, 'How're you doing? Are you on vacation? When was the last time you were here?' slow down their speech when they are listening more intently to something that places a heavier cognitive demand on informational content. Multitasking is demanding and slowing down the pace helps pacey-talk multitaskers mitigate the negative effects of overtasking themselves with talking while listening. It's true that listening slow allows for deeper listening in a number of different contexts.

Listening, though, isn't just about shutting up and giving someone your full attention. That makes listening a passive activity of just receiving speech – a highly impoverished form of listening of the kind people do when they are being scolded or bullied. In multitask listening, we might not be expressing all our thoughts out loud but we are actively encouraging the other person to speak in an interactive process. So rather than ban multitasking the way my mother banned code-switching at the dinner table, perhaps the more useful thing to do is ask what we can do to offset its negative effects. What strategies, other than slowing down, can we use to help each other while we're multitask listening?

Meta-Talk: Talk about Talk

Pacey talkers are actually not the only people who talk out loud about multitasking. Many queue talkers who like their talk organized in a formal structure and listener-talkers who like listeners to lead the conversation also talk out loud about multitasking. For example, in my bankers' study, I found that speakers voiced how they were listening at key junctures of the conversation, letting all listeners know they were changing topics, joining or leaving a conversation. I called this meta-talk – 'talk about talk'.

By telling someone about a switch in topics, the bankers

not only guided their listeners onto a new topic but also spotlighted their own conversational shift from listener to speaker – 'I'm not sure if we should talk about how the delay in the customer service response caused the dip in sales this week.' Notifying others about a switch not only announces the next topic but also helps relieve the cognitive load as it allows listeners to prepare for the new information. Talk about talk allows listeners to listen for the new topic, easing the transition and improving the quality of listening. This is a pro-listener communication device that is interestingly part of the advice given to those who want to assist the hearing impaired. By meta-talking about the imminent conversational topic shift the way the banker did, an abled listener-talker can help the hearing impaired as well as all participants in a meeting move forward in the conversation.

Talk about talk can also help direct future action and let conversationalists know that they have been heard. When we say things like, 'Okay, that's all from me for our weekly report. Anyone else?' the way the bankers in my study did, we not only make preparations to conclude the meeting but also acknowledge having heard others by offering the floor to someone else. By preparing listeners to navigate their next actions, meta talk can also be a listener talking out loud about their listening and works to demonstrate their listening the way the back-channel 'uhuh's do by making our listening explicit.

While we guide other listeners and smooth over transitions between topics and meetings as we move throughout the day, we not only ensure that everyone is ready to move on but also confirm they are satisfied with the informational language they have acquired. This example of listener talk shows how we can use multitasking to our benefit, as talking about talking reaffirms connections around our experience of listening together. While meta-talk helps conversationalists mind relationships when they are multitasking in conversation – i.e. speaking with listening – educational experts have suggested other conversational devices to help participants move through a conversation while multitasking to help us improve the quality of the content we hear.

Quality Questions

We know from search listening that one way to listen is by asking a question that elicits a reply. We learned before that in Japanese the same character that is used for listening for informational language, 聞, is also used to mean 'ask'. The meta-function of a question is that a speaker asks to be put in the listener's role to learn something they don't know. But asking a question in a culture that privileges speakers can be risky because by asking a question, a speaker makes explicit what they don't know. Leadership experts say that the number one reason why people don't ask questions is because it reveals what we don't know and we fear it makes us vulnerable or appear foolish.[2]

Despite the challenge of questioning, however, research also shows that asking questions has many relational benefits. Questions can initiate interaction, show interest, clarify understanding and encourage engagement. Not all questions have equal impact, though, and learning expert Jeff Wetzler advises us that while a quality question can show interest in a person and lead to a deepened understanding of them, others can disrupt the speaker's train of thought or put them on the defensive. Guiding communicators in the art of asking good questions, Wetzler encourages asking open-ended questions with the intention of listening to learn to hear what someone is really trying to tell you, rather than asking simple yes/no questions that don't invite a person to tell you about them or give you information about something you don't already know. The latter of these types of questioning can shut down a listener or put them on the defensive.[3]

Leading questions are a good example of questions that aren't actually questions but disguised reproaches. Questions such as 'What are you doing?' or 'Are you sure?' are usually respectively heard as *Stop doing that* and *I think you're wrong*. Instead, mashing our idea of the novice mindset we introduced in chapter three into quality questioning, we can ask quality questions that are grounded in a thoughtful and genuine question that seeks to learn something by asking 'how': 'How does that work?' How questions that ask someone to explain the process of something can often get them engaged in a response in a non-threatening way.

A novice mindset can help form quality questions that allow a listener to adjust their own conversational multitasking and join the conversation. Like meta talk, a quality question can help ease conversationalists through transitions where even the so-called quiet people can talk on a topic that interests them. A quality question is an example of a demonstrated listener-talk multitasked effort that contains the meta-message, *That's so interesting you know about that. Tell me more about it.* Good questions come from a listener-talker who optimises multitasking and includes people in the discussion.

Attributed Summaries

Another listener-assistance device that facilitators often advise to prevent response planning interference – thinking about the next comment rather than fully listening – is content summary. Like the academic summaries we made in our notes at school, speech summaries are the prototypical form of listening comprehension that checks to see if you've understood the content correctly. Summaries can help listeners retain key points by repeating and consolidating them to memory in their own words. It's a way for listeners to clarify their understanding by paraphrasing the speaker's message and asking the meta question, *Is this what you mean?*

Having said that, though, summaries can become a form of response planning interference if they are spoken out loud to inhibit the flow of conversation and/or make other listeners miss important details or even miss the point completely. Constantly interrupting the speaker with summaries about content can disrupt the speaker's train of thought and, worse, make it seem like you aren't really listening and just repeating back what you heard to demonstrate your listening competence. The best attributed summaries aren't a tally of key messages in the informational content but a practice that tunes into the experience of listening for the tones of cultures, genders and generations.

Attributed summaries work best when they are reflexive, working quietly as an inner voice that echolocates you in the conversation the way a bat hears echoes of their own sounds to navigate through the dark. A good summarizer is an echolocator who listens to their own summaries of the ongoing conversation to navigate their way through a conversation in which they are multitasking between speaking and listening. Ultimately, echolocators use conversational devices like meta talk, quality questions and attributed summaries to help other listener-talkers find their way through an interaction where everyone is multitasking multiple aspects of communication, including matching themselves to the tone of conversation.

In-Sync Tone Matching

While speaker-driven devices like quality questions and attributed summaries help guide listeners through the informational content of a conversation, listener-driven methods like tone matching help everyone stay in sync relationally. Tone matching is an important Listening with Fourteen Hearts device that allows listeners to set the right cultural tone for a conversation in progress. We often match our tones to the social formality of the register, using informal language, for example, when someone greets us with 'Hi, how's it going?' and we respond with, 'Yeah, not bad. You?', and more formal language for instance when a co-worker asks you something like, 'Can we discuss this quarterly report?' and you reply, 'Absolutely. I'll make time to look over it this afternoon and we can schedule a meeting with the other departments to go over the key issues tomorrow.'

Likewise, we also match our own tones to the emotional energy of a speaker in interpersonal communication. So, if you hear that someone has been having a challenging day, you probably wouldn't smack them on their back and say in a joking, upbeat tone, 'Ah, never mind, get over it!', as that would likely end the conversation. Instead you are probably more likely to say something along the lines of, 'Oh no, what's happening?' that is more likely to create space for them to talk about their day. Making an effort to match tones not only keeps us relevant in a conversation but also helps to extend the well-being to everyone involved and potentially longer into the future of an ongoing relationship. On the other hand, not noticing tone, in the way 1990s Japanese youth culture saw 'not being able to read the room', for example, by talking about work projects when everyone is just hanging out, can impair well-being and cost conversations not only in the immediate moment but impact relationships more widely.

Matching cultural tones can be challenging because it's another layer of multitasking that requires a listener to continue adjusting and readjusting their talk throughout a conversation. But activating the novice mindset and being in iterative beta mode can help motivate our intuition and provide powerful echolocation for tone adjustments in conversation. Guiding us towards the energy we need is a little-known fuel adaptor source called 'perpetual readiness'. This is part of the novice mindset that helps us remain open to match change and stay resilient throughout the process.

Perpetual Readiness

We rely on our listening to learn and to associate new learning with what we already know. Although the range and frequency may vary, associative learning helps us navigate new interactions, and it's particularly useful in seeing us through sticky situations. That answer you came up with in the interview when you had no idea what they were asking isn't so much a wild guess as an intuition informed by previous learning.

Intuition is one of four identifiable inner voices that psychologists identify as rational, self-critical, nurturing and intuitive. The rational voice is the voice we explored in chapter four on Credibility Listening. It's the voice that's necessary for critically distinguishing important information from unhelpful or misinformation. The rational voice is different from the self-critical inner voice, which psychologists suggest should be observed then challenged. By contrast, they advise embracing our nurturing and intuitive inner voices and using them as we navigate our way through conversations.

The semiotician and philosopher Charles Sanders Peirce suggested 'perpetual readiness' as a way of training the intuitive inner voice. Peirce's perpetual readiness is the intentional state of openness to engage with the world and meet any number of complex situations, many of which cannot be resolved through formal rational reasoning. The psychologist Daniel Kahneman argued that we aren't the rational decision-makers we sometimes believe we are, but it was Peirce who discussed a practical way to use perpetual readiness to adjust our interactions with the constantly evolving landscape of the world. Peirce said perpetual readiness is the intuition your inner voice uses to adapt to the environment and help you move forward.

One key benefit of perpetual readiness is adaptability. If you are ready, you have the potential to adapt to people in the moment and any number of things that can happen. As I moved countries, adaptability to a new environment was key to my survival, and lucky for me, being okay in beta was one of the charms of being a child. Awkwardness and discomfort gave way to a sense of openness and perpetual readiness, whether in New York City, Tokyo, or any new culture.

Perpetual readiness isn't just for kids. It's for adults who can reboot their novice mindset and listen with the adaptability that will allow them to quickly address unexpected circumstances or opportunities as they arise. That story about the young executive who mistook the CEO for a barman can actually be reframed as a story of perpetual readiness that helped Tak Watanabe adapt to the situation and fix the Singapore Sling. Perpetual readiness implies being mentally, emotionally and physically prepared to act, learn and grow in response to changing conditions or demands. It's about staying proactive in the face of uncertainty about what is going to happen next.

Perpetual readiness is a useful listening device in multitasking our way through conversations, especially when things aren't going to plan. In times of conflict or complementary schismogenesis when the opportunity for miscommunication is ripe, perpetual readiness can help guide us to listen for the challenges that are often the order of everyday life. Perpetual readiness facilitates navigation by not automatically turning down a challenge but by remaining open to the idea of taking it on. It's staying open and being prepared, the way retail shops present themselves in Japan when they display the signs that show that they are either *in preparation* or *in operation* rather than *open* or *closed*.

Listening is a way of harnessing perpetual readiness. When we are ready to recognize patterns such as verbosity in cover-ups, we can critically listen to our inner voices about the potential for misinformation in public. Likewise, when we're ready to visually listen for facial expressions, we can become aware of nonverbal cues of interaction and understand what they are saying. Our perpetual readiness listens to our own inner dialogue to categorize and sort through what is happening in any episodic interaction. When our Adaptive Listening connects with perpetual readiness, we can cast the widest net possible to adjust to our ever-changing landscape of interaction that will guide us in our listening journeys ahead.

Practising Adaptive Listening and Strengthening Associations

It's no secret that practice can make for better listening. In a simple study of word-pair recall, for example, ninety-six undergraduates who generated their own words in the pair recalled the pairs better than those who simply read out word pairs they were given.[4] Practising listening works similarly because every time we listen, we build our knowledge set and strengthen our intuition for future purposes, testing it again and again, updating past experiences through an association that strengthens recall. Neurologists tell us that intuition is likely processed in the hippocampus, the region of the brain that makes the connections between all the different things we see or hear and one that plays a crucial role in learning and memory. Every time we make a connection in our associative memories, we're practising a kind of Adaptive Listening that is perpetually ready for the next set of things that come our way.

In one study, volunteers were asked to play a virtual reality game where they heard a sound, such as running water, at the same time as they saw a colourful picture appear on the wall. In a following game, the same colourful picture was flashed up on the wall, only they were told this picture could help them win prize money. Although the sound was never directly connected to winning money, the volunteers began to associate the sound of running water with the prize. In a similar experiment conducted on mice, a sound was broadcast to the mice before they saw a picture made from LED lights. In a separate task, the mice were offered the reward of sugar water every time the lights were turned on. Like the human volunteers, the mice began connecting the sound they heard before with the reward as they went around hunting for it.[5]

Both humans and mice make associations with a variety of experiences we have banked in the past and use it towards our perpetual readiness in Adaptive Listening. David Dupret from the MRC Brain Network Dynamics Unit at the University of Oxford observes that as mice rest, their brains make new links between things they have not directly experienced. Simon Fisher, programme manager for the Neurosciences and Mental Health Board at the MRC also noted that humans put different memories together to help us in our everyday decision-making.[6]

A well-connected memory is a primary source for adaptability. As we auralize or visualize the associations we have made from past experience, we listen to our inner voices and join the dots about things we didn't know a moment ago to intuit what's happening in our current engagement. Adaptive Listening helps us make numerous associations and multitask all our efforts to adjust to life circumstances. Like the trimmer who adjusts the sails of a boat, we adapt our speaking and listening to the context of a conversation so the journey can continue. Adaptive Listening doesn't only help us join and adjust to conversations, it also helps us to learn from the environment and develop ourselves. I discovered this in the ICU but also back in the sunny nineties in Tucson, Arizona, where I was teaching. I just didn't know it then.

Practising Adaptive Listening at the Grand Canyon

I got a memo from our department head about a visiting Russian professor of Buddhism who had come to the university. The memo said the professor had become a Buddhist expert by covertly reading scriptures censored during the Soviet era and that, incredibly, he had learned Japanese on shortwave radio even when Soviet airwaves were jamming towers. Interest piqued, I read the part of the email from the department head that was personally addressed to me.

> This is the professor's first time out of the country and we want to bring him up to the canyons. However, I cannot convince him to take time away from reading Buddhist text in the archives. Please go talk to him. Maybe you could try reading some of the scriptures with him.

My first reaction was a hard no, which took the form of reminding the department head that I didn't read Pāli. Pāli is an ancient language that originated in the Indian subcontinent and is most famously known as the language of the Theravada Buddhist scriptures. But then he reminded me that there were Buddhist texts in Old Japanese, which, in the head's own words was, 'just like us reading Latin'. My second no was again based on language, that while the English language is connected to Latin in its Indo-European language heritage in both its written and spoken forms, the Japanese language is an orphan language related to Mandarin Chinese in only its written form. Brought over to Japan in the fourth to sixth centuries in waves, it was superimposed on the spoken language. 'Old Japanese is as related to modern Japanese as English', I contended, unable to hide the tone of an exclamation mark at the end of the sentence.

When the department head heard the tone, he checkmated me with the fact that the archives have translations in English. He then finished me off with his original motivation for asking me to meet the Russian Buddhist scholar in language and a tone of voice that expressed his authority and my mission in no uncertain terms: 'It's his FIRST visit outside the country. We NEED to get him up to the Grand Canyon. Just go read with him.'

Any Arizonan host feels they have the moral obligation to take a visitor to see the Grand Canyon, especially if it is the visitor's first trip to the US and likely the only one they'll make in their lifetime. So after I finished reading about the Grand Canyon's outstanding universal value as a UNESCO World Heritage Site, I took a breath and plotted archives avoidance routes so I could back out of my mission.

This worked well until three days later, I bumped into the Russian Buddhist scholar in the regular library in the adjacent building to the special collections archives. Now face-to-face, in-person, before in-person was even a thing, I had no choice but to sheepishly introduce myself. He didn't reciprocate but instead pointed at my lunch that I was going to eat as soon as I got out of the library. After a few more compliments on the sandwich, I offered it to him and, in keeping with the university's social etiquette regarding eating in the library, moved between him and the librarian to conceal him while he ate it. When he finished, he motioned for me to follow him. After uselessly mumbling that I had to go, I gave in and followed him. When we got to the archives, we walked in and he pointed to the floor in the universal gesture 'sit', which I did. I copied his cross-legged sitting style and tried not to show that I saw that one of his eyes was missing, a detail that had previously been relayed to me by several department members who had already met him.

Before I knew it, he had spread a giant book across his lap, and was reading what I assumed was Buddhist text. I stayed frozen, fearful of the moment he would try to get me to read it – but it never happened. Instead, at the end of what must have been ten minutes that had felt like a few days, he said something I'll never forget. The words weren't important but their meaning was: it was the first time anyone had ever listened to him read Buddhist text.

Not in a thousand reincarnations could I have known that my avoidance-fail that day would become the watershed moment when the professor would agree to go up to the Grand Canyon. The department head was also beside himself and couldn't believe his ears when he heard the news. He assumed I had read some Buddhist text which I tried to correct by saying something about a sandwich. But by then, the department head wasn't listening.

I assume that he must have been busy obtaining special privileges to copy some of the professor's beloved texts because that would have been preferable to bringing the texts out of the archives' air conditioning and into the desert heat. I never found out if that was what he did, but I imagined it, just like I imagined the professor reading the Buddhist texts in the Grand Canyon, his hair pulled back in a ponytail to reveal a contented face of someone who had been heard.

What I learned from the Russian Buddhist scholar was that opening yourself up to the challenge of listening can bring about real change. When the founder of the Center for Communicating Sciences at Stony Brook University, Alan Alda, said that listening is allowing ourselves to be changed by what is going on outside of us,[7] what I think he meant was that the real reason we often don't listen is because it can ignite the fear of change and make us vulnerable. We turn away from things we don't know and avoid things we fear may expose us, the way I naively thought reading ancient Buddhist texts might do. In reality, though, change can deepen your self-awareness and resilience, which in turn promotes your ability to adapt to the changing circumstances that lie ahead.

What I ultimately learned from the Russian Buddhist scholar was the power of adaptive listening in connecting listeners and speakers in the in-between space where we can hear both language and voice – the ancient Buddhist text and the Russian Buddhist scholar. Listening is multitasking. Although we can lose ourselves in conversation the way the young boy did in the church service that asked the children what they wanted for Christmas, a lot of the time we are talking while listening and listening while talking, and we are listening to others as we listen to ourselves. We enjoy talking to someone because of the joy of being listened to, and we enjoy listening to someone because of the joy it brings us both. Whether it's the department head talking about getting a visiting professor up to the Grand Canyon or the professor reading texts he loves, listening is sharing what's important to you with someone and enjoying together the charm it brings.

7 Keys to Adaptive Listening

- We code-switch and multitask between listening and speaking, sometimes speaking while listening to others and at other times listening to ourselves while others are speaking.

- Research shows that the vast majority of our workforce multitasks at some point in the day.

- Multitasking, including listening while talking and talking while listening, can incur a 'switching cost' in moving from one task to the next.

- The prescription from research into this area is to freely multitask for simple and routine tasks and use single focus for complex ones.

- One listening strategy we use for resolving complex tasks is adaptation.

- Adaptation draws on practice and a state of perpetual readiness that allows us to adjust to the conversation in progress.

- Adaptive Listening is important because every person has a unique voice that needs to be heard, and it's the Adaptive Listener that can show up for them.

3 Reflections on Adaptive Listening

- Think of ways you multitask at work and at home. Are these multitasks helpful or distracting to you? Can you think of ways of mitigating the distracting ones?

- Do a post-conversation check-in to notice your own communication multitasking of speaking while listening and listening while speaking and reflect on whether they are helpful or distracting. Being aware of your own multitasking can help you better navigate conversations.

- With perpetual readiness, basketball players can potentially score a basket by tipping in a ball to redirect a ball that is bouncing out. Do you use talk about talk to direct topics in your conversations? Listen for the next time you or someone else does and observe its efficacy.

Epilogue

As a person of a certain age settled in the European outpost of London, today, the seven-year-old lost on the first day of school in Tokyo seems a long time ago. The Japanese call getting lost 'direction deafness', and while I still get horribly lost, today I can thankfully navigate my way around with the click of a button on a wonderful app. That's one way technology has been incredibly helpful for humans, providing physical navigation for the directionally challenged, like me.

But for everything technology can do, including providing directions with pinpoint accuracy, there's still a need for human navigation fuelled by Listening with Fourteen Hearts. Machine-automated self-driving cars can load up real-time information that stop them from turning right because a car just ran a light, but they still can't tell you whether or not to cross the street because you just saw a friend on the other side. That's a decision only you and your fourteen listening hearts can make, and one we make as humans multiple times a day. For personal and relational matters, humans still have the edge on machines in navigational intelligence.

I was recently reminded of this by my late elderly neighbour, Milly, a descendant of the original builders of the five houses on our block in London, which were built in the early 1900s. When Milly died, her nephew, James, invited me into her house as a neighbourly gesture. I accepted because I had never been in Milly's house before – she wasn't too fond of the foreigners who had moved into her neighbourhood, especially as they had a cat that chased the pigeons she fed and loved, enough to complain to the council and have two armed bobbies come to interview the cat and its servants. We passed the investigation but never gained the connection we sought with her. Our annual New Year's card was returned through our letter box with a clear message on the envelope: 'Not Wanted'.

It was only through James's tour of the house that I learned how Milly had been living all these years. As I walked into the house, I sidestepped pieces of First World War memorabilia – just a week prior, James explained, the police were forced to close down the street for an afternoon because he had reported an old grenade with the pin still in it when clearing out the house. But for all the untold stories about undetonated bombs in the house, the tour changed tone when we went upstairs.

On the top floor was Milly's bedroom, in which a spartan single mattress by the window with a single fitted sheet was the feature piece. Next to this private bedroom was another room, filled to the brim with boxes – fifty-six of them, according to James. They contained unworn shoes in Milly's size, UK size eight. A shoe salesperson 'from the north' had apparently been selling Milly a pair every month.

'She loved hearing her voice,' said James.

Stunned by the story I wasn't expecting to hear, it felt as if the floor in Milly's two-storey house had subsided a little, the way our surveyor had warned us it might one day. Like me, the surveyor who referred to Milly as the 'spinster grouch' probably hadn't heard the shoebox story. If he had, he'd probably understand, as I finally did, that it's often when we're at our grumpiest that we need to be heard the most.

Epilogue

It feels like an understatement to say that the twenty-first digital century of isolated social bubbles designed in social media by AI-enhanced algorithms have created an even greater need for human listeners than we had before. Isolation has been exacerbated by the insufficiency of social housing and adequate social medical care. While loneliness has been primarily tackled in the traditional domains of government or privately funded means, loneliness today is also addressed by technology, which has the negative force of creating silos, but also the positive one of restoring health and even providing preventative health to our digital generation in novel ways. For example, in a fabulous mashup of technology and Listening with Fourteen Hearts, we now have games that help listeners stand in the shoes of characters we might not meet in live interaction, while anime and film characters break the fourth wall to simulate live interaction and make our audience listening more immersive.

As technology mixes into human channels of listening in ever more innovative ways, we are becoming, however incrementally, savvier Fourteen Heart Listeners. Young or old, at work or at home, bestie from school or absolute stranger, tele shoe salesperson or homebound pensioner, perfectly polite or grumpy, I hope you'll continue to enjoy expanding your listening practice with all your fourteen hearts to sustain our common human project so everyone can feel heard.

Although I still can't read ancient Buddhist texts and I no longer live in the state with the UNESCO World Heritage Site, I'm feeling what the Russian professor of Buddhism hopefully did at the Grand Canyon, having shared my thoughts on listening with you. Thank you all from the bottom of my fourteen hearts for listening.

Acknowledgements

In Japan, a film audience stays seated until every last credit rolls as a way of honouring all its contributors. Although a book might seem like it doesn't have the same magnitude of collaboration, for me, it certainly felt like it. It's hard to know where to begin my thanks, but I'll start with the people in the publishing community who supported me in the writing of this book.

Thank you to my agent Ben Clark for believing that there was something in the early listening proposal that readers could enjoy – it's a fact that I would not be here if you hadn't decided to read my query. Thank you also to HarperCollins Author and Design Academy who trained me and other authors from underrepresented groups and introduced us to the world of publishing. To Dr Sara Eusebi who pushed me to submit, thank you for your mighty encouragement and the tremendous support you provided. Sincerest appreciation to director and editor Bianca Bexton who teased out the things I wanted to say from my chaotic bilingual brain, thank you. To meticulous editor Liz Marvin who asked all manner of incisive questions, thank you so much. To the legal team, proofreaders, typesetters, assistant editor Ellie Harris who saw the book to its completion, thank you. To Audio Editor Rabeeah Moeen, Studio Manager Stefan Szwarc and voice actor Jacqui Bardelang – thank you for bringing listening to the ears of audio book lovers. And a big thanks to publicist Joe Thomas who, by reaching out and connecting listeners all

Acknowledgements

over the world, is responsible for helping us reconnect to our own listening practices every day. I still can't claim to understand the magic you all work, but thank you for making the process of publication feel that much more accessible.

Thank you to all researchers and contributors who helped with the scientific and ethnographic contents of the book. With deep gratitude to otolaryngologist Dr Kamal Batniji, Professors Emeritus of Nagoya University Foreign Studies Dr Douglas Wilkerson and Dr Kyoko Takashi Wilkerson, and Michael Heffner at Yale New Haven Hospital. Thank you to Minister of Digital Transformation, KONO Taro for being so relaxed about letting me use the photos of you in the book and for liaising with the photographers, despite your hefty schedule. Thank you to Dr Mazen Abudari and Mr UMEKI Takamori for granting me permission to reprint your photos.

Thank you also to all medical staff at the ICU at Charing Cross Hospital who looked after me when I fell off the scooter. You inspired me to explore listening in a different way and to see the hospital as more than clinical – a place that gives rise to the many listening opportunities I still get to experience in my own local hospital as a volunteer. Thank you to our special team at the Chelsea and Westminster Hospital headed by Nicolas Dreyfus. For a global nomad like me, you've given me a little home to come back to.

Thank you to family in Japan, the US and France, especially my late parents who began the process of putting me in so many intercultural listening experiences and my big sister, Kay Suzuki, who not only put up with my antics in our nomadic childhood, but also flew across oceans to become that 'forward family member' who risked her first week in a new position to fight my corner when I bonked my head.

Acknowledgements

Friends! Who needs them? Kyoko Takashi Wilkerson, Tomiko Kagei, Sally Mangum, Mag Combemale and Alice Kim, you know I do. Thank you for your many insights that have supported and fed my work, but also for showing up when I needed a listener even after long bouts of writing-incurred absence. Thank you too to all my childhood and college friends who have been key listeners at critical junctures. To Fiona Brady, Jennifer McCaffrey, Sangeeta Arora Shields, Kaori Nakajima and Karren Dickson, you have been, and are still part of, my listening journey everywhere I go – if your ears were burning during the writing of this book, you know some of that was me telling our stories.

And last but not least, thank you to my family in London: Bruno, Sébastien and Beni Mathieu. There may have been times when I thought our late cat Blaze exemplified superior listening, the way a third of the women in the Associated Press survey said when they confessed their pets were better listeners than their partners. But in my long road to getting to grips with listening, I've come to realise that that is just because humans can't do big goggle eyes or long-blink and purr like cats can. You each know this, but let me say it anyway, all of you are forever in my listening heart. Thank you.

Notes

Prologue

1 '1 in 3 married women say their pets are better listeners than their partners', *Mercury Tribune*, 28 April 2010. https://www.guelphmercury.com/news/1-in-3-married-women-say-pets-are-better-listeners-than-their-husbands-survey/article_50c4a225-511b-5f75-88fd-072dfd0b8285.html.

1: Listening with Fourteen Hearts

1 'The Harvard Study of Adult Development'. https://www.adultdevelopmentstudy.org/, viewed 27 May 2024.

2 Valtorta, Nicole K., Mona Kanaan, Simon Gilbody, Sara Ronzi and Barbara Hanratty. 2016. 'Loneliness and social isolation as risk factors for coronary heart disease and stroke: Systematic review and meta-analysis of longitudinal observational studies', *Heart*, 102.13, 1009–16. https://pubmed.ncbi.nlm.nih.gov/27091846/, viewed 27 May 2024.

3 Cutten, Dave. 2024. 'The top 10 animals with the best hearing', *Hidden Hearing*, 19 February 2024. https://www.hiddenhearing.co.uk/hearing-blog/case-studies/the-top-10-animals-with-the-best-hearing.

4 BioExplorer. 2024. 'Top 16 animals with the best hearing', reviewed 16 September 2024.

5 Kersken, Verena, Klaus Zuberbuhler and Juan-Carlos Gomez. 2017. 'Listeners can extract non-linguistic meaning from infant vocalisations cross-culturally', *Scientific Reports*, 7 41016. https://www.nature.com/articles/srep41016, retrieved 21 August 2023.

6 Victory, Joy. 2021. 'Hearing loss statistics at a glance', *Healthy Hearing*, 15 March 2021. https://www.healthyhearing.com/report/52814-Hearing-loss-statistics-at-a-glance.

7 RNID. 2019. 'Our social research and evidence: Facts and figures'. https://rnid.org.uk/about-us/research-and-policy/facts-and-

299

Notes

figures/#:~:text=In%20the%20UK%2C%20more%20than,the%20UK%20
living%20with%20tinnitus.

2: Informational Listening

1 McBaugh, James. 2013. 'Making Lasting Memories: Remembering
the Significant.' https://www.ncbi.nlm.nih.gov/pmc/articles/
PMC3690616/.
2 Cunningham, Sheila J. and David J. Turk. 2017. 'Editorial, a review of
self-processing biases in cognition', Volume 70, issue 6, June 1, 2017,
https://doi.org/10.1080/17470218.2016.1276609.
3 Ethnologue. 2023. Languages of the World. 24th Edition. As of
February 2023, there are 7,168 languages spoken in the world.
4 Brysbaert, Marc, Michaël Stevens, Paweł Mandela and Emmanuel
Keuleers. 2016. 'How many words do we know? Practical estimates of
vocabulary size dependent on word definition, the degree of language
input and the participant's age'. *Psychology of Language*, volume 7,
29 July 2016.
5 *Economist*. 2013. 'Lexical Facts', 29 May 2013.
6 Huld, Nickee Leon. 2017. 'How many words does a person know?'
Word Counter, viewed 21 June 2023, https://wordcounter.io/blog/
how-many-words-does-the-average-person-know#:~:text=According%20
to%20lexicographer%20and%20dictionary,vocabulary%20is%20
around%2040%2C000%20words.%E2%80%9D.
7 https://en.wikipedia.org/wiki/Most_common_words_in_English,
retrieved 2 September 2023.
8 Ethnologue. 2024. 'What are the top 200 most spoken languages?'
Retrieved 30 October 2024.
9 https://thelanguagenerds.com/category/facts/.
10 Kotz, Sonja A. and Burkhard Maess. 2022. 'Study researches to see
how the left and right halves of the human brain play a crucial role in
processing language'. Britannica transcript of conversation.

3: Soft Listening

1 Marler, Peter and Susan Peters. 1982. 'Long-term storage of learned
birdsong prior to production', *Animal Behaviour*, 30.2, 479–482. https://

www.sciencedirect.com/science/article/abs/pii/S0003347282800596, viewed 1 May 2024.

2 MacIntyre, P. D. and T. Gregersen. 2012. 'Emotional factors in L2 learning and use', *The Encyclopedia of Applied Linguistics*.

3 Doerksen, Sharon and Arthur Shimamura. 2001. 'Source memory enhancement for emotional words'. Emotion, 1.1, 5-11. doi: 10.1037/1528-3542.1.1.5.

4 Johnson, J. S. and E. L. Newport. 1989.. 'Critical period effects in second language learning: The influence of maturational state on the acquisition of English as a second Language.' *Cognitive Psychology*, 21.1, 60–99.

5 Lenneberg, Eric Heinz. 1967. *Biological Foundations of Language*. New York: John Wiley & Sons.

6 Crystal, David. 2006. *How Language Works*. London: Penguin.

4: Credibility Listening

1 Evans, Robert. 1994. *The Kid Stays in the Picture*. Hyperion. Preface, 1.

2 Tannen, Deborah. 1984. *Conversational Style*. New Jersey: Ablex.

3 Yamada, Haru. 1997. *Different Games Different Rules: Why Americans and Japanese Misunderstand Each Other*. Oxford: Oxford University Press.

4 For a comprehensive study of frames, see sociologist Erving Goffman's 1974 book, *Frame Analysis: An Essay on the Organization of Experience*.

5 Lakoff, George and Mark Johnson. 1980. *Metaphors We Live By*. Chicago: The University of Chicago Press.

6 See short video of this, for example, https://www.youtube.com/watch?v=Fg3DsTuG7yY.

5: Nonverbal Listening

1 Willis, Janine and Alexander Todorov. 2006. 'First Impressions: Making up your mind after a 100-ms exposure to a face', *Psychological Science*, 17(7), 592–8, 1 July 2006.

2 Jiang, Jing, Kamila Borowiak, Luke Tudge, Carolin Otto and Katharina von Kriegstein. 2017. 'Neural mechanisms of eye-contact when listening to another person talking'. *Social Cognitive Affective*

Notes

Neuroscience, 12(2), 319–28, 20 October, 2016. https://www.ncbi.nlm. nih.gov/pmc/articles/PMC5390711/, viewed 19 September, 2023.

3 Sheikh, Knuval. 2017. 'How We Save Face--Researchers Crack the Facial-Recognition Code'. *Scientific American*, 1 June 2017. https://www. scientificamerican.com/article/how-we-save-face-researchers-crack-the-brains-facial-recognition-code/.

4 Masuda, Takahiko, P. C. Ellsworth, B. Mesquita, J. Leu, S. Tanida and E. Van de Veerdonk. 2008. 'Placing the face in context: Cultural differences in the perception of facial emotion', *Journal of Personality and Social Psychology: Attitudes and Social Cognition*, 94(3).

5 Binetti, Nicola, Charlotte Harrison, Alan Johnston and Isabelle Mareschal. 2016. 'Pupil dilation as an index of preferred mutual gaze duration'. The Royal Society, https://royalsocietypublishing.org/ doi/10.1098/rsos.160086, 1 July 2016.

6 Masuda, et al, 'Placing the face in context'.

7 Altieri, N. A., D. B. Pisoni and J. T. Townsend. 2011. 'Some normative data on lip-reading skills (L)', The *Journal of Acoustical Society of America*, 130, 1:1-4. viewed 6 April 2024.

8 Rule, Nicholas O. and Nalini Ambady. 2009. 'When two smiles are better than one: Enhancing the persuasive appeal of dual-smile requests', *Psychological Science*, 2009: 20, 8, 1029–31.

9 Ohira, Hideki, Maki Oribe, Mitsuhiro Takenaka and Shinobu Osanai. 2011. 'Effects of speaker's smiling expressions on free recall and recognition of narratives', *Japanese Psychological Research*, 2011, Volume 53, Issue 2, 175–83.

10 For example, Meltzoff, Andrew and M. Keith Moore. 1977. 'Infants' understanding of people and things: From body imitation to folk psychology', in *Social Development*, Vol. 6, Issue 328–39.

11 Jones, Colin. 2022. Edited by Sam Dresser. 'The smile: a history', Aeon, June 10, 2022. https://aeon.co/essays/a-history-of-the-smile-through-art-culture-and-etiquette, viewed 25 September 2023.

12 Collett, Peter. 2018. *Uncovered: The body language secrets of the key players involved in Brexit*. YouTube, 22 December 2018, https://www.youtube. com/watch?v=KHNyMtZk_jk.

13 Bogodistov, Yevgen and Florian Dost. 2017. 'Proximity begins with a smile, but which one? Associating non-duchenne smiles with higher

psychological distance', *Frontiers in Psychology*, 10 August, 2017. https://www.frontiersin.org/articles/10.3389/fpsyg.2017.01374/full, viewed 25 September 2023.

6: Cultural Listening

1 Wikipedia. https://en.wikipedia.org/wiki/List_of_countries_and_territories_where_English_is_an_official_language, reviewed 12 September 2024.

2 Wikipedia. https://en.wikipedia.org/wiki/List_of_multilingual_countries_and_regions, reviewed 17 September 2024.

3 Collins, Hanne K., Serena F. Hagerty, Jordi Quoidbach, Michael I. Norton, and Alison Wood Brooks. 2022. 'Relational diversity in social portfolios predicts well-being'. Proceedings of the National Academy of Sciences of the United States of America (PNAS), 22 October, 2022, Vol. 119, No. 43, https://www.pnas.org/doi/full/10.1073/pnas.2120668119.

4 Granovetter, Mark S. 1972. 'The strength of weak ties,' *American Journal of Sociology*, Vol. 78, No. 6, 1360–80.

5 Tannen, Deborah. 1984. *Conversational Styles: Analyzing Talk Among Friends*. Norwood, NJ: Ablex Publishing Corp.

6 Yamada, Haru. 1997. *Different Games Different Rules: How Americans and Japanese Misunderstand Each Other*. Oxford: Oxford University Press.

7 Ibid.

8 Bounds, Paulina, Jennifer Cramer and Susan Tamasi. 2020. *Linguistic Planets of Belief: Mapping Language Attitudes in the American South*. London: Routledge.

9 For colourful maps of regional language in Britain, see https://starkeycomics.com/2023/11/07/map-of-british-english-dialects/.

10 *Saturday Night Live*. 2019. Air Traffic Control – SNL. [Video], January 27, 2019. https://www.youtube.com/watch?v=UGRcJQ9tMbY.

7: Social Listening

1 Tannen, Deborah. 1990. *You Just Don't Understand: Women and Men in Conversation*. New York: William Morrow, 280–1.

Notes

2   Mehrabian, Albert. 1981. *Silent Messages: Implicit Communication of Emotions and Attitudes*. Wadsworth Publishing Co. Inc., second edition.

3   Floyd, Kory. 2024. *Interpersonal Communication*. New York: McGraw Hill.

4   Guy, Gregory, B. Horvath, J. Vonwiller, E. Daisley and I. Rogers. 1986. 'An intonational change in progress in Australian English'. *Language in Society*. 15: 23–52.

5   Linneman, Thomas J. 2012. 'Gender in Jeopardy!: Intonation Variation on a Television Game Show', *Gender & Society*, Vol. 27, Issue 1, 30 October, 2012.

6   See for example, sociolinguist, William Labov's studies in, *Sociolinguistic Patterns*, 1984, Philadelphia: University of Pennsylvania Press.

7   Tannen, Deborah. 1990. *You Just Don't Understand: Women and Men in Conversation*. New York: William Morrow, 226.

8   Ibid.

9   Miller, Anne Neville. 2011. 'Men and women's communication is different – sometimes', National Communication Association, 1 February, 2011, https://www.natcom.org/communication-currents/men-and-women's-communication-different—sometimes.

10 Jehn, Karen A. 1995. 'A multimethod examination of the benefits and detriments of intragroup conflict', *Administrative Science Quarterly*, 40m 256–82.

11 Proyer, Rene, T., Fabian Gander, Emma J. Bertenshaw and Kay Brauer. 2018. 'The positive relationships of playfulness with indicators of health, activity, and physical fitness', *Frontiers in Psychology*, 14 August 2018, Vol. 9. https://doi.org/10.3389/fpsyg.2018.01440.

12 Yip, Jeremy, Maurice E. Schweitzer, Samir Nurmohamed. 2018. 'Trash-talking: Competitive incivility motivates rivalry, performance and unethical behavior'. *Elsevier*, Vol. 144, January, 2018, 125–44.

13 Ibid.

14 Ibid.

15 Brusoe, Peter W. 2020. 'I didn't realize you were on a first-name basis?' *Pulse*, 13 December 2020. https://www.linkedin.com/pulse/i-didnt-realize-you-were-first-name-basis-her-peter-w-brusoe/.

16 Lambert, Mike. 2015. 'Identifying gender when you're blind'. BBC News, https://www.bbc.co.uk/news/disability-34776343, 11 November 2015.

Notes

8: Work Listening

1 Dhawan, Erica. 2021. 'The digital communication crisis and steps to the solution'. https://ericadhawan.com/wp-content/uploads/2021/05/The-Digital-Communication-Crisis.pdf?utm_source=email&utm_medium=KIT&utm_campaign=ECON_BSW_KIT4_8/10/2024.

2 Grant, Adam. 2021. *Think Again*, London: WH Allen, p.158.

3 Brunner, Briggita R. 2008. 'Listening, communication and trust: Practitioners' perspectives of business/organizational relationships'. *International Journal of Listening*, 22.1, 73–82.

4 Ibid.

5 Chokshi, Niraj, Sydney Ember and Santul Nerkar. 2024. 'Shortcuts everywhere: How Boeing Favored Speed over Quality', *New York Times*, 28 March 2024.

6 Larker, David F. and Brian Tayan. 2024. 'Boeing 737 MAX'. Harvard Law School Forum on Corporate Governance, 6 June 2024. https://corpgov.law.harvard.edu/2024/06/06/boeing-737-max.

7 O'Connell, Andrew. 2009. 'LEGO CEO Jørgen Vig Knudstorp on leading through survival and growth', *Harvard Business Review*, January 2009.

8 Sombret, Paulyne. 2023. 'Employee disengagement: an increasing issue for HR to tackle', deskbird, 28 June 2023, http://www.deskbird.com/, viewed 20 May 2024.

9 Johnston, Michelle Kirtley and Kendra Reed. 2017. 'Listening environment and the bottom line: How a positive environment can improve financial outcomes', *International Journal of Listening*, 31.2, 71–9.

10 Dewhurst, Martin, Matthew Guthridge and Elizabeth Mohr. 2009. 'Motivating people: Getting beyond money', *McKinsey Quarterly*, 1 November 2009.

11 Novak, David. 2018. 'Follow Indra Nooyi's example: Be a leader people are excited to follow', CNBC, 12 September 2018, viewed 19 April 2024. https://www.cnbc.com/2018/09/12/pepsico-indra-nooyi-be-a-leader-people-want-to-follow.html.

12 Gentry, William. A. and Claire M. Harbour. 2018. 'Always On, Never Done? Don't Blame the Smartphone', Greensboro, NC: The Center for Creative Leadership (CCL).

Notes

13 Nawaz, Sabina. 2017. 'Become a better listener by taking notes',
    Harvard Business Review. https://hbr.org/2017/03/become-a-better-
    listener-by-taking-notes, retrieved 19 April 2024.

14 Janusik, Laura and Andrew Wolvin. 2006. '24 hours in a day: A
    listening update in the time studies', paper presented at the meeting of
    International Listening Association, Salem, Oregon.

9: Generational Listening

1   Sky Mobile Research. 2023. 'CALL DECLINED. A quarter of 18-24s say
    they refuse to pick up the phone says new research', 12 October 2023.
    https://www.skygroup.sky/article/call-declined- viewed 15 February
    2024.

2   Wise, Alyssa Friend, Simone Nicole Hausknecht and Yuting Zhao.
    2014. 'Attending to others' posts in asynchronous discussions:
    Learners' online "listening" and its relationship to speaking',
    International Journal of Computer-Supported Collaborative Learning, 9.2,
    185–209.

3   Wise, Alyssa Friend, Jennifer Speer, Farshid Marbouti and Ying-
    ting Hsiao. 2013. 'Broadening the notion of participation in online
    listening behaviors', *Instructional Science*, 41, 2, 323–43.

4   Storch, Sharon L. and Anna V. Ortiz Jarez-Paz. 2018. 'Family
    communication: Exploring the dynamics of listening with mobile
    devices'. *International Journal of Listening*, 32.2, 115–26.

5   Maben, Sarah K. and Christopher C. Gearhart. 2018. 'Organizational
    social media accounts: Moving toward listening competency',
    International Journal of Listening, 32.2, 101–14.

6   Crawford, Kate. 2009. 'Following you: Disciplines of listening in
    social media', *Continuum: Journal of Media and Cultural Studies*, 23.4,
    525–35.

7   Lacey, Kate. 2014. 'Smart radio and audio apps: The politics and
    paradoxes of listening to anti-social media'. *Australian Journalism
    Review*, 36.2, 77–90.

8   Maben, Sarah K. and Christopher C. Gearhart. 2018. 'Organizational
    social media accounts: Moving toward listening competency'.
    International Journal of Listening, 32.2, 101–14.

Notes

9 Wheatley-Hawkins, Raven. 2022. 'Top 10 "Should I" Google Suggestions' following 10th May UK government announcement', Adroit Data and Insight, site visited 19 August 2022.

10: Adaptive Listening

1 Accenture Newsroom. 2015. 'Accenture finds listening more difficult in today's digital workplace', 26 February 2015. https://newsroom. accenture.com/news/2015/accenture-research-finds-listening-more-difficult-in-todays-digital-workplace.

2 Maxwell, John C. 2014. *Good Leaders Ask Great Questions*. New York: Center Street.

3 Wetzler, Jeff. 2024. *Ask*. London: Hachette Go.

4 Slamecka, Norman J. and Peter Graf. 1978. 'The generation effect: delineation of a phenomenon', *Journal of Experimental Psychology, Human Learning and Memory*, 4, 6, 592–604.

5 Barron, Helen C., Hayley M. Reeve, Renee S. Koolschiin, David M. Bannerman, Timothy E. J. Behrens, and David Dupret. 2020. 'Neuronal computation underlying inferential reasoning in humans and mice', Vol. 183, Issue 1, 17 September 2020, https://doi.org/10.1016/j.cell.2020.08.035, viewed 19 September 2023.

6 Ibid.

7 Alda, Alan. 2018. *If I Understood You Would I Have This Look on My Face?: My Adventures in the Art and Science of Relating and Communicating*. Random House.